INGMAR BERGMAN

Geoffrey Macnab writes on film for the *Guardian*, the *Independent* and *Screen International*. He is the author of *The Making of Taxi Driver* (2006), *Key Moments in Cinema* (2001), *Searching for Stars: Stardom and Screenwriting in British Cinema* (2000), and *J. Arthur Rank and the British Film Industry* (1993).

INGMAR BERGMAN

The Life and Films of the Last Great European Director

Geoffrey Macnab

I.B. TAURIS
LONDON · NEW YORK

Sheila Whitaker: Advisory Editor

Published in 2009 by I.B.Tauris & Co Ltd
6 Salem Road, London W2 4BU
175 Fifth Avenue, New York NY 10010
www.ibtauris.com

Distributed in the United States and Canada Exclusively by
Palgrave Macmillan 175 Fifth Avenue,
New York NY 10010

ISBN: 978 1 84885 046 0

A full CIP record for this book is available from the British Library
A full CIP record is available from the Library of Congress

Library of Congress Catalog Card Number: available

Printed and bound in Great Britain by CPI Antony Rowe, Chippenham

FSC
Mixed Sources
Product group from well-managed
forests and other controlled sources
Cert no. SGS-COC-2953
www.fsc.org
© 1996 Forest Stewardship Council

To Finlay, Francis and Catriona

Contents

Illustrations

Acknowledgements

I WOULD LIKE to acknowledge the help given to me in the writing of this book by Jannike Ahlund, who organises the 'Bergman Week' on what was Bergman's home island, Faro, every year, and invited me on to the island in 2007. I would like to thank Fredrik Gustafson at the Bergman Archive, housed in the Swedish Film Institute in Stockholm, for helping me negotiate my way through the archive's holdings. Thanks also to David Thompson of BBC's Arena for providing me with old documentaries about Bergman. Thanks to Paul Smith too of the (sadly now defunct) Tartan Films for sending me DVDs of the films in Tartan's Bergman Collection. My thanks, also, to Danish journalist Jorn Rossing Jensen for his suggestions and help with contacts.

My thanks to those who gave me special interviews for the book: Barbro Hiort af Ornas, Bertil Guve, Katinka Farago, Kabi Laretei, Marie Nyrerod and various others.

I am grateful to the book's editor Philippa Brewster and to the assistant editor Eloise Villez for their patience. Thanks, also, to Payal Malik for her diligent copy editing.

Introduction

Lord, let my soul come to maturity before it is reaped.
(DAVID HOLM, in *The Phantom Carriage*)

IT WAS A MIDSUMMER evening in 2007 on Faro, a small windswept island in the Baltic Sea, and a group of film enthusiasts were climbing aboard a bus for the 'Bergman Safari', a tour of landmarks where the island's most famous resident, Ingmar Bergman, had shot scenes from some of his best-known films. The mood was enthusiastic and a little raucous, as if we were going on a school trip. I was sitting in the back seat alongside Japanese, French, Russian and American admirers of Bergman as the bus set off from Strandskogen at 5.30 pm.

The light was grey and overcast (just as Bergman and his cinematographer Sven Nykvist used to like it). 'When it rains, we call that Bergman weather', locals remark.[1] (Popular belief has it that in the wet air, the spirits can be felt.) Our tour guides were Arne Carlsson, a bluntly spoken islander who worked as a truck driver and cameraman for Bergman, and the formidable Katinka Farago, who was an assistant and production manager on many of his films. The three-hour outing was a little like the Universal Studios' tour, but instead of seeing the shark from *Jaws*, we wandered across *Persona* beach, were shown just where Liv Ullmann and Max Von Sydow's farmhouse was razed in *Shame* (Bergman's only action movie) and drove past many of the houses that Bergman built for his family and collaborators. As the tour party trundled around the island, the guides revealed how Bergman and Sven Nykvist achieved the trompe l'oeil effects on *Shame*, burning down miniature churches and making tiny streams into turbulent rivers. They stopped briefly on the north side of the island, within sight of a series of looming rocks by the seashore, allowing the bus passengers off for a 'Bergman burger' and a low-alcohol beer.

Faro is a magical place full of myth and history. The light and atmosphere are constantly changing. The island can seem grey and brooding, but when the sun shines, it suddenly becomes idyllic. Residents tell colourful stories about buried Viking princesses, pirates, boat wrecks and fishermen on daredevil trips. The local lore – recounted in one of Bergman's documentaries – is that seal hunters discovered the island by accident, when they were swept away by a chunk of drifting ice.

Despite the thousands of tourists who visit here in summer, the 600 or so locals face a fierce struggle to survive. The fishing industry is all but dead. This is a harsh place on which to farm and there are few jobs outside tourism. While we were on Faro, we learned that the only school on the island was threatened with closure. That is one of the reasons why the residents were so protective of Bergman. One of the world's most celebrated filmmakers was living in their midst, and they saw it as their duty to protect him. It was as if they had struck an informal pact together. He poured investment into Faro. (It used to be said that his tax bill was as big as those of the rest of the islanders put together.) He always used many local craftsmen on his films and made angry documentaries – Faro Document 1969 and Faro Document 1979 – about Sweden's neglect of the island. In return, the islanders went to extreme lengths to preserve Bergman's privacy. When visitors asked where Bergman lived, they either said they had no idea or pointed them in the wrong direction. There was a sign on his gate, 'Beware Of Killer Dog', to frighten away anyone uninvited who somehow tracked him down. Locals told a story – perhaps apocryphal – about a young French woman who located his house. When Bergman opened the door, he was brandishing a gun and made sure that she was promptly escorted off the island.

Foreigners have only recently been allowed here. In the past, there was a military base on the island and only Swedes were permitted to catch the ferry across Faro. That was one of the reasons why Andrei Tarkovsky was not able to make his 1986 film *The Sacrifice* here as he had originally planned.

It was late June. Bergman was 88 years old. He had stayed out of sight as we blundered around the settings from some of his films. We were told he was in a wheelchair. Earlier in the year, he had made a final trip to Stockholm for a hip operation and was too proud to be seen in public when he couldn't stand on his own legs.

Bergman first came to the island well over 40 years before, when he was scouting locations for *Through a Glass Darkly*, and instantly fell in love with it. It wasn't just the brooding landscape and the ever-changing light that attracted him – it was the solitude. This was one place where he could escape the rest of the world. Here, the politicking and backbiting in the film community in Stockholm seemed very far away.

'The air is different, the light is different. There is a peace you can get here – an absolute peace. No one to see you and nothing to disturb you – just nature', his fellow Faro resident and former Bergman actress Barbro Hjort af Ornas told me when I spoke to her in a cafe beside the Sudersand Cinema, the tiny converted barn where Bergman used to show his rushes and which now functioned as a cinema for the island.[2]

You could understand why Bergman had looked askance when some local enthusiasts started a mini-festival – the Bergman Week – in his honour four years before. He reluctantly gave the event his blessing, but vowed he would not join in. In 2006, when the filmmakers Ang Lee and James Schamus, and Bergman's old muse Harriet Andersson, were visitors, Bergman surprised everyone by actively participating in discussions and lectures that were about him and his work. By 2007, though, Bergman was in frail health. He was beginning to waver from that rigorous routine that he had adhered to for so long in order to work productively and keep his many demons at bay. The routine consisted of a brisk morning walk of around 45 minutes, a fixed stint of writing – around three hours – and then a light lunch and time to read and perhaps watch a film. His main solace now was music. On Sunday evenings, he would visit his former wife Kabi Laretei (an acclaimed concert pianist) to listen to her perform on one of the two grand pianos in the house he lent her for the summer.

'He comes every Sunday evening and I play for him', Laretei told me over tea and biscuits. 'Last week, he came. I had my friend here. We played Brahms waltzes together. That is the only thing he misses here in Faro, to have live music in concert halls.'[3]

When he finished his final film, *Saraband*, Bergman had declared that he never wanted to leave the island again. It was here he had come to die.

Twenty years before, Bergman had – as he put it – 'hung up his camera' after completing his final theatrical feature, *Fanny and Alexander*. His relentless artistic drive hadn't abated. In the intervening years, he remained as prolific as ever, writing and directing stage plays and TV dramas. Nonetheless, Bergman would not make his own feature films any more.

'The pressure was too high. *Fanny and Alexander* was very difficult for him. In many ways, it was a summing up, a final word. He just cannot stand the pressure because he is a perfectionist. He wants everything to be just the way he asked for it. Too often, there are unpleasant surprises and he just can't take it', actor Max Von Sydow noted of the director's self-enforced retirement.[4]

Bergman epitomised a brand of auterial arthouse cinema that was beginning to seem very old-fashioned by the end of the twentieth century. In 1997, at the 50th Cannes Film Festival, when he had been awarded (in absentia) the 'Palme of Palmes', it had seemed as much a valediction as a tribute to a working filmmaker. In Sweden itself, he was regarded with a mixture of reverence and disdain. Swedish audiences hadn't much cared for his last TV film as a director, *Saraband* (2003), objecting to the stagey performance style. Swedish filmmakers felt oppressed by him. He cast a long shadow and had no natural successors. He was a victim of what one of his collaborators (the actress Lena Olin) called 'the royal Swedish envy'. He stood out too much and his achievements were too substantial for his fellow Swedes to appreciate. Bergman wasn't exactly ignored, but he wasn't cherished either.

In the summer of 2007, when tourists arrived at Stockholm's airport Arlanda, they were greeted by a gallery of portraits of notable Swedes, including scientists, artists, golfers, playwrights and clothes designers. Among the many headshots of luminaries living and dead, it was telling no sign was to be found of Bergman, arguably the most famous Swede of his generation. Maybe – as it was suggested to the visitors to Bergman Week – this had been a simple oversight attributable to worries about copyright, indecision about which image of Bergman should be used and the fact that the authorities were nervous about asking the great man (whose temper almost matched his fame) for permission to use his portrait. Even so, it was a glaring omission. Once Bergman was dead, it was easy enough to predict, the Swedes would begin to feel much more comfortably and affectionately about him, but while still alive, he continued to frighten them.

In 2002, Bergman donated his vast 'archive' to the Swedish Film Institute. This was an astonishing collection, stored on shelves and cabinets in a fireproof vault at the Film House in Stockholm. There were over 7000 letters as well as home movie footage. The archive stretched from the late 1930s, when Bergman was starting out as a theatre director, right through to the workbook for his final film, *Saraband* in 2003. It included hundreds of scripts, many photograph albums, home movie footage, fan letters and requests for photographs from as far afield as Pakistan and even unlikely bits of bric-a-brac (e.g. a cigarette holder that he might once have used).

After five years, the collection had neither been digitised nor been made widely available to Bergman scholars. In certain official quarters, it was clear that Bergman vexed his fellow Swedes. Rather than welcoming the gift of the archive as a unique historical resource, public funders regarded it as a burden and groaned at the prospect of having to collate and protect the material. Younger Swedes didn't seem especially interested in Bergman. Their parents might have known about him and felt a vestigial pride in his achievements, but the younger ones often regarded his work as too dark and forbidding to watch, except under sufferance. The one Bergman movie received with real public affection was his adaptation of Mozart's *The Magic Flute*, which had screened for the first time on Swedish television on New Year's Day in 1975 and had reached a huge audience. This, though, was hardly a characteristic Bergman project.

Bergman had helped fix the image of Swedes abroad. Films like *The Seventh Seal*, *Fanny and Alexander* and *Wild Strawberries* were an immediate point of reference for the outside world when it came to pinpointing national characteristics. Whether gloomy knights playing chess with death or wild and defiant women (like Harriet Andersson in *Summer with Monika*), Bergman provided a series of characters who are seen by outsiders as national archetypes. As filmmaker Marie Nyrerod (who made an excellent series of documentaries based on 30 hours of interviews with the filmmaker) remarked: 'we Swedes are so often described through the eyes of Ingmar Bergman that we have to say "no, we're not like that".'[5]

Other Swedish filmmakers objected to his influence and to the way he sucked up attention and resources that might otherwise have come to them. There was also the sense of an Oedipal battle. He was the father figure that the younger generation wanted (at least symbolically) to slay. In the 1960s, the era of the counter-culture, Bergman already seemed part of the Old Guard. During this period, when *Cahiers du Cinema* published a series of anti-Bergman articles, he contributed a piece himself under the pseudonym of Ernest Riffe (apparently the name of his then wife's hairdresser). 'It was severe and well-written', Bergman expert Stig Bjorkman remembers of Bergman's attack on himself.[6]

Forty years later, there was still the same animus against Bergman. In 2001, when Lukas Moodysson emerged as the latest new hope of Swedish cinema, there was a spate of articles suggesting that his well-received films *Fucking Amal* and *Together* had at last enabled Swedish cinema to escape from under the yoke of Bergman. Journalists began to talk about 'the Moodysson effect'.

'I think it is really sad today that there is a tendency in Sweden to talk badly about Bergman and to say that finally his role is over', Moodysson reflected at the time. 'To me, it seems he is just a very lonely old sad person, who sits in his big house and reads in the papers that his days are over. I wrote a letter to him two weeks ago. I didn't know what to say so I just said that I liked *Fanny and Alexander* and that it was one of the best films I had ever seen.'[7]

Ironically, Bergman himself was an early champion of Moodysson, calling *Fucking Amal* 'a young master's first masterpiece'.[8] That didn't stop critics from using Moodysson's success as an excuse for attacking him.

The relationship between Bergman and new generations of filmmakers had a competitive edge. As Lars Von Trier put it: 'Bergman was also an artist to prove yourself against. A filmmaker to admire but also someone towards whom one had to adopt a critical wait-and-see attitude.'[9]

The doubts and suspicion were felt on both sides. It wasn't just a case of younger directors confronting and challenging the old master, but of the old master trying desperately to ensure his work was still relevant to them. The Bergman of the early 1960s was so lionised that – at least in the eyes of younger filmmakers – he was in imminent danger of being co-opted by the establishment. His image had been on the front cover of *Time* magazine in March 1960, at around the time of *The Virgin Spring*. He is shown stern-faced, standing in front of a sun-dappled wood, holding up the thumb and forefinger of his left hand to his face as if they are a viewfinder. Behind him, a woman hides as a shadowy figure in the distance comes looking for her. Bergman had won the Oscars and major awards in Cannes and Berlin. He was an international celebrity. The American magazines were fawning over him. In the summer of 1961, US weekly magazine *Look*, then about to celebrate its 25th anniversary, tried (unsuccessfully) to recruit him alongside a gallery of other international celebrities for a special issue in which prominent men and women of 1961 were invited to tell the magazine's readers briefly what they imagined – or hoped – the world would be like in 25 years time. *Esquire* offered him thousands of dollars for pre-publication rights to his screenplays.

In the 1960s, newly radicalised Swedish filmmakers didn't care at all for the lionised and pampered Bergman, a filmmaker who appeared uninterested in the political and social struggles of the period. Bo Widerberg (the director of *Elvira Madigan*) was especially trenchant in his attacks on Bergman. 'Nor me or my friends saw very much in him. We didn't find the issue of god's existence that damn important. But it's safe to say you'd be putting yourself in a bad position if you're trying to slit the throat of the father figure before your own debut,'[10] Widerberg commented on the low regard in which he and his contemporaries held Bergman. They accused him of looking inward – of engaging in solipsistic soul searching – instead of paying attention to the world around him.

In films like *The Silence* and *Shame*, Bergman responded, touching, however obliquely, on militarism and totalitarianism. When Bergman did make concessions to his era, he often regretted it. In 1968, a seismic year of student riots across Europe, he was on Faro, making *The Passion of Anna*. Against his better judgement, he allowed his actors to talk him into allowing them to wear the clothes and hairdos of the time – something which he later thought made the film look horribly specific and dated. (We have Bibi Andersson and Liv Ullmann wearing mini-skirts and behaving as if they are on leave from swinging London, although this is a dark and oppressive film set on a remote island.) Bergman – as if in deference to Brecht and Godard – was even ready to 'lay bare the device' and include sequences in which the four principal actors stepped out of character and talked directly to the camera about the movie they were appearing in. What seemed like an interesting formal experiment then appeared horribly self-indulgent when the director revisited the film during the preparation for his book, *Images*.[11]

It would be stretching it to say that Bergman was forgotten or neglected by the end of his life, whatever the Swedes' ambivalence to this mercurial titan in their midst. In the summer of 2007, plans were already well underway for a series of international retrospectives and special events to mark his 90th birthday (due to fall in July 2008). Nonetheless, his status was ambiguous. The tourists aboard the bus for the 'Bergman Safari' that Saturday evening on Faro were hoping for a glimpse of him in the same way that naturalists might hope to see an exotic panda during a field trip. They may have been passionate about his life and work, but Bergmanophilia seemed very much a special interest.

A month later, on July 30, when Bergman died less than a fortnight after his 89th birthday, the perception that the Swedish director was a forgotten old Prospero from another era of world cinema was conclusively shattered. His death was front-page news all over the world. In the

UK, the reaction was especially pronounced. The cartoonists in every British broadsheet newspaper drew images of the grim reaper playing chess on the beach in Bergman's *The Seventh Seal* which – coincidentally – had just been re-released in Britain. *The Independent* had an image of US President George Bush (in grim reaper outfit) playing snakes and ladders with the new British Prime Minister Gordon Brown. 'NO EXIT STRATEGY ...BACK DOWN THE BIG SNAKE FOR YOU!' read the caption, in reference to the continuing quagmire of the Iraq War. News programmes, which would not normally have mentioned the death of a foreign-language film director, covered Bergman's passing in great detail.

As the rash of obituaries and tributes attested, Bergman was far more widely known and appreciated internationally than his grudging Swedish detractors had realised. Tributes were announced; retrospectives rapidly planned. They seemed to go on all year. Every major festival had its Bergman homage. In May 2008, Martin Scorsese's World Cinema Foundation (WCF) and Ingmar Bergman Foundation announced a joint project aimed at preserving, editing and revealing several hours of behind-the-screen footage from the Ingmar Bergman Foundation Archives, in total 18 films, ranging from *Sawdust* and *Tinsel* in 1953 via *The Seventh Seal*, *Persona* and *Cries and Whispers* to *After the Rehearsal* in 1984. Founded and officially announced by Martin Scorsese in 2007, WCF is dedicated to the preservation and restoration of neglected films from around the world. It helps support and encourage efforts to ensure that these films are preserved, seen and shared.

Bergman's influence, it was clear, was far more pervasive than the many critics bemoaning the death of old-style auteur cinema and the 'dumbing down' of film culture could have imagined. In Britain, the old-style repertory cinemas that used to show his work were long since closed or had been turned into pubs, offices or new multiplexes, but awareness of Bergman's films had not diminished in the slightest. The influence stretched into some surprising corners. Scandinavian, French, Hollywood, Asian and British directors, alike all, acknowledged a significant debt towards Bergman. There were many, often contradictory, reasons why they had responded so forcefully to his work. Some liked its literary quality. Others responded to its theatricality. Some relished his willingness to tackle big eschatological questions. Others enjoyed the uninhibited way in which he dealt with sexuality and the many beautiful actresses he cast over the years. Some saw him as the great chronicler of childhood. Others responded to the acute way in which he dealt with old age and the fear of death. His films are full of both couples and loners. The invocation of seasons in some of their titles hints at their changing moods – the sunniness of *Summer with Monika* to the chill of *Winter Light*.

In Billy Wilder's *Sunset Boulevard*, Norma Desmond, the decaying old actress played by Gloria Swanson, famously said of the silent era: 'we didn't need dialogue. We had faces.' Bergman was one director who treated the human face with the same rapt curiosity as any filmmakers in the silent era. 'The human face is the most cinematographic thing that exists', he once observed.[12] For him, the ability to scrutinise the human face was what distinguished cinema from any other art.

By the end of his career, it was as if faces were all Bergman cared about. In his remarkable, elegiac 1986 film, *Karin's Face*, he told the story of his mother's life through a selection of still images of her taken from family albums. Karin is a very beautiful young woman. Her story is familiar enough from Bergman's fictional films and from his autobiographical novel, *Best Intentions*. Here, Bergman tells it, stripped down to essentials. We know that she married young, against her mother's wishes, to Lutheran pastor Erik Bergman, and that the marriage was stormy. In *Karin's Face*, there is no need for long, dramatic scenes or descriptions of the joys and sorrows of their marriage. Their peculiar engagement photograph, in which Erik is pictured looking down at a book as Karin stares nervously at the camera, is all that is needed to hint at the tensions between them. Over the course of the 14 minutes of the film, as Bergman's ex-wife Kabi Laretei's simple piano music is heard on the soundtrack, we see Karin being transformed. In a parade of family images, the beautiful young woman becomes an old lady. Soon, as Bergman's voice-over puts it, she begins to disappear into group photographs. She suffers illness. The film ends with the same image with which it started – of Karin as an old lady, clearly close to death.

In this short documentary, Bergman is playing a variation on an old childhood game. As a young kid, he worshipped his mother and craved her attention. In order to get it, he would switch from fawning affection to hostility towards her – anything to make her notice him. In *Karin's Face*, he is again oscillating between devotion and provocation. He is able to show her at her best and also at her frailest. She is the lead player who, in old age, retreats into the chorus. Curiously, although Bergman wrote about his mother and referenced her in his work frequently, she remains an opaque presence, far less sharply drawn than Bergman's father. She was beautiful, well-born and had a strong personality. That much he tells us but we still have very little sense of what she was really like. The documentary shows Bergman still puzzling over her, as if he feels that by showing her face in magnified close-up, he can get closer to her. However, she remains the same inscrutable and elusive presence.

When Bergman died, his own face was everywhere in newspapers and magazines. There was the young Bergman with his round, arched back and trademark beret, communing with black-caped Death (Bengt Ekerot) on the set of *The Seventh Seal*; there were those much later portraits of Bergman taken when he was directing plays at the Royal Dramatic Theatre: the lean-faced Magus.

In Sweden itself, the old man who had been living neglected on the island, suddenly, in death, became a subject of huge fascination: written about in the tabloids as well as in the more serious newspapers. For example, in the mass circulation *Aftonbladet*, next to the stories about the missing English girl Madeleine McCann (whose alleged abduction from a Portuguese holiday resort had turned into a media phenomenon), a feature writer pondered just whom Bergman's money would benefit. His children, the paper suggested, were set to become millionaires. You could be forgiven for thinking you were reading about a wealthy, old industrialist or someone who had scooped the pools rather than a leading European filmmaker as the journalist dissected his will, asking just where all those millions of Swedish kronors were going to be dispensed.

While the Swedish tabloids gossiped about what would become of Bergman's fortune, the weighty European film journals ran long, searching features, asking whether Bergman's death (followed on the same day by that of the almost equally revered Italian director Michelangelo Antonioni) marked the death knell of European auteur cinema.

Cahiers du Cinema asked what was most worth savouring in Bergman. French critical orthodoxy had it that his best work was all done in the 1950s, when the magazine 'thrust him to the forefront of the struggle of Auteur politics'. By contrast, his later work, as Cyril Neyrat wrote, was generally deemed to have sunk into 'narcissistic and crude psychological theatre, with the grand support of auteur effects for the helots'.[13]

Amid the eulogies, there were one or two pointed attacks on Bergman after his death. The distinguished American critic, Jonathan Rosenbaum, contested that Bergman used film simply to 'translate shadow-plays staged in his mind; that he was in retreat from the modern world; that cruelty and spite were wellsprings of his work and that theatre (not cinema) claimed most of his genius.'[14] In his essay, 'Scenes from an Overrated Career', the critic made the familiar charge that Bergman was the laureate of pampered, bourgeois angst. His films, Rosenbaum asserted,

were mannered, self-absorbed and too narrow in focus to have much resonance in the 'larger world'. His work was – and this was probably the
most damning world the critic had in his arsenal – 'chic'.[15]

'His artfully presented traumas became so respectable they could
help to sell espresso in the lobby of the Fifth Avenue Cinema', Rosenbaum wrote. 'Mr Bergman, famously, not only helped fuel the art-house
aspirations of Woody Allen but Mr Allen's class aspirations as well – the
dual yearnings ultimately becoming so intertwined that they seemed
identical.'[16]

Rosenbaum, it seemed, had not noticed Bergman's fascination with
the human face or his intensely filmic use of close-ups. Nor had he paid
attention to the rawness of the director's work or Bergman's willingness
to probe into intensely uncomfortable areas. He downplayed the self-
lacerating honesty that always characterised Bergman by writing dismis-
sively about his 'bitter and pinched emotions' and the 'antiseptic and upscale look' of his interiors. What was most egregious about Rosenbaum's
observations was how selective they were. There are films in Bergman's
filmography that support his contentions – handsomely mounted costume dramas or intimately focused studies of bourgeois marriages
coming apart at the seams. However, Bergman was a far more protean
filmmaker than what a narrow dismissal of his 'theatrical ... homemade
cinema' allows. The rebelliousness and flirtatiousness of Monika in *Summer with Monika* has more in common with 1950s US movies about defiant teenagers than with any overly tasteful European theatrical tradition.
The violence and desolation shown in films like *The Virgin Spring* and
The Serpent's Egg and the humiliation endured by the circus manager in
Sawdust and *Tinsel* have nothing antiseptic or upscale about them.

Those making the familiar criticisms about the theatrical nature of
Bergman's creativity risked overlooking his sheer technical mastery of
the filmic medium. After his difficulties with his first films (as he writes
in *The Magic Lantern*:[17] 'I had landed myself in an apparatus I had by
no means mastered'), he made a conscious decision to learn his craft.
He knew as much about lenses and lighting as his cinematographers. As
he put it to those who disliked or criticised his work, a Bergman movie
was invariably put together extremely carefully, 'My films involve good
craftsmanship, I am conscientious, industrious and extremely careful. I
do my work for everyday purposes and not for eternity and my pride is
the pride of a good craftsman.'[18]

It is worth noting too that Bergman's original interest was in the
magic of the machine. 'When I was 10 years old I received my first

rattling film projector with its chimney and lamp which went round and round and round. I found it both mystifying and fascinating.'[19]

In a very curious obituary in the *Guardian*, Brian Baxter placed Bergman on 'the second rung' of directors, below such true geniuses as Ozu and Rossellini. He complained about Bergman's 'lack of spontaneity', his heartlessness and his 'grim obsession with physical confrontation'.[20]

Depending on critics' points of view, Bergman's work was either too tasteful or not tasteful enough.

The year before Bergman died, filmmaker Alex Cox had fiercely attacked *Fanny and Alexander* (briefly re-released in Britain) as 'a mishmash of posh tosh' and as a filmic equivalent to the 'well-made play', hidebound theatre by and for the upper middle-class.[21] It is ironic, then, that you can trace a direct link from Bergman's tormented heroes to the supreme anti-hero of 1970s American cinema, Travis Bickle, in Martin Scorsese's *Taxi Driver*. 'I would not have made any of my films or written scripts such as Taxi Driver had it not been for Ingmar Bergman', Paul Schrader wrote after Bergman's death. 'He made filmmaking a serious and introspective enterprise. No one had been able to pull that off until he showed up.'[22]

Woody Allen, meanwhile, was equally effusive, calling Bergman 'the finest filmmaker of my generation' and pointing out that despite his forbidding reputation, he 'was a born spinner of tales who couldn't help being entertaining even when all on his mind was dramatizing the ideas of Nietzsche or Kierkegaard'.[23]

For Allen, Bergman's importance lay not just in his films, but also in his method, in particular, in his husbanding of his own gifts and in his ferocious work ethic. Bergman had the discipline to make a movie and move on to the next one without being sidetracked.

'I think it is very important for both me and you to use our time well, because we only have it on loan', Bergman told the Icelandic filmmaker Hrafn Gunnlaugsson in an interview in 1987. 'We have our creativity on loan and we can spoil or destroy it through compromises. We can kill it in other ways. Creativity can be killed in so many ways. We can also waste it by not making use of time.'[24]

Filmmaking is such an embroiled and difficult process, pitched between art and industry and dependent on collaboration, that it is a small miracle that Bergman managed to keep on working at such pace. Regardless of its quality, the sheer size of his filmography is astounding. If his work for television is included, he directed more than 60 films. The secret was always to decide the next project before the current one was finished. 'It has to be before. Then the big decisions are already made', Danish director Thomas Vinterberg recalls the advice that Bergman gave him when his career briefly lost momentum between his second feature *Festen* and its follow-up *It's All About Love*. By knowing what you are going to do next, 'you are not provoked by either the fiasco of the film – or even worse – the success of the film'.[25]

British director Michael Winterbottom made two documentaries about Bergman for BBC early in his career. He, too, was immediately struck by Bergman's work ethic and intense practicality. In his own career, Winterbottom has tried to embrace similar principles, making sure that there is never a hiatus between his projects.

'In the autumn, he (Bergman) would write the scripts already knowing who the actors and crew were going to be', Winterbottom notes. 'He would know he already had the finance because he kept things very small and simple. In a sense, his career and way of making films got simpler and simpler. He tried to get rid of anything unnecessary and focus on the essential. It is easier to borrow from his way of working than from his films themselves. You just can't beat his films, no-one can copy his films, but if you want to continue making the films you want to make, his method of working is a brilliant method.'[26]

Bergman's technique too is frequently cited by younger filmmakers as something to aspire to. The Swedish director's mantra 'love your actors' has been especially influential.

For some younger filmmakers, what was inspiring about Bergman was seeing his failures and his false turns. Vinterberg talks about his time as a film student, watching Bergman's first 12 films and realising that they weren't all masterpieces. Bergman, like every other director before or since, had to reach for a style and to learn his medium.

An older British director Michael Apted (whose credits range from James Bond's movie *The World is Not Enough* to *Coal Miner's Daughter*) expresses well just why Bergman appeared so attractive to a young bookish student growing up in 1950s' Britain. As a 16-year-old pupil at the City of London School, Apted sneaked off to a screening of Bergman's *Wild Strawberries* at the Academy Cinema on Oxford Street.

'I realised that a film could carry serious ideas', Apted remembers. 'Up till then, movies to me had been about following girls and having popcorn entertainment. This, in a sense, changed my whole life. I don't know whether the film itself was something I would consider to be a powerful influence on the sort of work I ended up doing, but it was certainly a life-changing experience being in that cinema, watching that movie.'[27]

Apted was enthusiastic about theatre, literature and ideas. In Bergman's work, he saw a way in which film could combine his different passions. Up till then, his cinemagoing had been about 'following girls' and enjoying 'popcorn entertainment'.

'It seemed a natural progression from the theatre and books into movies, via that', Apted recalls. 'I began to investigate more of Bergman – I remember *The Seventh Seal* vividly, *The Virgin Spring* and the more psychological ones that followed, but *Wild Strawberries* was the key to the door. I think it was the literary power of Bergman that transfixed me. I could see that film was a poetic and visual medium but my access to it was through my literary instincts.'[28]

The Italian director Bernardo Bertolucci shared Apted's sense that Bergman in the late 1950s was using cinema in a way that had once been the preserve of novelists. 'I'm talking about the depths of the human spirit, going even further into the interiors of men and women, in a black and white that turned his characters into ghosts and his ghosts into characters', Bertolucci suggested in an interview with Stig Bjorkman just after Bergman's death.[29]

Bergman was a far more protean and contradictory figure that either his admirers or detractors allowed. 'Bergmanesque' was an adjective used indiscriminately to describe dark, brooding arthouse movies. Motifs and themes recur across his films. However, their differences outweigh their similarities. He continually experimented with different genres and storytelling styles. His range is testified by the large number of different filmmakers influenced by him.

Alexander Payne's road movie *About Schmidt*, about a widowed insurance salesman Warren Schmidt (Jack Nicholson) travelling across country en route to a family wedding, plays like a barbed, Nebraskan version of Bergman's *Wild Strawberries*. An old man in the twilight of his life is confronted by a difficult family. Payne's film is satirical and ironic and has little of the warmth of Bergman's movie. The director acknowledges that he is 'woefully underexposed to Bergman'.[30] Nonetheless, he acknowledges that his film was directly influenced by *Wild Strawberries*.

The LA-based feminist director Nina Menkes freely admits that her feature *Phantom Love* was inspired by *Persona* and *The Silence*. This is an eerie, dream-like drama, sleekly shot in black and white, about an alienated woman. Lula (Marina Shoif) lives alone and works in a gruelling job in a casino. She has a younger boyfriend (Bobby Naderi), but when they make love, she remains aloof and entirely in her own world. Lula also has a sister with whom she has a fraught relationship. Menkes has described the film as being about 'descent into self' and as 'a surreal drama about a woman trapped within an enmeshed family'.[31]

'The emotions are so wrenching in this film', Menkes remarked. '*Persona* tried to deal with two sides of the female psyche. When I saw it first, I was really affected and I didn't even know why ... it's that split of the female psyche into the wounded one and the functioning one.'[32]

On that Saturday evening in June 2007, when the Bergman tour bus trundled around Faro, Arne Carlsson and Katinka Farago joked that *Shame* was Bergman's only 'action movie'. In a way, it was. An allegory about a bourgeois couple (Max Von Sydow and Liv Ullmann) caught up in a war zone, it features soldiers, explosions, burning buildings and interrogation sequences.

Bergman's *The Hour of the Wolf*, about an artist (Max Von Sydow) losing his sanity, might equally be described as a horror film. You could argue that Bergman has also made teen movies (*Summer with Monika*), family films (*Fanny and Alexander*), musicals (*The Magic Flute*), circus movies (*Sawdust and Tinsel*), political dramas (*This Couldn't Happen Here*), historical films (*The Virgin Spring, The Seventh Seal*), hospital dramas (*So Close to Life*) and crime thrillers (*From The Life of the Marionettes*). Jean-Luc Godard, who called him 'the most original auteur in European cinema', rhapsodised about the 'classically romantic' quality of Bergman's work.

Bergman was there at the birth of the French New Wave. Watch François Truffaut's seminal film, *The 400 Blows* (1959), and about an hour into the film, you will see rebellious kid Antoine Doinel (Jean-Pierre Leaud) and his friend rip down and steal a poster of Harriet Andersson in Bergman's *Summer with Monika*. This is Truffaut's little homage to Bergman. It is not arch or self-conscious. Harriet Andersson was a pin-up. The idea that horny young adolescents might want to steal an image of her was perfectly plausible. Moreover, as played by Anderssen, Monika has precisely that sense of mischief and defiance that define Doinel too. Truffaut also borrowed one of Bergman's daring formal devices, having Doinel talk directly to camera, just as Monika does in Bergman's movie.

James Schamus, the screenwriter of *The Incredible Hulk* and *The Ice Storm* and the boss of Focus Features, points to Bergman's mastery of screen violence and the way that his work transcended the high-culture/low-culture divide.

'I first became aware of his work when I was a teenager. If you're a cinephile, anti-social freak as I was, Bergman was pretty much your common vocabulary with all the other cinephile, anti-social freaks', Schamus recalls. '*The Virgin Spring* locked me in. I felt great excitement years later when I saw Wes Craven's first movie, *Last House on the Left*, and realised it was a remake of *Virgin Spring*. It was a high-culture/low-culture moment I realised that what I thought was high culture was just culture. People forget just how visceral a filmmaker Bergman is. You think of the more symbolist films like *Seventh Seal*, but the fact is that this guy was a master of things we associate with the Hollywood canon, like screen violence.'[33]

It may be prurient and reductive to pore over the private life of an artist like Bergman, but he drew so heavily on his personal experiences in his films and talked so much about his background in interviews and books that it is impossible to separate the work and the biography. Some Bergman admirers were drawn to him precisely because they could identify with elements in his background. For example, the Oscar-winning Taiwanese director Ang Lee was drawn initially to Bergman by parallels in their family circumstances.

'The way I was raised, there was no way to approach art', Lee recalled. 'I have a very stern dad, like Bergman. That's why I felt so close to him.' As a teenage art school student, the young Taiwanese would-be filmmaker saw Bergman's *Virgin Spring*. 'And I was struck, I didn't know what to make of it. How dare someone ask the question where God is, with such beauty. I just couldn't get over it. I stayed on in the cinema, watching it one more time. I think the world changed for me, ever since. That was the epiphany for me, not as an artist, but as a person. I became a thinker.'[34]

In a telling aside in his book *Images*, Bergman reflects on watching 40 years of his work in a single year, a process that turned out to be 'unexpectedly upsetting, at times unbearable. I suddenly realised that my movies had been mostly conceived in the depths of my soul, in my heart, my brain, my nerves, my sex, and not least, in my guts.'[35]

This primal quality can make his films so resonant and sometimes painful for certain viewers too. When director Terence Davies was growing up in an impoverished working-class background in Liverpool, between the ages of 5 and 7, he witnessed his father die at home of cancer.

'It took him two years to die. So I saw someone in agony, dying over two years', Davies recalls. 'It had a very, very profound effect on me. When he died, my mother was a widow. He hadn't paid any National Insurance and so she did not get any (welfare) benefit. I had to sleep in the bed he died in, which was quite traumatic for a seven year old.'[36]

Later, when Davies was a student at the National Film School and saw Bergman's *Cries and Whispers*, the terror he felt as a child was reawakened. This is the film about women in a red room waiting for their sister to die. She endures a grim and painful death. Once she finally dies, she seems to spring back again briefly to life.

'What Bergman does is three things', Davies suggests, 'he shows us the actual death, which is very, very painful and not an easy death. Then, the dead sister is washed and dressed and everything is made to look perfect, as if she is merely asleep. Death becomes decorous. But then that decorousness is broken because she appears to come back to life. It is those three things he is showing the actual agony of death, the way we try to prettify it because it is too horrible to contemplate and then the dead coming back to haunt us and exercise their power over us.'[37]

Death was Bergman's subject. As he told the filmmaker Marie Nyrerod, 'not a day has gone by in my life when I haven't thought about death.'[38] It is there in almost all his work. You find it most famously in the overly familiar image of Max Von Sydow's knight, playing chess with Death on the beach. There are many other embodiments of death in his films: the silent old woman in black who walks past Maj-Britt Nilsson's bereaved lover in *Summer Interlude* or the same actress seeing the blurred outline of a man in a bowler hat in *Waiting Women* 'I had a horrible feeling of death itself waiting for me outside the door', her character Marla recounts. 'A poor pedlar or a friend of the family. It could be explained away. Still I was overcome by a paralysing fear of death and my loneliness became the loneliness of death. It was like in a dream where you try to shout but can't utter a sound.'

In September 2007, two months after my trip to Faro, I visited the Bergman Archive at The Swedish Film Institute. 'I never save anything, out of superstition', Bergman once wrote. 'Others have saved things for me.'[39] The shelves crammed with boxes in a fireproof vault make Bergman's claim seem absurd. He saved everything, including copies of his own correspondence. The records of 65 years of artistic work are stored on shelves and cabinets.

Bergman used his workbooks as diaries; they include drawings and even shopping lists. From the beginning, he frets about his stomach. He often draws images of demons (he-devils and she-devils which are now treated almost as if they are his personal trademark) in the margins. Much of the material is in a very fragile state. Much of it is written in Bergman's hard-to-decipher handwriting.

Just before Bergman died, the Ingmar Bergman Archive received 'Memory Of The World Status' from the Unesco International Advisory Committee.

The archive – whose full contents won't be made available to scholars for another 50 years – is an extraordinary resource. You can't help but wonder why Bergman left this material – much of it deeply personal – behind him if it was not to influence the way in which his reputation was assessed. He was determined to exercise as much control over his life and work as he could. That was part of the allure of the 'magic lantern' right at the outset. Bergman had bribed his older brother with toy soldiers in order to be allowed to take possession of his first movie projector. He was awestruck when the woman in the film moved: 'woke up, sat up, slowly got up, stretched her arms out, swung around and disappeared. If I went on turning, she would again lie there, then make exactly the same movements all over again.'[40] He was somewhere between God and puppet master.

It is telling and poignant that Bergman even sought to choreograph his own funeral. 'People kept the secret from the press until the grave was dug the night before', Faro resident Thomas Soderlund, who provided the wood for Bergman's coffin, told *The International Herald Tribune*. 'These were his instructions. He directed his own funeral.'[41]

Bergman attempted to control which of his films remained in circulation. In Sweden itself, his work was not especially widely distributed. He forbade certain of his films, for example *This Can't Happen Here*, to be shown.

On that bright but cold day in September when I visited the Archive, The Swedish Film Institute was nearly deserted. The students weren't yet back for the autumn term. The restaurant was empty. It is a curious, rectangular building which houses academics, producers, bureaucrats and archivists. The studio space (where Bergman shot *Fanny and Alexander*) is the heart of the building. Everything else has been designed around it. As a result, the building is full of immensely long corridors.

The Film Institute was founded in 1963 and its present building completed seven years later, in 1970. The driving force behind it was its first managing director, former film critic Harry Schein, who was a friend of Bergman. (Schein was married to one of Bergman's 'actresses', Ingrid Thulin. In his earlier days as a journalist, he had also been one of the director's most perceptive and caustic critics.) Schein knew well what drove Bergman. 'If I would tell him I have a cancer and was going to die, he would be extremely sorry, but also extremely curious', he once remarked.

'He (Bergman) is interested in the unhappiness of his friends. He dwells on it – he can get material. We often have long phone calls, and if he asks, "How are you?" and I say, "Fine", he would be extremely disappointed. A human being in pain – he can learn much more.'[42]

Fredrik Gustafson, the young film enthusiast working at the archive, showed me around. One of the boxes we looked at contained material from the very start of Bergman's directorial career. An old notebook from a 1939 stage production of Strindberg's *Lucky Peter's Journey* featured pencil sketches from the young director. Most strikingly, on the top of the page, just above the printed dramatis personae, was an image of a scythe wielding grim reaper. The edge of the reaper's blade touches the face of a bare-breasted woman, who is drawn as if she is a vamp in a George Grosz caricature. There are other doodles in the margins, including an angelic figure with a halo above her head and a prim, ferocious-looking matriarch. What is intriguing about the graffiti-strewn notebook is that all Bergman's pet themes seem to be present here in miniature form.

Bergman is often praised for his naturalistic approach to filmmaking and his ability to elicit raw, unaffected performances from actors who seemed at their most exposed. However, there was always contrivance and sleight of hand in his work. He was never simply, and artlessly, record-ing reality but was moulding the events he depicted. Right from the out-set, Bergman was a puppeteer. He was the creator behind the scenes. On the one hand, this was to do with showmanship and magic. He liked to emphasise the dream-like quality of cinema – the fact that when you are watching a film, you are not watching real movement but an illusion.

The metaphor of the marionette is used again and again in his work. One of his last films was called *From the Life of the Marionettes*, and many of his movies involve puppet shows, dream sequences and mes-merism. On a formal level, there is the sense of the director as a magician, using trompe l'oeil effects to bewilder and enrapture his audiences. On a philosophical level, Bergman's protagonists often appear to be caught by forces beyond their control. They believe that they are acting with free will, but like archetypes in the classical tragedies that Bergman so often called upon, their behaviour seems pre-determined. They can't escape the fates.

1

A Portrait of the Young Filmmaker

THE LOCATION IS the Hedvig Eleanora Church Hall in Stockholm in 1933. A group of teenagers has been meeting regularly in the hall to discuss religion. They are all shortly due to be confirmed into the church. The pastor is encouraging them to discuss what faith means to them. Among the students is the pastor's son: a gangly 15-year-old. Once a year, the pastor organises a film screening for his confirmation class. On this occasion, the film that has been chosen is Victor Sjostrom's *The Phantom Carriage* (1921). An elderly man from the film company Svensk's school department turns up with a projector and several reels of film under his arm. Using some white sheeting, he improvises a cinema screen and begins to show the movie. The 15-year-old kid looks on, enthralled.

To anyone who knows Bergman's work well and believes that it is firmly rooted in his own childhood experiences, a viewing of *The Phantom Carriage* can't help but come as a surprise. The film offers a repository of ideas and themes that Bergman would draw on again and again in his own movies.

Bergman freely acknowledged that watching the film was a key formative experience in his adolescence. 'I remember it as one of the great emotional and artistic experiences of my life', he later wrote.[1]

The Phantom Carriage was to be a constant companion throughout Bergman's career. He would watch it again and again. As a young would-be film director working for Svensk in the early 1940s, long before the era of video and DVD, he paid a small fortune for his own 16-mm copy of the film. Sjostrom was to become an important mentor to him and was to appear in his films *To Joy* and (most famously) *Wild Strawberries*.

That day, watching the silent movie on a big white sheet in a church hall was an epiphany for the teenage Bergman.

What drew him to *The Phantom Carriage*? Why did his father – towards whom he was so hostile – choose that movie to show? Did the film just happen to chime perfectly with his own pet obsessions or did it help create those obsessions?

It is not just the now cliched image of the scythe-wielding 'Death' going on his rounds that anticipates Bergman's work. Perhaps more significant is the way the film treats illness, family discord, guilt and unhappy marriage. The opening scenes of Sister Edit (Astrid Holm), the woman in her bed, dying of consumption, echo moments in Bergman's great film about illness and death, *Cries and Whispers*. The main character David Holm (played by Sjostrom himself) is a quintessentially Bergmanesque figure: tortured, self-destructive, stubborn and cruel.

Like Bergman, Sjostrom is fascinated by the magical, showground side of filmmaking. His cinematographer Julius Jaenzon contrives some startling effects, for example the early sequence in which we first see Death on New Year's Eve, harvesting souls. 'Whoever dies on this Eve must drive the cart of death. For him, a single night is as long as 100 years on earth ... wherever he goes, he is greeted with sorrow and despair.' A businessman is shown committing suicide in his library. He takes a pistol out of the drawer of his desk and holds it to his head. The next moment, the spirit of Death walks through the walls to his slumped body and carries off his soul. The next stop is a drowning man at sea. Jaenzon's camera shows the carriage driving through the water to pick him up.

David Holm (played by Sjostrom himself) is a drunkard living in a hostel. It's almost midnight on New Year's Eve, the moment when the man who dies as the bell chimes will be condemned to take over Death's carriage. He resists pleas to visit the ailing Sister Edit, gets into a drunken brawl and is seemingly killed. At this point, inevitably, the clock strikes 12 and the carriage appears. Death has a very familiar face: it is his old friend Georges. The message for him is that he must face the consequences of the 'evil of his life'.

There is a flashback to idyllic scenes of David as a husband and father. We see David in prison for his drunken behaviour and then learn that his brother is also in jail for killing a man while intoxicated. Grief-stricken and feeling responsible, David agrees to serve the sentence in his brother's stead. When he is finally released from prison and heads for a joyful reunion with his wife, he discovers that she has abandoned him, leaving him to come home to an empty house. He is furious and vengeful.

We next see a scene that is pure Bergman in its unbridled malice. The year before his death, on New Year's Eve, David Holm had turned up at a Salvation Army hostel. There, he had found Sister Edit, working as a nurse. She had taken his germ-ridden coat and tried to sew it together. All night long, she had laboured over the repairs to the coat. David Holm reacted by ripping out the stitches and reducing the coat to its old, torn and tattered state. Sister Edit begged him to visit her the following New Year's Eve.

A year on, we discover that David has given her the disease that is ending her life. She is the first spirit he will have to collect as Death's driver. The reaper ties him up and drags him to Sister Edit's bed. 'It is Death but too soon', she says in words which prefigure the famous scene between the knight and the reaper in *The Seventh Seal*. Holm is the man Sister Edit loves, but he neither knows her nor recognises her. In flash-backs, we see him rebuffing her as he sits drinking. He is a consumptive who coughs in people's faces in the 'hope of finishing them off'. Hatred consumes him. All he wants is to find the wife who abandoned him. Sister Edit has met the wife. She tells her that she must take Holm back and engineers a reunion between them. It is disastrous. He is still brutal, still a drunkard – and still consumptive. At one stage, looking like Jack Nicholson in Stanley Kubrick's *The Shining*, he hacks at his wife's locked door with an axe as she cowers behind it. The wife ends up impoverished and alone with her two children, contemplating suicide. Now on her own deathbed, all Sister Edit wants from the Reaper is a few minutes' grace so she can see David mend his ways. There is a Dickensian-style finale in which this finally happens. David saves his wife from poisoning herself. They are reconciled and the wife accepts that he has finally reformed. As they embrace, David utters the lines that are the film's motto: 'Lord please let my soul come to maturity before it is reaped'.

The Phantom Carriage may be wildly melodramatic, but it is worth dwelling on at length. The prayer that comes at the end, just before the final reel redemption, 'let my soul come to maturity before it is reaped', could stand as a mantra for Bergman's work. Guilt, cruelty, humiliation, death – it is all there.

There is an irony in Bergman seeing what he has called 'one of the greatest of all films'[2] thanks to his father. In most accounts of Bergman's life, Erik Bergman, the Lutheran pastor, is portrayed in a resolutely neg-ative way. He is the distant and aloof figure who used the carpet beater to thrash his children when they stepped out of line. 'After the strokes had been administered, you had to kiss Father's hand, at which forgiveness was declared and the burden of sin fell away,[3] Bergman writes – a telling detail that found its way into his 'ferociously autobiographical' *Fanny and Alexander* (1982).

According to the director's own and others' accounts, his father was a vain and narcissistic pastor who had an actor's ability to captivate an audience when he was in the pulpit but quickly grew moody and depressed when he wasn't performing. He was the martinet with right-wing views. He was the usurper who dragged Bergman's beloved upper-class mother down and stole away the attention and affection that the son felt should be rightly his. He humiliated Bergman – and Bergman hated humiliation. Finally, when he was a young man, beginning his career as a director, Bergman had a stand-up fight with his father. He wrote him a letter, saying they would never see one another again.

Doubtless, Bergman's portrayal of his father is rooted in truth. However, as he acknowledged himself, it was a partial and unfair representation of a man with whom he had much in common. Bergman, too, liked to take to the pulpit. That fearsome temper of his to which all his contemporaries testify and the tendency – at least occasionally – to bully his collaborators may well have had their roots in the parsonage.

The actress Barbro Hiort af Ornas, who first worked with Bergman in student plays in the late 1930s, met the director's father and corroborates some of the testimony about him. 'I didn't like him very much', she recalled during an interview with the author on Faro in the summer of 2007. 'He was very famous as a priest. He was good looking and expressed himself in a poetical manner but as a 16-year-old girl, you see through people. To me, it didn't sound honest. There was a dishonesty about his way. I didn't like him. If Ingmar was harsh with him afterward, that was natural.'[4]

However, Hiort af Ornas makes a crucial point about Bergman that hints at why he was so antagonistic towards his father. 'He (Bergman) dramatised everything – he made the most of it. If you get cross with something, either you try not to think about it or you confront it. That is what Ingmar did. He loved drama, even in his life.'[5]

His former wife, the Estonian concert pianist Kabi Laretei, likewise testifies to Bergman's habit of dramatising his life. She calls him a fantasist. 'They (his parents) had no understanding for his fantasy. They always said he was lying because he had these fantasies.'[6]

In Bergman's own accounts, what must have seemed like minor domestic incidents – everyday rows between father and son – assume a huge symbolic importance. His language – as he writes about his family life – is that of the resistance fighter, pitted against a regime he loathes. It is worth noting, too, that his own record as a father was chequered. As he admitted in a late interview, 'I've been family-lazy. It's quite simply that. I haven't put an ounce of effort into my families.'[7]

There is a very telling detail in a Bergman essay/interview written by the critic John Lahr for *The New Yorker* in the late 1990s. As Lahr was told by Liv Ullmann, Bergman was meeting his youngest daughter Linn Ullmann, then around seven years old, for the first time in four years. '"Oh, Linn," he said, and swung her around in his arms for half a minute. Then he said, "You know, Linn, Daddy has work, too. He has other things to do." And then he left the room. That was it.'[8]

It is noticeable how much more forgiving Bergman became about his father towards the end of his own life. This was not because of any new-found mellowness in old age. His last film *Saraband* (2003) features scenes between a father and a son as raw and brutal as anything found in his earlier work. We see the elderly father Johan (Erland Josephson) humiliate his cash-strapped 61-year-old son Henrik (Borje Ahlstedt) in utterly vicious fashion. Johan radiates contempt as he tells his son: 'I don't give a damn if you hate me. You barely exist. If you didn't have Karin (his daughter), who thank God takes after her mother, you wouldn't exist for me at all.' Bergman shows the son's face in huge close-up, looking crestfallen and utterly bewildered that his father, even after all these years, won't accept him or try to effect a rapprochement with him.

In Bergman's own case, the tone of his observations about his father gradually grew warmer and more understanding. Belatedly, he attempted to see events from his father's perspective as well as his own. In his autobiographical novel *Sunday's Children*, for example, he explores the circumstances in which his father married into his mother's family.

> In himself, the future pastor might have been a mother-in-law's dream: ambitious, well brought up, tidy and relatively handsome. In addition to that, the promise of a decent future in the service of the state. But Mrs Anna had an eye for people. She saw something below the irreproachable surface: moodiness, oversensitivity, a violent temper and sudden emotional coldness.[9]

Intriguingly, Bergman ascribes to his father some of his own temperamental qualities. The Erik he portrays is thin-skinned and suspicious. 'He never forgot a real or imagined injury.'[10]

There is a devastating moment in the book when Erik finds his wife's diaries and realises how little he knows about her, despite having lived with her for 50 years. When father and son talk and discuss Erik's fits of rage and his abusive behaviour towards Bergman and his brother as children, the father tells him: 'Don't you think it punishment enough to sit here at my desk, day after day, reading mother's diaries. She even complains about my sermons.'[11]

Bergman's resentment of his father is at least partly rooted in his recognition of himself in his father. There was a side of him that was ordered and conventional. He had a fetish for punctuality and could not bear actors or journalists who turned up late. As he writes witheringly in *The Magic Lantern*, 'I despise Walter, who appears slightly drunk at half-past ten in the morning and spews out his private complications. I am disgusted by Teresa, who rushes up and embraces me in a cloud of sweat and perfume ... I want calm, order and friendliness.'[12]

As a child growing up in a parsonage, Bergman was on permanent display. His father's parishioners naturally expected Erik Bergman's family to behave in a certain way. Whatever battles the family may have fought in private, the evidence is that they did not let the father down in public. They kept up appearances.

Bergman shared many of his father's demons. 'I am an irascible person with a terrible temper', he admitted in a late interview.[13] He was choleric as a child and still capable of throwing huge tantrums towards the end of his life. Those who have witnessed his fits of temper at first hand speak of them with a mix of awe and affectionate amusement. 'He had it all from the start – the personality and gifts and his talents were obvious at an early age. Of course, he has learned a lot along the way, but the ground for it was all there – even when he was a young boy,' remembers Barbro Hiort af Ornas of her experiences working as an actress in his stage productions in the late 1930s.

> Sometimes, he could grow so angry. If you were late, he got angry. If the sets weren't good enough or ready in time, he got very angry – very angry, indeed! When something went wrong, he went mad! He would shout and leave us dramatically. He had a very bad temper and even fainted on several occasions of rage![14]

Actors browbeaten by him must have felt very similarly to the little boys in the parsonage who were the butt of their father's wrath.

Kabi Laretei believes that after Erik Bergman's death in 1970 (following on from that of Bergman's mother in 1966), Bergman began to think about his parents in a more forgiving way. Laretei had noticed that whenever he was in their presence, his personality changed: he became more nervous, less at ease. She talks about the stiff, formal way in which they approached life. 'There was nothing spontaneous about that family.'[15]

Laretei's own family communicated in an easy, informal way – so she was startled by just how aloof the Bergmans' behaviour often appeared to be. 'At the table, there was all this discipline and a certain kind of respect that children had to show to parents, which was completely strange to me,' Laretei recalls. 'His father liked me. I felt he liked me as a musician and a person. (But) I had heard from Ingmar how he was treated as a child and I could never get over that.'[16]

As harsh as he was to his father, Bergman was rhapsodic about his mother. 'Mother is beautiful, really the most beautiful of all imaginable people, more beautiful than the Virgin Mary and Lillian Gish', he writes in *Sunday's Children*. In *The Magic Lantern*, he talked about his little ruses to win her attention and the way he used to cling to her. 'My four-year-old heart was consumed with dog-like devotion.'

Bergman firmly believed that his artistic gifts came from his mother. This was surely because he idealised her and liked her considerably more than he did his father. There was little to suggest that she was especially artistic. Her biggest stimulus to her son's budding career was to force him to use such ingenuity to win her attention. As was underlined when her diaries were discovered after her death, she shared her son's quality of brute honesty. There was no self-deception or gilding in her account of her family life and frequently unhappy marriage.

The Oedipal strain in his relationship with his parents is self-evident. What is also clear is his talent and need for self-dramatisation. The notion that he, like most other children, had a sometimes tempestuous relationship with his parents wasn't acceptable to him. He needed to create an epic narrative and to ascribe weighty, symbolic significance to incidents that others might see simply as the abrasion of a typical family life. In particular, he liked to view himself as a victim. He was self-obsessed. 'I considered myself to be a piece of shit, a real good for nothing',[18] he told his friend Jorn Donner, but low self-esteem didn't seem to affect his opinion of his own creative gifts or his intolerance of others' perceived shortcomings.

'I was appallingly introspective during a great part of my early life, totally closed up', he told Swedish Television in a 1975 interview.

'I fought like mad to get out of this prison. A prison probably built up in childhood as a protective layer against a reality which was too horrific and brutal
for me. In that prison, I performed ritualistic acts to exorcise my loneliness
and confusion. It often became sterile and pretentious but the more I managed to pull down these walls, both with my work and through the help of
my friends, the closer reality came to me.'[19]

Reality may have been horrific and brutal, but he later accepted that
his parents weren't wilfully sadistic: they were simply reacting as best
they could to the way in which their children behaved. There were happy
times – parties and theatre trips. Erik Bergman wasn't an entirely oppressive figure. He had at least some capacity for joy. As Bergman later
conceded, his parents were basically decent people, doing the best that
they could. It wasn't their fault or intention that the children's upbringing
was 'sheer hell'.[20]

Ernest Ingmar Bergman was born on 14 July 1918 in Uppsala. Given
his obsession with death, it is perversely fitting that his mother was suffering from Spanish influenza at the time of his birth. She was one of the
victims of the pandemic which is estimated to have killed over 50 million people between the spring of 1918 and the summer of 1920. The
idea that death could come calling for anyone at any time, an underly-
ing theme in *The Phantom Carriage* and in Bergman's work as a whole,
wasn't just an abstraction in Europe in this period. It was something that
almost every family had experienced directly.

Bergman's parents were not entirely confident that he would survive.
They quickly had him baptised at the hospital just in case he didn't pull
through. 'I suffered from several indefinable illnesses and could never
really decide whether I wanted to live at all',[21] he recalls on the very
first page of *The Magic Lantern*, clearly relishing the drama surround-
ing his birth. It was only fitting that he should make an eye-catching
entrance.

Bergman's reminiscences of his childhood, growing up in the grace
and favour parsonage of Sophiahemmet in the heart of Stockholm, are
predictably ambivalent. (His father was appointed chaplain to the Royal
Hospital in Sophiahemmet in 1924.) Joy and misery are always intertwined. 'I think that anything I have done of any value is rooted in my
childhood. Or in dialectic terms, it is a dialogue with my childhood,' he
told Jorn Donner. 'I've never distanced myself from my childhood but
have continued a dialogue with it.'[22]

His memories of his early years are incredibly precise. He can describe smells, sights and sounds from a time that predates his ability to

talk or write. It was his proud boast, often repeated, that he could remember every last detail about his beloved grandmother's flat in Uppsala. He knows somehow that his wet nurse was fair and blonde. The image he presents of himself is complicated and contradictory. On the one hand, he was a little terrorist, plotting mischief, bitterly competitive with his older brother Dag. On the other hand, he was a sensitive and forlorn boy with an imagination which had the ability to fill him with dread. The fear of betrayal was with him right from the outset. In particular, he had an early terror that his mother was trying to abandon him and clung to her as a consequence. Desperate for her attention, he would feign indifference to her or pretend to be ill in order to ensure that she doted on him. The passage in his autobiography in which he recounts how he and his brother tried to kill their younger sister, the 'fat, monstrous creature' who had usurped their place in their mother's affections, seems only partly tongue-in-cheek.

The cruel and elaborate games he played with his mother and the constant oscillation in their relationship – the sudden lurches between tenderness and antagonism – anticipate the often similarly vexed relationships between lovers, spouses, parents and children in his films.

Hearing Bergman's descriptions of his childhood, it is easy to be reminded of Freud's phrase 'his majesty the child'. Bergman behaved like a little monarch. One can't help but also be reminded of William Blake's *Songs of Innocence* and *Songs of Experience*, his visionary poetry portraying childhood both as a state of pre-lapserian innocence and wonder and as a time of intense suffering. In his autobiography, Bergman writes about his own childhood as a time of 'delight and curiosity', when the world around him was exploding with 'wonders, unexpected sights and magical moments'.[23] Joy and terror nestled side by side.

Again and again in Bergman's films, we are presented with a character who yearns after some lost age of innocence – a time in which (at least in symbolic fashion) the child was still doted on by its mother. There is the buffoonish circus master Albert Johnasson (Ake Gronberg) in *Sawdust and Tinsel* (1953), hankering again after all the years on the road for the comfort of a domestic life with Agda, the wife he abandoned so long before. Equally consumed with longing is the elderly professor Isak Borg (Victor Sjostrom) in *Wild Strawberries* (1957), lost in the memories of the summers of his childhood. The warmth and humour of the prolonged Christmas celebrations that open *Fanny and Alexander* (1982) provide a stark counterpoint to the bleakness of so much that follows.

One of the most glaring paradoxes about Bergman was that such a supreme chronicler of children's lives in all their terror and joy was so uninterested in kids. Bergman had an uncanny knack for capturing a child-eye view of the world, but the only childhood he really seemed curious about was his own. There are other filmmmakers who stood up fervently for children. For example, François Truffaut could not bear cruelty against children. Films like *The 400 Blows* or *L'Argent du Poche* weren't simply about the suffering of some sensitive young protagonist but about the plight of children as a whole. That Dickensian-like affinity for kids and determination to stand up for them was not something that Bergman shared.

'He has a wonderful way with children and he talks to them in a magic way', Kabi Laretei observed of him shortly before his death. 'With his grandchildren, he tells them stories and he is great fun – but he gets very easily tired of them – so he doesn't want too much. He is wonderful with children but he can't have them too near. It is simply his way of getting his mood of solitude for creative thinking – and when children come in, you can't (think creatively).'[24]

Bergman's childhood was the acknowledged wellspring of his creativity. However, it is striking how rarely children feature in his films about marriages coming apart at the seams. Whether in *Scenes from a Marriage* or *From the Life of the Marionettes*, when the adults rage against one another, we don't see kids on the edge of frame, begging their parents to stop arguing. They are simply not there. Only in his script for *Faithless* (2000), which was directed by Liv Ullmann, was the break-up of a marriage seen (at least partly) from a child's perspective.

When Ullmann was asked how men and women had reacted differently to *Faithless*, she pointed out that men were far more upset than women about how the child suffered as a result of the marriage break-up.[25] This may have been a factor of the times. In the late 1990s, the era of the 'new man', fathers were very conscious of their responsibilities to their children. In the 1940s and 1950s, when Bergman was a young man, such responsibilities did not seem paramount. Bergman had several broken marriages and fathered several children, but he didn't go on to make films about the dilemmas of parenthood.

Ullmann contends that you can't damage a grown-up life. It is children who suffer in the fallout when their parents' relationships falter, but only rarely was Bergman interested in telling their stories.

As a husband, Laretei recalls, Bergman needed reassurance and pampering. Children would threaten that security. He would grow intensely jealous when Laretei was away on a concert tour. 'There were too much misunderstandings when I was on trips with him wanting me to ring him, and a hotel in Italy would say that I hadn't come – he was always thinking I was unfaithful.'[26]

It should also be added that Bergman's private life was constantly in upheaval. He was married five times and had several other serious relationships, often with actresses with whom he worked. Laretei speculates that his was yet another case of a man looking for his mother in the women he married.

'There was a great longing in him for security – for someone who took care (of him) and was secure', Laretei says. Their own marriage in 1959 represented Bergman's self-conscious quest for bourgeois stability. At times, he appears to have overlooked the fact that she was an artist too. 'Everyone thought I came into Ingmar's life as a bourgeois person. My father was a diplomat and so on. It was exactly the other way round. And he wanted absolutely to have a church marriage etc. and the house bought. I was scared to death. I thought we don't know each other that well. Can we really live together? He was very dependent to build up something he had had as a child – a bourgeois (life) with a maid who was cooking and so on and hardly meeting anyone.'[27]

Meanwhile, he was so devoted to his profession that there was little space for a conventional bourgeois family life. Ironically, one of the reasons that he spent so little time with his children was that there were so many of them. He had so many families and children to provide for that he could not afford to take time off to act the model father.

When he was the artistic director of the Royal Dramatic Theatre in Stockholm in the early 1960s, Bergman would begin work before 8 am and would not arrive home until close to midnight. Summer holidays weren't easy to take for an artist who often worked in the theatre during the autumn and spring and then shot his movies when the light improved (and he had time off) in May, June and July.

'I lived very simply', he told Jorn Donner in a revealing interview he gave late in his life. 'I always had some flat or other. And they were always furnished. And then I got married very often. I don't remember much about my private life, to be honest. When I want to date something, I refer to films or plays. I can't remember when my children were born. I know their ages roughly.'[28]

Only with his final marriage, to Ingrid Von Rosen in 1971, did he finally achieve the domestic security that he had so long been yearning for. 'She was all that he needed – a housewife and a practical person.

She arranged things', Laretei observes. 'I think that Ingrid in a way was almost a portrait of his mother.'[29]

In Bergman's late workbooks, you can find occasional hints as to how domestic concerns entered into his professional life. For example, in the workbook for *The Serpent's Egg* (1976), the first film he made during his 'exile' in Munich, there is a poignant little passage written by Ingrid herself about what the couple planned to eat for dinner on New Year's Day. This entry, entitled *History about a Duck*, nestles next to all the diary-like observations that Bergman makes about his bad stomach (one of his constant preoccupations), his sleeplessness and his hypochondria. 'This is a true story viewed from the wife's perspective of how it can turn out when you are married to a genius. It swam. It just happened,' Ingrid observes. Her tone is affectionate and gently ironic.

> The day before New Year's Eve I thought I would do all my shopping on New Year's Eve. The shops closed early and there are a lot of people. What shall we eat on New Year's Eve! I would like to have salmon from Sweden or caviar, turkey and chocolate mousse. But the turkey was so very big, I thought that since Ingmar only eats the same thing twice, it's a pity. So I bought a duck instead. Added to that, I bought apple jam, red cabbage – although I know Ingmar doesn't eat that – I also bought veal and some raw meat. New Year's Day. In the morning, I say we will have duck but Ingmar says he can't eat it. It is too fat. I had forgotten. He goes to Bavaria. I run to the oven and fry the duck so it will not smell in the afternoon.... I take out the veal so Ingmar will get that instead. I see that the duck is actually rather fat but I fry it anyway and put it out on the balcony. In fact, I am rather angry because there is something that you can never do with Ingmar.
>
> Now I am going to Bavaria where at the strike of 12.15, I have fried Ingmar's two eggs and squeezed out his sour cream in a paper cup. Now it gets boring. Ingmar thinks that I made the duck out of aggression. We argue. I begin to laugh but Ingmar is still not laughing. In the end, Ingmar decides to – with death in his heart – eat the duck and be happy. I have suddenly developed a feeling of disgust toward the duck and I put it in a plastic bag and throw it away. Quickly, I defrost some more veal and make a very good dinner.'[30]

The anecdote about the duck testifies to Bergman's extraordinary particularity: his insistence that in his private life, as in his professional life, everything has to be 'just so'. It also hints at the way that Ingrid mollycoddled her husband, almost as if he was still a kid. When you are married to a genius and he wants his eggs on the stroke of 12.15, you had better make sure you provide them. The humour is revealing too. In Bergman's work, couples have momentous rows about their re-lationships and behave as if on leave from Strindberg plays. Here, the focus of the drama is simply a duck that Bergman may or may not eat for lunch.

The story also testifies to how easily Bergman (admittedly abetted here by his wife) could make a simple, everyday incident assume a weighty symbolic significance.

In the mythology Bergman created around his own early life, one incident stands out. 'Then came the cinematograph', reads the single sentence paragraph in his autobiography announcing the arrival of cinema in his young life.[31] He was around eight years old when he spotted the projector in the photographic store, Forsners, on Hamngatan, one of Stockholm's main shopping streets. He yearned to own such a magical piece of equipment. A year or so before, he had seen his first movie, an adaptation of *Black Beauty*. What struck in his memory was the dramatic fire sequence in which the horses have to be rescued from the burning stables. Bergman doesn't specify which version of Anna Sewell's much-filmed novel he saw. It was probably the 1921 Vitagraph production, starring Jean Paige – a big Hollywood success of the period. Whatever the case, this early cinema-going experience made a strong impression.

Bergman had a Proust-like capacity to re-invoke what he called the landscape of his childhood. In interviews, he often talked about his grandmother, who lived in a big flat in Uppsala and often used to take him to the cinema. He could still recall the precise sound she made when she rubbed her galoshes together during lovemaking scenes, of which she disapproved. He had equally vivid recollections of his wealthy Aunt Anna. She was the relative most generous with her largesse at Christmas time. One Christmas, he spotted a parcel from Forsners among the presents she had brought. This, he hoped, was the projector that he so badly wanted. It was indeed the projector, but by one of those reversals we encounter so often in his work, he was not the recipient. This was yet another occasion on which the young Ingmar was humiliated. All he received from his wealthy aunt was a teddy bear, a present he was already far too old for. His brother Dag, four years older than him, was given the projector. Bergman's initial reaction to the injustice of it all was to retreat under the table and howl away in self-pity. Then, showing the resourcefulness and cunning later to become his hallmark, he entered into negotiations with Dag. In return for half his toy soldiers, Dag agreed to give him the projector.

The ecstasy Bergman felt in using his magic lantern can still be felt years later, in the many descriptions he gave in interviews or in his own writing about his early experiments in film projection. It wasn't just the machinery itself he took joy in – the metal box with mirrors, lenses and lights that allowed him to watch images in the safety of the nursery wardrobe. The images too enraptured him. They were a voyeur's delight. There was a hint of the forbidden in what he was looking at. By cranking the handle on the projector, he could make a woman asleep in a meadow miraculously spring to life and move. He was in control. If he repeated his mechanical actions, she would dance her pretty arabesque for him all over again.

Who was this woman? On the box in which the film came was an etching and the words Frau Holle. 'Who Frau Holle was, nobody among my acquaintances knew but that did not matter very much, the film was a great success and was projected every night till it broke and could not be mended any more.'[32]

The magic lantern is one of the key motifs in Bergman's life and work. It gave the name to his autobiography. On both literal and metaphorical levels, his movies are full of puppeteers and magicians, manipulating characters just as Bergman manipulated that woman in the meadow the first time he started using his cinematograph.

The opening images of *Fanny and Alexander* (1982), his most openly autobiographical film, are of the boy Alexander playing with his puppet theatre. We see his face framed through the curtains of the puppet theatre. Later, at the end of the Christmas party, as the children are sent to bed, Alexander is shown setting up his magic lantern in the dark. We see him dismantle the projector. Lovingly but furtively, he feeds the coloured lantern slides into the machine. His sister wakes up and joins him in his illicit game. The first images are of a beautiful girl (the poor Arabella) alone in a big, dark house. 'Her mother is dead and her father is carousing with loose companions', Alexander narrates the film show. As midnight strikes, a ghost enters the frame. The terrifying figure floating on moonbeams by Arabella's bed is her dead mother's ghost. (The plot for this performance seems like a mix of *Hamlet* and *The Phantom Carriage*.) Noises and the smell of paraffin attract the attention of Alexander's father (later to die on stage during an amateur production of *Hamlet*). Rather than punish the children, he puts on his own performance using as his central prop a chair, about which he spins a far-fetched story.

Variations on magic lantern shows – some innocent, some sinister in the extreme – are found again and again in his movies. In *The Serpent's Egg* (1976), we see sequences from the films of patients being tortured by the Josef Mengele-like scientist, Vergerus. In *Hour of the Wolf* (1966), we see *The Magic Flute* performed in miniature. In *Persona* (1965), there is the prologue which pastiches early silent comedy.

Bergman often described directing as being like necromancy.

> I work like a conjurer. The basic thing in cinematography is the perforated film containing 52 frames per metre, each separated by a thick black line. On closer study we see that these small frames, which at first glance seem to be similar photographs of the same subject, are slightly different to each other due to movement of the subject. By means of projection, when each of these small frames appears on the screen for a twenty-fourth of a second, we are given the illusion of movement.[33]

As a storyteller, Bergman was at liberty to invent and embellish. He is not always consistent in his accounts of his childhood. In some interviews, he says that he first received the magic lantern as an eight-year-old. In *What It Means to Make a Film*, a revealing lecture he gave at the University of Lund, Sweden, in 1959, the chronology has changed. He says that he was ten years old when he received his 'first rattling film projector with its chimney and lamp which went round and round and round. [He] found it both mystifying and fascinating'.[34]

In this lecture, he draws connections between what he witnessed every day as the son of a parson and the wondrous world projected through the cinematograph.

'If one is born and brought up in a vicarage one gets an early picture of behind the scenes of life and death', he told his audience of students. 'Father performed funerals, marriages, baptisms, gave advice and prepared sermons. The devil was an early acquaintance and in the child's mind there was the need to personify him. This was how the magic lantern came in. It consisted of a little metal box with a carbide lamp (I can still remember the smell of the hot metal) and coloured glass slides. Red Riding Hood and the Wolf and all the others. And the Wolf was the Devil, without horns, but it had a tail and a gaping red mouth, strangely real but yet inapprehensible, a picture of wickedness and temptation on the flowered wall of the nursery.'[35]

It is fascinating how Bergman ascribes religious and eschatological meanings to cinema right from the outset. That 'little metal box', as he called the projector, wasn't just a fairground attraction for him: a piece of apparatus that made pretty and diverting patterns. It was far more subversive than that. The cinematograph projected images of innocence and temptation, of life and death. For Bergman, it also became a metaphor for memory. In much of his fiction, autobiographical writing and

interviews, he describes incidents – especially those from his childhood –
as if he is seeing them projected through that magic lantern. The impressions they leave are fractured, dreamlike, sometimes magical and sometimes deeply disturbing. Morbidity and eroticism go hand in hand. The
young Bergman was proud of his friendship with hospital workers and
morticians. He loved to see the corpses, the amputated limbs and bloody
organs. Death obsessed him. In *The Magic Lantern*, there is Uncle Carl
'lying between the tracks with multiple injuries'[36] after being crushed in
a railway tunnel; there is the boy who drowns and whose body is discovered months later, 'his stomach full of eels and eels coming out of his
mouth and backside';[37] and there is the account of being locked inside
the mortuary as a ten-year-old. Death is associated with sexuality. When
he was a boy just on the threshold of puberty, he claims in an anecdote
which may have been apocryphal but clearly had an immense symbolic
resonance for him, he was locked inside the mortuary at the Sophiahemmet. In the inner room, among the other corpses, was the body of a recently deceased and very beautiful young woman. He was drawn towards
her by some morbid, voyeuristic urge. He pulled back the sheet that covered her.

> She was quite naked apart from a plaster that ran from throat to pudenda. I
> lifted a hand and touched her shoulder. I had heard about the chill of death,
> but the girl's skin was not cold, but hot. I moved my hand to her breast, which
> was small and slack, with an erect black nipple ... I could see her sex, which
> I wanted to touch but did not dare.[38]

Bergman tells this story in such a way that we are not sure whether
this is a real memory or a fantasy. He even wonders if the girl was playing
a practical joke on him. The scene is recreated in fictional form in *Hour
of the Wolf*. Here, the scene is deliberately stylised and dreamlike. The
artist Johan Borg (Max Von Sydow) is shown being made up (symbolically humiliated) by the rich aristocrats on the island. He walks down the
castle's long, bird-filled corridors and finds an empty room with a sheet-
covered table in the middle. He slowly pulls the sheet back, revealing
the naked, seemingly dead, body of the beautiful Veronica Vogler
(Ingrid Thulin), the former lover with whom he is obsessed. He traces
her features with his hand, working his way down from her breast to her
sex. Suddenly, she leaps up laughing grotesquely and tries to kiss him.
The cackles of the aristocrats, secretly watching, reveal that this has all
been an elaborate ruse. He is being mocked. As the camera trains on his
face, his voice becomes inaudible.

What is intriguing is how unreliable Bergman's memory appears to be and how he deliberately blurs lines between his experiences and his fantasies, his real life and his films. It is as if each feeds off the other. In chronicling his own life, he is a deceptive narrator, playful and sombre by turns. He seems to be brutally honest about everything: ready to expose everything from his bad digestion to his adolescent sexual fantasies, from his political mis-steps (e.g. his adolescent Nazism) to the flagrant lies he often told as a kid. It is surely surprising that someone who described himself as a shy, self-conscious and isolated child is so ready to bare his secrets. However, there is always the sense that he is holding something back. His anecdotes, even the ones most damning of his own behaviour, don't have the air of spontaneity. They are as carefully crafted as the storylines in his screenplays. They are drawn from real life and yet are at a distance from it.

Moreover, he clearly found it therapeutic to reveal the most intimate aspects of his own life in the most public way – as incidents to be watched on screen. He testified again and again to how introspective he was as a young adolescent. His own temperament was like a prison to him. He struggled to escape this prison, fighting against his taciturnity and mood swings. Closing himself to the outside world was, on the one hand, a protective measure. He could retreat from people and events that threatened him. On the other hand, it was obvious how much he yearned to escape his self-constructed prison and to engage with the outside world.

> The more I managed to pull down these walls, both with my work and through the help of my friends, the closer reality came to me.[39]

What was Bergman's memory really like? He claimed that he had a very poor memory and that was why he kept a 'black book' in which he wrote down the names of people he didn't like. Others suggest that his memory was incredibly precise. He would never forget a slight or a bad review – he didn't need to take notes to remind him of aggravating events or circumstances in his past but could hold on, vice-like, to all the bleakest details. Meanwhile, sounds or smells could trigger off those involuntary memories of childhood that he refers to again and again in self-consciously Proustian fashion: for instance his grandmother's apartment or the family's summer house or the first time he visited the island of Faro, when scouting for *Through a Glass Darkly*.

It is striking how often his memories appeared to be wrapped up with guilt and regret. There is sometimes something self-indulgent about his relish in prostrating himself and the glee with which he basks in his own wretchedness. As the critic Gabriele Annan wrote of *The Magic Lantern*, 'the autobiography is exactly like the films, beautiful and repulsive; truthful and phoney, constantly startling and occasionally embarrassing'.[40]

Bergman used to joke that he didn't leave puberty until he reached his late 50s. In his films and writing, there are often traces of an adolescent desire to shock. Not many other major artists are so frank in sharing details of their teenage masturbatory habits. 'My nice little willie, which I had previously regarded with absent-minded interest, had suddenly been transformed into a throbbing demon sending violent sensations of pain up towards my stomach and down towards my thighs', he writes in a tone that is both comic and grotesque – and exaggerated for maximum effect. 'I didn't know what to do with this mighty enemy. I took a firm hold of him with my hand and the detonation occurred simultaneously. To my dismay, an unknown fluid spurted out over my hands, my trousers, the toilet seat, the net curtain over the window, the walls and the blue towelling mat on the floor.'[41] In other words, this wasn't so much an orgasm as a dam bursting.

Jean-Luc Godard is said to have called film history 'a history of boys photographing girls'. This may not have been a thesis that Bergman endorsed, but it was surely one part of his fascination with the celluloid muse.

'Drama and film are incontrovertibly two professions that are immensely erotically charged', he told the interviewer Marie Nyrerod in a late interview, talking of the 'incredibly pleasurable tensions' that the quest for perfection shared by him and his actors could cause.[42] As is well chronicled, he had several affairs with his collaborators, in particular his actresses – Harriet Andersson, Bibi Andersson, Liv Ullmann and others.

In Bergman's cosmos, flesh, the devil and God always sit side by side. Describing his attraction for cinema, he uses an extraordinary array of metaphors. One moment, he is the wizard. The next, he is the humble artisan. One of his favourite claims for himself is that he was skilled: like or dislike his work, you can't deny that it is well put together.

'I want to be one of the artists on the Cathedral on the great plain', he declared in a rousing (if not altogether honest) lecture that he gave in the late 1950s. (He may have paid lip service to the idea of being the anonymous craftsman, but he was always interested in recognition too.)

> I want to make a dragon's head, an angel or a devil or perhaps a saint out of stone, it does not matter which: it is the feeling of contentment that matters. Regardless whether I believe or not, regardless whether I am a Christian or

not, I play my part at the collective building of the Cathedral for I am an artist and a craftsman and I know how to chisel stones into faces and figures. I never need to concern myself about present opinion or the judgement of the after world, I am a name which has not been recorded anywhere and which will disappear when I myself disappear, but a little part of me will live on in the triumphant masterwork of the anonymous builders. A dragon, a devil or perhaps a saint, it does not matter which.[43]

He saw something sacral in filmmaking. This son of a chaplain who had grown up in the shadow of the church was fascinated by religious art. His father, with whom he had such a vexed relationship, not only introduced him to Victor Sjostrom's *The Phantom Carriage* but also would take him to visit churches. Bergman's admiration for the work of the ecclesiastical painter Albertus Pictor is well chronicled. It was in a church in Uppland that he saw the image that inspired one of his best-known films, *The Seventh Seal*. This image showed Death playing chess with a knight. Admittedly, the image is a long way removed from the ghoul in the black cape playing chess on the beach with Max Von Sydow in the film. The knight is not a gaunt, blond-haired Scandinavian, but wears a green tunic and white stockings and has red hair. Death, meanwhile, is a reddish skeleton.

Bergman was open to a unique range of influences: everything from the Swedish fad of the 1940s for naturism and summer movies to the pull of the church, in all its pomp and formality. His interest in the church and in showmanship and magic went hand in hand. This mix of influences partly explains why his films so often wrong-foot viewers: they are solemn when you don't expect it and playful when you expect them to be solemn. They can be both austere and flamboyantly melodramatic. There is a mercurial quality to the work which reveals the personality behind it.

What is also evident is an extreme recklessness. This is both formal and thematic. Bergman's characters may be bourgeois couples, but he is ready to push beyond the boundaries of 'good taste' in the way he anatomises their relationships. 'What I learned from Bergman is that you can explore human relationships with a certain level of brutality and crudity as long as you love your characters', French director Olivier Assayas noted of him.[44] He was also willing to throw in complex dream sequences and flashbacks and to lay bare his own devices. (This happens most disconcertingly in *The Passion of Anna*, in which the four main actors are all shown on camera, discussing their roles.)

In his descriptions of himself as a director working with his actors, Bergman can sometimes sound more like a doctor (or a priest with his parishioners) than an artist. After some grim experiences early in his career, when he tried to behave like a great maestro and ended up alienating his colleagues, the more mature Bergman would go to extreme lengths to create a pleasant and professional atmosphere. During rehearsals, he would ask for plentiful supplies of fruits and flowers. His own feelings would be kept strictly under wraps. Although he was still capable of throwing huge tantrums when props weren't delivered or technicians let him down, he endeavoured to maintain an even-handed and professional demeanour. Method and discipline were everything. 'I am first and foremost a craftsman and I make fine goods for people's use. And I'd be very upset if it should ever come to pass that no one wanted to use my goods,' he once stated.[45]

As his former wife Kabi Laretei testifies, Bergman relished the objectivity and professionalism of classically trained musicians and yearned for his actors to show the same discipline. 'He often said that as musicians start when they are children and they have work severely. Actors become actors when they are grown up and there is no precision in what they do. I have terrific precision if I play Bach. He (Bergman) said music is much more precise than words.'[46]

As rigorous as he was, Bergman realised that creativity required intuition, indulgence and a degree of disorder. In a telling passage in *The Magic Lantern*, he recalls his relationship as a young director with a much older actress. 'She scorned my cleanliness theory and maintained that theatre is shit, lust, rage and wickedness', he writes. The actress used to taunt him about his 'passion for the wholesome' and to encourage him to seek out his 'syphilitic whore'. He adds a coda to the anecdote, pointing out that this actress, so in touch with her raw emotions and so disdainful towards order and conventional thought, ended up dying a squalid and premature death.[47] Bergman was determined not to go the same way. He could draw on his demons for inspiration, but he would never allow them to take over.

His ability to remain analytical even in the most extreme circumstances was made evident in the wake of his battles with the Swedish tax authorities in the mid-1970s. Exhausted and close to nervous breakdown, he spent almost a fortnight in a mental clinic. Even here, he was able to distance himself from his own problems and to observe what was going on around him. 'I tell you, the time at the clinic was very fascinating. They took me to the clinic. There I lived with 12 other patients, day after day, night after night. I learned a lot. It was an enormous experience of human experience. That time – ten days I think it was – are the most important days of my life,' he later boasted.[48]

The story illustrates perfectly Bergman's uncanny ability to keep life and work separate. His domestic life may have been in upheaval and his finances in a parlous state; he may have been in dispute with critics and potential financiers. Whatever the case, nothing distracted him from his relentless focus on the script he was writing or the play he was rehearsing or the film he was shooting. The work was the one fixed point in his otherwise often chaotic and turbulent existence.

2

Early Work

'SOMEWHERE IN THE depths of my conceited soul, I nurture one conceited notion. One day, perhaps, one day something shining and beautiful will be prised out of all this wretchedness. Like a tiny, tiny pearl and a big, black ugly mussel shell. If one day something beautiful might come from me, then I will have answered my calling in life.' Thus wrote the 20-year-old Bergman in a notebook in 1938. The tone may be affected, but the would-be artist knew his mission right from the outset.[1]

Five years later, when he took his first teetering steps in the film business, he turned to his school days in search of inspiration. His experiences at Palmgren's School in Ostermalm, Stockholm, provided the inspiration for his first filmed screenplay, *Frenzy*, a.k.a. *Torment* (1944), directed by Alf Sjoberg. As if as a foretaste of Bergman's films to come, the very first image of the film is a huge close-up of a wretchedly unhappy couple.

By late 1944, Bergman had spent close to two years in the script department at Svensk Filmindustri, the leading Swedish film company. By his own admission, he was considered 'talented but difficult'. He already had extensive experience as a stage director, both from his student days at Stockholm University, where he had studied art and literature between 1938 and 1941, and from the host of amateur productions he had directed at Master Olofsgarden, a youth centre in Stockholm. He had tackled Shakespeare and Strindberg. He had written and staged several stage plays of his own. He had also run Sagoteatern, one of Sweden's leading children's theatres. These flickerings of early talent had brought him to the attention of Stina Bergman (no relation), who headed Svensk's script department. She was the widow of Hjalmar Bergman, a major Swedish novelist and playwright.

For Bergman's development as a filmmaker and screenwriter, the key fact about Stina Bergman was that she had spent time in Hollywood. Her husband was Victor Sjostrom's favourite screenwriter. When Sjostrom was hired by Louis B. Mayer at MGM in 1923, Hjalmar Bergman travelled with him. Hjalmar may not have prospered in Hollywood, but his wife was able to witness the Hollywood machine at first hand. Back in Europe two decades later, she was trying to apply some of what she had learned from the studio system.

There is a certain irony in the fact that Bergman's screenwriting apprenticeship was so influenced by the Hollywood studio model. He is seen now as the quintessential European auteur: an artist and a filmmaker who spoke always in his own voice. However, he freely admitted the benefits of Stina Bergman's methods. Through her, he developed a special admiration for filmmakers like Billy Wilder, William Wellman and George Cukor. Her emphasis was on clarity. As he writes in *Images: My Life in Film*, the techniques she encouraged were formulaic.

'The audience must never have the slightest doubt where they were in a story. Nor could there be any doubt about who was who, and the transitions between various points of the story were to be treated with care. High points should be allotted and placed at specific points in the script.'[2] Stina Bergman distrusted literary affectation and insisted that dialogue be kept as terse as possible.

Bergman's experiences as a young, desk-bound scriptwriter, working to order and often revising others' original ideas, provided a stark contrast to his writing for the theatre. In the early 1940s, when he was convalescing from the ulcer which had given him exemption from military service, he had completed a dozen stage plays and an operetta. Now, the precocious would-be genius was learning to buckle down. He likened Stina Bergman's regime at Svensk to a 'slaveship', but he saw its benefit too.

Throughout his filmmaking career, Bergman took an extraordinarily disciplined approach to screenwriting, setting aside a specific amount of time each day and working to clear targets. He was always aware of story structure.

Frenzy is a fascinating affair betraying a range of often contradictory influences on its impressionable young writer. On the one hand, it is a 'school days' drama, about rebellious pupils and a sadistic teacher. On the other, it is a tortuous and dark love triangle drama, as much about sexual jealousy and class and generational conflict as it is about scrapes in the classroom. Sjoberg shoots in a self-consciously expressionistic fashion. The school's corridors and staircases are often shown bathed in shadows. There are swooping camera movements, high-angle shots, constant use of staircases, jarring close-ups and strong melodramatic elements.

Bergman had written *Frenzy* as a short story after his baccalaureate exam, during a period of convalescence in hospital. The main character is Jan-Erik (Alf Kjellin), a good-looking, highly strung student with more than a trace of Bergman about him. He is pitted against a sinister father figure, the sadistic teacher 'Caligula' (Stig Jarrel). Their antagonism becomes horribly fraught when both realise that they are in relationships with the same girl – the flirtatious, working-class Bertha (Mai Zetterling). All the familiar Bergman themes are here in roughened form: family discord, sexual jealousy and Oedipal tension.

Much in the screenplay was autobiographical. The character of Caligula really existed. He was called the jockey because he rode Bergman and his fellow school pupils so hard that they lost confidence and risked becoming failures. He was their English teacher and had a special animus against Bergman.

However, as so often in Bergman's subsequent works, Bergman dramatised and exaggerated the elements from his own life. Henning L. Hakanson, headmaster at the Palmgren's School, was both offended and surprised by comments Bergman made at the time of the film's release, suggesting that his school days had been hellish.

'Mr Bergman's statement, that his entire time at school was hell, surprises me', Hakanson wrote to the newspaper *Aftonbladet*. 'I clearly recall that he, his brother and his father were all very satisfied with the school. After his final examinations, Ingmar Bergman came back to school to attend our Christmas party, bright and cheery as far as one could tell, and not seeming to harbour any grudge, either against the school or its teachers. In all probability, the fact of the matter lies elsewhere. Our friend Ingmar was a problem child, lazy yet rather gifted, and the fact that such a person does not easily adapt to the daily routines of study is quite natural. A school cannot be adapted to suit bohemian dreamers, but to suit normally constituted, hard working people.'[3]

Bergman replied that he had not set out to criticise just his own school, but schools in general. He claimed that he hated the institutional life with its rigid routines and emphasis on homework, punctuality and exams. Given his own later reputation as someone obsessed with discipline and routine, his remarks take on a certain ironic resonance.

Certain elements of *Frenzy* are generic. Others feel fresh and ahead of their time. The character of Jan-Erik, the introspective rebel loner, anticipates all those equally disaffected and misunderstood heroes found in US teen movies such as *Rebel Without a Cause* or *East of Eden* a generation later. The scenes between Jan-Erik and Bertha have a roughness and

spontaneity later to be found in the early films of French New Wave directors. Whatever else, the film has Bergman's imprint on it. The young
writer was hired by Svensk in a dual capacity – as assistant director as
well as director. Svensk executives decided that the original ending of
the film was too bleak. With Sjoberg otherwise engaged, Bergman was
assigned to direct the sentimental coda to the film in which the student
has a final confrontation with 'Caligula' before marching away into the
dawn. Despite a near mutiny from the crew at being told what to do by
a lanky young tyro, Bergman managed to get the footage in the can.

There is the sense of a baton being passed down. Three of the major
figures in early Swedish cinema were involved in different capacities in
the film. Not only was Sjoberg the director and Victor Sjostrom one of
the producers (he is credited as an artistic consultant); but Gustaf Molander, another major director, also championed the screenplay, telling Carl-
Anders Dymling, then the head of Svensk, that this was a film the company should make, regardless of its 'objectionable' and 'unpleasant'
elements. These three peers all had an immense influence on Bergman.
They weren't only figures to emulate. Their experiences also hinted at
some of the challenges that lay ahead for Bergman. What compromises
might be entailed in trying to make movies in Hollywood, as Sjostrom had
done? How easily could a director balance the demands of both theatre
and cinema, as Sjoberg had tried to do with varying degrees of success?
How could Bergman avoid the mawkishness that sometimes clouded the
work of Gustaf Molander, who is better known to film historians today
for 'discovering' the young Ingrid Bergman than for his own movies?

Frenzy was a useful calling card for its young writer. Critics noticed
his screenplay. 'The young man of the theatre, Ingmar Bergman, has
written *Torment*. He must be a film talent!' enthused Stig Almqvist in
Aftontidningen.[4] 'Visual narration comes naturally to him, the screenplay has focus, rhythm and vigour.' Thanks to the theatre critic and playwright Herbert Grevenius, he was offered a job as the artistic director of
the Helsingborg City Theatre. It may not have been the grandest job in
the Swedish dramatic world – he later complained that the theatre was
full of fleas – but it was still a singular achievement for a 26-year-old.
He was joined in Helsingborg by Erland Josephson, an actor who had
played Antonio in Bergman's 1940 student production of *The Merchant
of Venice* and who would still be working with him more than 60 years
later.

Bergman felt ambivalent about the posting in Helsingborg. On the
one hand, he was the youngest artistic director of a theatre in Sweden

and justly proud of his achievement. On the other, he was stuck in the provinces, and his film career – after all the expectation created by *Frenzy* – appeared to have stalled. 'No one got in touch with me', he recalled.[5] Therefore, when Svensk gave him the chance to adapt Leck Fischer's play *The Maternal Heart* for the screen, he leaped at the opportunity. This was to become his directorial debut *Crisis* (1946).

Film historians especially haven't been kind to Bergman's early work. 'Bergman's early films are in themselves largely insignificant', the historian Ephraim Katz has written in what passes as received wisdom, 'but they are interesting from a film historian's point of view as works that contain the seeds of the director's artistic development and hint at greatness to come'.[6]

This was a verdict that Bergman himself largely shared, at least as far as *Crisis* was concerned. In later years, he was quick to distance himself from the film and to portray it as a complete artistic disaster. 'If someone had asked me to film the telephone book I would have done so. The result might possibly have been better. I knew nothing, could do nothing and felt like a crazy cat in a ball of yarn', he stated.[7] *Crisis* certainly was not a happy film to shoot. Its young director was at odds with his cinematographer Gosta Roosling, a documentary specialist foisted on him by the studio. He drank heavily. He despised his source material. To compensate for his lack of technical knowledge and inexperience, he behaved in a temperamental and headstrong way.

Seen today, *Crisis* does not appear quite the artistic disaster that Bergman later claimed. Formally, the film is often clumsy. The all-knowing voice-over, with its asides about old ladies gossiping and boiling kettles, is grating. The way Bergman uses music to signal emotion is surprisingly heavy handed. However, for all the film's melodramatic lurches, it addresses themes that would become familiar in the director's later works, notably bereavement, sexual jealousy and family tensions. Bergman effectively contrasts sleepy rural life with the excitement and alienation of the big city. He shows the contradictory impulses driving the impressionable young heroine. We are always aware of the director's hand, seeking to galvanise his source material. There is a creative intelligence at work here trying – and sometimes succeeding in – turning a trite yarn about a country lass adrift in the city into a moody, fatalistic drama about love and death. The filmmaking may be raw, but it has an adolescent energy about it.

The story is largely set in a sleepy, provincial town. Here, the beautiful but ingenuous young Nelly (Inga Landgre) lives with her foster

mother Miss Ingeborg (Dagny Lind) – a decent, hard-working piano
teacher. Into this idyllic world comes Nelly's real mother Jenny
(Marianne Lofgren) – a blousy, big-city woman who now wants her daughter back, but who (we all know) will corrupt her. The plot is hackneyed in
the extreme and most of the characters are stock types. At the town ball,
Nelly is seduced by gigolo Jack (Stig Olin), who is also her mother's lover.
She does indeed end up going to the big city. Her new life in the bright
lights – working in her mother's beauty salon – is every bit as wretched
as the audience guesses it will be. In the most fraught and emotionally
charged sequence of the film, Jack commits suicide. Nelly returns to the
tranquillity of her home town and her childhood sweetheart Ulf.

The most intriguing character is Jack, the city slicker/poet maudit
played by Stig Olin. Bergman apparently saw Olin as a kind of alter ego.
Jack here is a perverse and contradictory character. Like his director, he
aspires to be worldly wise but appears callow and very young. He wants
to project an air of world-weary decadence, but despite his moustache,
felt hat, spiv's suit and affected way of smoking cigarettes, he looks as if
he has barely left school. He has a streak of malice about him, but he is as
much victim as victimiser. He is also full of self-pity. 'I'll live under some
stairs where the moon will shine in', he declares, absurdly, when Nelly's
foster mother comes to visit Stockholm and tries to make him reveal his
intentions.

'Poor Jack' eventually carries through his threat to kill himself, but
not before he has made love to Nelly.

Cue swirling music and Nelly's rapid return to the warmth of her
provincial home.

At the time he made *Crisis*, Bergman was fascinated by Jack The
Ripper and the idea of the villain tormented by his own misdeeds. As
he confided to a notebook of the period: 'The truly awful thing is that
the villain Jack is constantly forced to tear open his own heart and show
himself as he really is to the audience. That is what they are paying
for.'[8]

Crisis also boasts Bergman's first dream sequence. Formally, this is
the most innovative moment in the movie. The stepmother is returning
home from the city. As she lies on her bunk bed in the railway carriage,
she thinks back to moments in Nelly's childhood. There is even one shot
anticipating the famous moment in *Persona* where Bibi Andersson's and
Liv Ullmann's faces seem to merge. We see Nelly's face projected onto
that of her stepmother. The stepmother wakes from her dream shrieking,
'I don't want to be dead!'

Unlike *Frenzy*, *Crisis* was not well received by critics. One or two reviewers spotted promise. Some were viciously hostile. 'This writer must, for his own part, declare that seldom has he seen anything more abortive, spurious and tedious', complained a reviewer Georg Svensson in *Bonniers Litterära Magasin*.[9] Even Bergman's champions were aware of the film's shortcomings. His source material was crude and homely and yet – in a pretentious way – he had tried to graft experimental ideas onto it. He wasn't serving his story so much as showing off his own prowess as a director. This was why he was later so appreciative of the advice that Victor Sjostrom gave him in a paternal way during the shooting of *Crisis*: keep it simple, film the actors from front. Like Stine Bergman in the Svensk script department, Sjostrom knew from first-hand experience how the Hollywood system emphasised clarity, pragmatism and teamwork. There was no point in picking unwinnable or unnecessary battles or in digging your heels in over-trivialities. Sjostrom advised the young director to keep his temper in check, warning him that raging at his collaborators only succeeded in making them angry and therefore more difficult to work with.

By the same token, Bergman didn't want to accept the role of hack director, in thrall to second-rate material. The best moments in *Crisis* are the most ambitious ones, where the young director is at least trying to impose his vision on the story.

Despite the underwhelming reception that *Crisis* received, Bergman's stock had not altogether sunk. Independent producer Lorens Marmstedt of Terrafilm clearly saw a chance to secure the young director's services. An ex-film critic and one-time film director, Marmstedt, was a much-loved figure in the Swedish film industry. Although he could be acerbic and harsh towards filmmakers, he was prepared to give young talent its head. Once they realised he was not going to throw empty compliments in their direction, they grew to respect and even revere him.

Marmstedt correctly guessed that Svensk would not be hurrying to offer Bergman new directing opportunities. Marmstedt had a project – a chance to direct an adaptation of the Norwegian play *Good People*, by Oskar Braaten. Marmstedt had been commissioned by exhibitor-producer Sveriges Folkbiografer AB to produce two movies. This was to be one of them.

Herbert Grevenius, the critic who had helped him land his post in Helsingborg, had written a first draft of the screenplay for what became *It Rains on Our Love*.

As in *Crisis*, the narrative structure is self-conscious and cumbersome. After the opening credits (which unfold over a high-angle shot of passers-by in the rain getting on a bus), we meet our narrator. 'It is my duty to acquaint you with what's about to take place', a mischievous old man under an umbrella tells us. He sets the scene – it is a Wednesday in October, chilly and wet – and introduces us to one of the main characters – Maggi (Barbro Kollberg). She is a young woman desperate to catch a train. Her missing it throws her together with David (Birger Malmsten), the man she meets at the railway station. The two decide to spend the night in a hotel together. She is a would-be drama student who has been working as a maid. He is an ex-con. They have only a few cents between them.

'This bloody society', David rails. He is another of Bergman's young rebels without a cause. Bergman was an avowed fan of the work of the French director Marcel Carne, who, in collaboration with the writer Jacques Prevert, had made a series of dark and lyrical films about doomed lovers. He aspired to match the so-called poetic realism of such Carne classics as *Le Jour se Leve* or *Quai des Brumes*. It was hard, though, for a young Swedish director, living in a neutral country and without great wells of personal experience to draw on, to match the work of filmmakers working in the build-up to the Second World War and then in occupied Paris. Nor did he have actors with the experience and charisma of the stars Carne used: icons like Jean Gabin, Michele Morgan and Michel Simon.

The nods in the direction of Marcel Carne in *It Rains on Our Love* are self-evident. The couple are like a juvenile version of Jean Gabin and Michele Morgan. Bergman films their relationship in a naturalistic, freewheeling way. The scene in the hotel room where they make love is remarkably frank for its period. Like Jean-Paul Belmondo and Jean Seberg in Godard's *Breathless*, they try to create their own magical, self-enclosed world and to keep outside events and responsibilities at bay. They are helped in this ambition when they are allowed to stay in a small cottage in the countryside for a minimal rent.

As in *Crisis*, there is again a maudlin quality which Bergman's more mature work would shed. When David confesses to Maggi that he has spent time in prison, Bergman underpins the scene with quiet but syrupy music. There are several shots showing a lovable dog. The humour is quirky and sometimes a little feeble, taking its tone from the narrator who reappears mid-way through. Like Clarence, the angel in *It's a Wonderful Life*, or the ghost in a Charles Dickens story, he confronts David with the consequences of his actions. Again, the plotting is melodramatic in the extreme. Just when David and Maggi seem to have achieved the perfect rural idyll, they are evicted from their cottage and she reveals that she is pregnant – and became so before she met David.

David and Maggi want to live honestly and legally together, but circumstances (and the authorities) keep on getting in the way. 'Decent people with principles' disapprove of the cohabiting couple. David is accused of petty theft. During the court case that ends the film, they are accused of every kind of delinquency. Their real crime – it quickly becomes evident – is to be poor, young and non-conformist. Their awkward but sincere attempts to fit into society are constantly rebuffed.

Despite its wildly uneven quality and many contrivances, *It Rains on Our Love* was warmly enough received by critics. 'A breath of fresh air in Swedish cinema', enthused one critic in Swedish newspaper *Aftontidningen*. 'So longed for, so welcome![10]' Reviewers warmed to the warmth, charm and lyricism of the film – the fact that it wasn't as confrontational as *Frenzy* or *Crisis*. There wasn't, they felt, the same adolescent desire to shock as in Bergman's previous films.

As academic Birgitta Steene pointed out in a lecture on 'The Landscapes of Ingmar Bergman', there was a fad in the post-war Swedish industry for making 'summer movies': films with titles like *Short Summer*, *Young Summer*, *Summer in Sin*, *One Summer of Happiness* and *In the Realm of the Rye*.[11]

At one level, these films were precursors to the teen movies that began to be made in earnest in the 1950s. In the countryside, as the experiences of the couple in *It Rains on Our Love* showed, youngsters were free from the constrictions placed on them by their parents or teachers. They could have love affairs. This was one of the reasons for the immense enthusiasm of international audiences for films like Arne Mattsson's *One Summer of Happiness* (1951), which won the Golden Bear at the Berlin Film Festival. Audiences not only responded to the landscapes – the beautifully shot forests and meadows – or the scenes of the youngsters making hay on the farm, but were also intrigued by the sexual tension at the heart of the film. In one famous scene towards the end of the film, the lovers are shown frolicking naked in a lake. Through the rushes, we see them embrace and kiss. Then, they are shown naked from the waist up, making love.

The same symbolism that Mattsson uses here was often found in Bergman's work. The youthful exuberance and lust for life is juxtaposed with scenes of death and decay. Throughout Mattsson's film, we are made aware that the characters' happiness is provisional and short lasting. Soon the summer will be over. Mattsson begins the film just as Bergman might have done with a funeral sequence. He ends the film in apocalyptic fashion with first a fire (which the local priest ascribes to God's wrath at the corruption in his midst) and then a fatal motorbike crash.

After her summer of happiness, Kerstin (the female protagonist) dies. The community blames her death on Goran, the distraught boyfriend. 'She sacrificed her life on the altar of aberration', the priest declaims, although we suspect that he might have been driving the car that (seemingly deliberately) forced the motorbike off the road.

To watch a film like *One Summer of Happiness* is to realise that Bergman was not alone in his obsessions as a young filmmaker. Other Swedish writers and directors had similar preoccupations with love and death, the transitory nature of happiness, the conflict between generations and the attritional attitude of youngsters towards the church.

Not only did Bergman make several of his own films during the summer (in breaks from his theatre work), but he also made films which fall loosely into the 'Swedish summer' genre: for example, *Summer with Monika*, *Smiles of a Summer Night* and *Summer Interlude*. The genre had its own hallmarks and visual motifs. As Steene put it, these were films filled with 'placid lakes, birch trees with filtering sunlight and hills and meadows'.[12] They presented an idealised vision of the Swedish countryside.

'To Town, to Countryside' reads the signpost at the crossroads where David and Maggi are found at the end of *It Rains on Our Love*. The tension between town and country was a constant in Swedish cinema of the period – and Bergman was far from unique in exploring it.

As Bergman delved into this most quintessentially Swedish of genres, there was still the sense that he was a filmmaker in search of his own style. The goal – as he had written in his notebook when he was 18 – to prise 'something beautiful and shiny' out of the 'wretchedness' of life was clearly there, but he was not yet sure how he was going to do it. As a result, his early films were often mannered and self-conscious.

A Ship Bound for India (1947), Bergman's next feature as a director after *It Rains on Our Love*, was also for Marmstedt and Sveriges Folkbiografer AB.

'When I had finished *A Ship Bound for India*, I was swimming in euphoria. It was great. I thought I was terrific, just as good as the French directors who were my idols',[13] Bergman self-mockingly reminisced years after completing the film. He and Marmstedt had gone to the

French Riviera to work on the screenplay, an adaptation of a play by the Finnish-Swedish author Martin Soderhjelm. (While Bergman wrote, Marmstedt played roulette.) Again, Birger Malmsten played the lead – a sailor in awe of his brutal father. Again, Bergman tried to make the film as lyrical and moody as Marcel Carne's studies of romantic losers or as Jean Vigo's tale of love on the barges, *L'Atalante*. Again, the result was fitfully effective and showed plenty of promise without there being much sense that Bergman was in full mastery of his medium.

The casting was perverse. Hiring Malmsten – by consensus the best-looking juvenile lead in Swedish cinema – to play the humpback Johannes is a strange choice. (Not that Malmsten looked misshapen in the Quasimodo mould, just a little round shouldered.)

This was an embroiled Oedipal melodrama. The story unfolds in flashback as Johannes, freshly arrived in port, remembers how he first met the beautiful singer Sally (Gertrud Fridh). At the time, he was living with his family on a salvage vessel. His father, Captain Blom (Holger Lowendadler), is a tyrant – a brawling, bullying figure in whose presence Johannes is utterly cowed. At a fairground cabaret where the captain muscled his way into the front row, he encounters Sally. After provoking a mass brawl, he blunders his way into her dressing room.

The captain is a more sympathetic figure than his behaviour initially suggests. For all his boorishness, he displays an unexpected sensitivity and even vulnerability. After he brings Sally on board, we learn that his eyesight is fading. ('It is to do with some nerve and some fluid that is drying up ... then everything will go dark.') He yearns to run away with Sally to Ceylon or Tahiti: one of those exotic places from where he claims he has culled his collection of coral, seashells and shark skin.

Lowendadler, in his early 40s when he played the role, is arguably too young to play Malmsten's father (the actor was only 15 years his junior). Even so, it is an impressive performance, combining machismo and melancholy. From his own vexed relationship with his father, Bergman knew all about the bitterness and humiliation that can go hand in hand with family life. Here, in the first of those father–son conflicts that were often to be found in his subsequent work, we see the captain slapping his son around, browbeating him and contemptuously knocking a knife out of his hands when the son attacks him. There is a poignant scene in which the captain tells his wife, Alice, in a matter-of-fact way, that he is planning on leaving her. Already, the director is probing away at what would become one of his key themes – the misery caused when a marriage goes wrong.

Johannes, meanwhile, is another of Bergman's gimlet-eyed delinquent anti-heroes. Inevitably, he also becomes close to Sally. After as-
saulting her and demanding that she acknowledge he is a freak, they
make up. He rows her ashore, and they walk together to Johannes'
favourite hiding place – the inside of a windmill. They end up making love. Bergman throws in footage of the couple together against the
backdrop of beautiful rural landscapes that could easily come from one
of those summer movies the Swedish were making in such profusion
during this era.

This prompts the furiously jealous captain to come close to drowning
his son during a diving expedition.

There is a carnivalesque strain to the storytelling that would be found
in many of the director's latest films: a fascination with the magic and
vulgarity of the fairground and the cheap vaudeville performance. We
see footage of a puppet theatre and are taken backstage.

Bergman may have broken some new ground in *A Ship Bound for
India*, but his direction betrayed a stylistic uncertainty and an over-
reliance on show and even kitsch effects. The film, he latest testified in
Images, was 'a major disaster'. It didn't help that the sound quality on
the print projected at the premiere was very poor or that two of the reels
were shown the wrong way round. Bergman was so humiliated at what
had happened that he drank himself comatose.

Still, like *Crisis*, *A Ship Bound for India* wasn't quite the catastrophe
that Bergman later claimed. Some of the reviews were relatively sympathetic. It was apparent that the press was already beginning to notice the
first signs of a Bergman style. One newspaper even described the film as
'Bergmanesque', an early sign of his ability to put his own imprint on his
work.

What was also clear was Bergman's pragmatism. He reacted to the
technical problems that the film endured in the lab by making sure that in
future, he knew as much about sound, lenses and editing as his collaborators. When the film failed to perform at the box-office, he was prepared
to move more towards the mainstream, even if it entailed making some
surprising compromises.

'In spite of all that happened, Lorens Marmstedt did not throw me
out', he recalls in *Images* of how his long-suffering producer reacted to
the failure of *A Ship Bound for India*. 'With great diplomacy he pointed
out that now would be the perfect time for at least one modest audience
success. Otherwise my days as a movie director might be numbered. *A
Ship Bound for India* as well as *It Rains on Our Love* had been made

for Sweden's Folkbiografer. Now Marmstedt suggested that I make a film for his own company, Terrafilm. It must be noted that Lorens was a passionate gambler, able to put his money on the same number a whole evening.'[14]

Music in Darkness (1948) was Bergman's first box-office hit, but it was also one of his least distinguished films.

The source material was a novel about a blind musician by Dagmar Enqvist. Bergman hated it on a first reading, but then he met the author, a pretty and charming woman who quickly won him over. They collaborated happily on the screenplay.

For once, Bergman was a director-for-hire. He talked about 'stuffing his demons into an old sack' because this wasn't a project on which he would have any use for them. These demons may have tormented him, but they were also the source of his inspiration. When he discarded them, his work invariably lacked its usual intensity.

What the film makes clear is a growing formal confidence on the director's behalf, even if he uses his skills in a showy and meretricious way. *Music in Darkness* opens with an impressive set-piece. Soldiers are on a firing range, practicing their target shooting. A little white labrador puppy suddenly appears in their sights. One soldier Bengt (Birger Malmsten) clambers onto the bank to rescue the dog but is shot down in a hail of bullets.

This may be melodrama, but that doesn't stop Bergman from throwing in expressionistic dream sequences which look as if they have been culled from some old B horror movie. As Bengt lies unconscious, we see an anvil being hammered in front of a huge close-up of an eye. Then, we see him crawling through what looks like lava. Out of the bubbling mud, several filthy hands emerge and try to drag him down. Then, he floats up through a pool of fish. A beautiful blonde nymph is sitting on a rock, combing her hair. The sequence is both trite and absurd. It ends with Bengt waking from his reverie, lamenting the fact that he is not dead. Slowly, he realises he has lost his sight.

The trajectory of the film is utterly predictable. At first, Bengt is filled with self-pity and reacts with hostility and disdain to any attempts to help him. Gradually, though, he finds purpose in his life after falling in love with the servant girl Ingrid (Mai Zetterling). 'Make sure there are no tedious parts. Keep it entertaining' were Bergman's instructions to himself while shooting.

The motif of blindness allowed Bergman to explore one of his pet obsessions: the power of music to express feelings.

'My idea is that they (film and music) are much the same', Bergman told the journalist Oscar Hedlund. 'They are means of expression and communication that bypass man's reason and touch his emotional centres. The film isn't just a picture. Music isn't just a sound. Both of them work with rhythmic sequences, harmonies, colours, relations, forms ... it (film) should communicate psychic states, not merely project pictures of external actions. Communication of this kind has always been the basic function of music.'[15]

One rhetorical question Bergman returned to again and again was, why is there music? He saw music as the most unexplainable and miraculous art. In *Music in Darkness*, he tries to express how music can transcend the grind of everyday life and provide reason and consolation even to a character as despairing as the blind protagonist. We see the film's benighted anti-hero sitting in the darkness, playing Beethoven and finally achieving the peace that has eluded him. He applies to the Royal Music Academy but is turned down and ends up as a cabaret pianist in a cheap restaurant with an unscrupulous owner. He is reduced to finding work as a piano tuner. Then he meets Ingrid again. She is on her way up the social ladder. He is on the way down. She has a boyfriend, a macho type who humiliates him by beating him at arm wrestling. Inevitably, though, by the final reel, he manages to win Ingrid's love and they have the chance for a new life together.

Bergman was praised for the sensitive way in which he depicted the plight of the blind hero. 'The subject of the film would have been completely repellent had Bergman not carried over so much of Dagmar Edqvist's unsentimental sympathy for the world of blind people and his portrayal of their rational view of what is a particularly complicated, yet otherwise universal human existence', stated one reviewer in *Aftonbladet*.[16]

Even so, this was a very conventional melodrama, as saccharine and manipulative in its way as any Hollywood equivalent. The film proved a modest box-office success. This strengthened Bergman's position at Svensk.

As if in reaction against the contrivances of *Music in Darkness*, Bergman next directed a film in a far harsher, more realist groove. Even so, traces of affectation and self-consciousness remained. To some, *Port of Call* (1948) seemed like pastiche neo-realism, but at least it had a grit missing in his previous feature. Again, the opening is abrupt, but this time, instead of a soldier rescuing a fluffy little puppy, we see a young woman (Nine-Christine Jonsson) in the docks plunging into the water in a clear attempt to commit suicide. At the same time that she is rescued, Gosta (Bengt Eklund) is returning home to Stockholm from his latest voyage. After eight years at sea, he wants to end his roaming ways. A job in the docks might be his best prospect.

The casting itself is a departure. Instead of the epicene good looks of Birger Malmsten, Bergman opts for the far more rugged Eklund (who had also played Mai Zetterling's boyfriend in *Music in Darkness*). He also went out of his way to use real locations rather than the stylised studio sets he had used in his previous feature. Certain sequences of workers operating cranes, loading and emptying ships, or working on noisy factory floors could have been taken wholesale from a documentary. Gosta meets Berit, the suicidal young woman from the docks, at a dance hall. She is from a broken family, browbeaten by her mother, and has already spent time in reform school. Two lonely, marginalised figures, they fall in love.

Bergman later sought to distance himself from *Port of Call*, suggesting that he was 'a technical half-wit' flailing around, in search of a style, when he made it. If there was a rawness and authenticity to the storytelling, he attributed this to his collaborator Olle Lansberg. 'The only bit of *Harbour City* (*Port of Call*) which I wrote – and which is bad anyway and clashes with the rest of the film – is the hero's experiences when he gets drunk with a whore', Bergman told Stig Bjorkman. 'It's a really miserable piece of work, thoroughly stylized and semi-literary, utterly out of tune with the rest of the film.'[17]

Despite the director's scathing remarks about it, *Port of Call* is strikingly shot by Gunnar Fischer (working for the first time with Bergman on a feature having been removed from *Crisis* before production began). Nine-Christine Jonsson gives a lively and affecting performance as the young woman terrified of being locked away in an institution again. She is still traumatised by her childhood memories of the violent break-up of her parents' marriage. For all her seeming worldliness and her very chequered past, she has an ingenuous, childlike quality. There is quiet heroism in the way she confesses her former misdeeds to Gosta, even though she is terrified that he will leave her. This is another of Bergman's stories of love against the odds.

Like *Music in Darkness*, *Port of Call* chimed with audiences. Whatever compromises Bergman had made by shooting some of the film on studio sets rather than on locations, this was still earthier and more intense than many other melodramas of its era. It exposed the cruelty with which the state treated problem kids, hauling them off into reform schools. Some scenes, for instance when Gosta is beaten up after taking Berit to the cinema, have the intensity you expect to find in noirish B gangster movies. There was also the sense of the parson's son chafing against his bourgeois background, desperate to see life from a dirty, street eye view. Bergman was building a reputation as a filmmaker ready to take the outsider's point of view. He didn't patronise his mixed-up young protagonists because he clearly felt a strong affinity with them. He was the rebel of Swedish cinema and recognised as such.

'Bergman has continued to be a rebel', noted Carl-Anders Dymling, the president of Svensk. 'He has always been a problem, not only to others but to himself, and I think he will remain so. He is a high-strung personality, passionately alive, enormously sensitive, very short-tempered, sometimes quite ruthless in the pursuit of his own goals, suspicious, stubborn, capricious, most unpredictable. His will power is extraordinary.'[18]

Along with the rebelliousness was a capacity for an extraordinary lyricism. This was evident in *Eva*, a screenplay he wrote that ended up being shot at the same time as *Port of Call*. Like many of his early projects, *Eva* was begun first as a novella. He would present the Svensk bosses with a piece of prose fiction which would then be worked into script form. In this case, the source material was his story *The Little Trumpeter and the Lord*. The film, again starring his alter ego Birger Malmsten, was another of his evocations of childhood in all its joy and darkness.

In his autobiography *The Magic Lantern*, Bergman writes evocatively about his childhood memories of the family summer house in Dalarna and of the small country railway station at Dufnas. This is the same world that *Eva* seeks to rekindle. Ironically, the film is more 'Bergmanesque' than many other movies of the period that Bergman himself directed. It begins with Bo Fredriksson (Birger Malmsten) returning home on the train for a few days' leave from his service in the navy. As the train wends its way through gorgeous forests and around lakes, he is delighted to be going back to the world of his childhood, but the closer he gets to home, the more perturbed he becomes. There is a shadow hanging over him – a dark memory which has haunted him since he was 12 years old.

Cue a flashback.

The depiction of the little railway station is comic and affectionate. At first, we seem to be plunged into a world of endless summer. The light is bright. The kids are contented and mischievous. The adults cleave to long-established routines.

As a kid, Bo (played by Lasse Sarri) is already rebellious. He is at odds with his stationmaster father, who is forever threatening to thrash him. 'I hate you all! I hate everyone! I don't give a damn about you!' he shrieks after the latest altercation at the family dining table. It seems no coincidence that the stationmaster shares Bergman's own father's name, Erik.

Eva sees Bergman giving his childhood an improbable Huck Finn-like spin. Bo runs away from home with his Rin Tin Tin-like dog in tow and takes up with Austrian gypsies he meets, who are travelling hobo-like on a goods train. Again, blindness features prominently in the story. The dimple-chinned, accordion-playing, Heidi-lookalike Marthe has lost her sight. Bo delights in describing the world to her, explaining colours (red is 'angry and happy') and trying to tell her what it is like to look at fields and flowers. There is fortune-telling too. The gypsies, who might have been forecasting Bergman's own career, tell Bo that love and death will be intertwined throughout his life. As in the summer movies then so popular with Swedish audiences, director Molander, following Bergman's screenplay, goes to exhaustive lengths to depict the Swedish countryside in the most idyllic light possible. We are always aware, though, that those balmy moments enjoyed by Bo and Marthe in the woods are only the precursors to the tragedy that will follow. This comes soon enough when Bo takes Marthe aboard the train.

The childhood sequences are intercut with Bo as an adult, returning home and revisiting the old sites. Death is never far away. It is not just the memory of the death of Marthe, for which he was directly responsible, that torments him. An old family friend is on his deathbed. The man's wife is inconsolable. She solemnly reads her dying spouse passages from the Bible but tells him all the joy will go out of her life with his passing. There are some very Bergmanesque touches – the candles flickering and the old man in the glass of the clock as the pendulum swings back and forth, counting down his few remaining hours.

Still riddled with guilt, Bo is beginning to think about his own mortality too. 'It's like a shadow behind you that grasps at everything and crushes it', he laments as he sees death all around him. He has rejected God and takes no consolation in religion.

There are some familiar oppositions. The innocence and simplicity of country living are contrasted with the cynicism that Bo, now a successful jazz trumpeter, encounters in the city with his worldly friends, Goran (Stig Olin) and Susanne (Eva Dahlbeck). Bergman's screenplay explores tentatively what were to become some of his key themes: betrayal and sexual jealousy. Suzanne is like a femme fatale in a James M. Cain story: flirtatious and conspiratorial.

Death is always present, even when Bo and Eva (Eva Stiberg) seem to have built an idyllic life for themselves on a remote island. One morning, Bo finds the corpse of a soldier, washed ashore. The body is that of a young man about his own age. He doesn't tell Eva, but when she discovers the corpse, she is horrified. Pregnant herself, she is appalled at the idea of bringing a baby into the world.

Eva is a fascinating hybrid: a film by a young, neurotic writer but directed by a mature (if conventional) filmmaker. It is more solidly crafted than Bergman's own work as a director in this period. The affectations are kept in check. The ending is trite: by accepting the responsibilities of fatherhood, Bo overcomes his narcissistic fear of death. It is no longer a shadow behind his back, 'but a part of life and its waves'. Even so, there is an emotional depth here lacking in such posturing work as *A Ship Bound for India* or *It Rains on Our Love*.

Bergman's next film as a director, *Prison* (1949), was his first in which he had total control over the screenplay as well as direction. This wasn't an adaptation of someone else's novel or play or a script written to order, but a project that Bergman devised himself. Terrafilm's Lorens Marmstedt gave him the chance to make what can fairly be described as his first film as a full-blown auteur on the condition that he shot quickly, deferred his own fee and worked on a small budget.

'Make a cheap film, make the cheapest film that has ever been made in a Swedish studio and you will be given great freedom to create according to your own conscience and as you know best', Bergman was told by his loyal and caustic producer.[19]

Prison is a striking but affected piece of work, combining moments of raw intensity with pretentious symbolism. Bergman touches on some very dark subjects – poverty, prostitution, the killing of a child. The film opens with an old man (Anders Henrikson) walking over wasteland and into a film set. Fresh out of the asylum, he is the former teacher of a now successful film director. He wants to propose a movie to his former pupil – a film about hell. 'It should open with a proclamation by the devil himself . . . everything will remain the same.'

The director mentions this stranger encounter to a journalist friend, Thomas (Birger Malmsten). Thomas has recently been researching a story about a teenage prostitute. Seen from her perspective, he suggests, the contemporary world could indeed seem like hell.

With its elaborate narrative structure and conceit of a film within a film, this is Bergman at his most self-reflexive. A narrator tells us that we are watching a film called *Prison* 'produced by Lorens Marmstedt of Terrafilm at Sandrew Studios' and then proceeds to list the actors as the camera wends its way down a narrow Stockholm street. Six months, we are told, have passed since the day the old director came into the film studio.

The prostitute, Birgitta Karolina (Doris Svedlund), is now in a wretched situation. She has just had a baby, but her ne'er-do-well boyfriend wants her to get rid of it.

The journalist, looking at her life as if he is an anthropologist studying a subject, has his own problems. He drinks heavily and is at odds with his girlfriend. They are a prototypical Bergman couple: attractive and super-ficially happy but inwardly miserable. Drinking heavily and talking con-stantly of suicide, they are successfully making their own hell on earth.

Prison sees Bergman experimenting with longer takes than he had used hitherto. Certain scenes – for example, the encounter between Thomas and Birgitta Karolina on the Stockhom streets – are studio bound. Nonetheless, their scenes together are among the most affecting in the film. He confesses to her that his relationship with his wife is breaking down. She talks of her loneliness. In a heartbreaking monologue, she reminisces about the lost world of her childhood and of a dream she has had of walking through the sunlight, feeling so joyful it hurt and being approached by a woman in mourning. This is the prelude to the couple sleeping together, a tryst that Bergman accompanies with some heavy-handed symbolism of two logs burning in the fire. Birgitta Karolina then has a nightmare. It is not one of the director's most distinctive sequences. Shot on a sound stage, showing the poor lost girl wandering through a forest filled with silent, hostile faces, it comes across like a student's self-conscious foray into avant-gardism.

Even so, Bergman's affection for *Prison* is self-evident. Two decades later, when he made *Persona*, he quoted directly from it. The silent slap-stick sequence that Thomas and Birgitta Karolina watch together, with its Charlie Chaplin-like visual gags and playful evocations of the Grim Reaper and the devil, is included in the prologue to *Persona*. Malmsten has grown into the role of the tormented anti-hero: he brings a ferocity to his role not always evident in his earlier films with Bergman. Svedlund, meanwhile, gives an utterly haunting performance. With her huge eyes and mobile, sensitive face, she registers her character's extreme vulner-ability in the face of a world that has treated her so cruelly.

As Bergman's fellow filmmaker Vilgot Sjoman later revealed, the writer–director made one significant and surprising compromise during the making of *Prison*. Belying his later reputation as a purveyor of dark, morbid tales, Bergman ended his original story about Birgitta Karolina on an upbeat note. The one-time prostitute had found redemption by joining the Salvation Army. Like a character in a Christian morality tale, she had transcended the squalor and degradation of her background and achieved a kind of grace. Bergman's mentor Herbert Grevenius read the original treatment and heaped scorn on it, calling it 'religious sentimentality'. Bergman deferred to Grevenius, ending the movie instead with Birgitta Karolina's suicide.[20] The irony was that this grim Bergmanesque finale wasn't at all what he had originally planned.

Grevenius scripted Bergman's next film as a director, *Törst* (1949) (released in English as *Three Strange Loves*). His screenplay knitted together a series of short stories by Birgit Tengroth, who also appeared in the film in the role of Viola. What is immediately striking is the visual confidence of the direction. None of those cumbersome framing devices or voice-overs are found in some of his early features. Instead, the film begins with a woman waking up at night in a hotel room in Basle. Bergman shows Ruth (Eva Henning), a former ballet dancer, fidgeting around, smoking a cigarette and brushing her teeth as her boyfriend Bertil (Birger Malmsten) sleeps on. Then, with no fuss, there is a flashback to a beautiful summer day. She is sunbathing on a yacht, and all seems idyllic. Then, we see her almost stepping on a snake in the woods – an intimation of unhappinesses to come. Her soldier lover Raoul belatedly confides that he is a married man with children. In the next scene, she is confronted by his wife, Astrid. Then, Raoul learns that she is pregnant, calls her a whore and says he will have nothing to do with the child. The next scene shows her waking from what we assume must have been the abortion of her child.

We are then whisked forward in time to the hotel room. Ruth and Bertil are in love, but they are impoverished and there are tensions pulling them apart. They are on their way back home to Stockholm from a romantic holiday in Italy. By chance, they meet Raoul at the railway station. Ruth makes small talk with her former lover. Then, as their train sets off, there is another flashback, this time showing another ill-starred love affair, between a psychiatrist, Dr Rosengren, and his unhappy, neurotic patient, the widow Viola. He is preying on her, taking advantage of her weaknesses. 'You belong with the incurables. Your breakdown is imminent', he sneers at her when she tries to split with him. 'As usual, you'll end up at the asylum.'

In another flashback, we are shown Ruth's struggles as a ballet student.

Bergman is dealing with sensationalist material (abortion, lesbianism), but does so in restrained fashion. This is a study of a series of unhappy relationships. The director later credited writer-actress Tengroth with teaching him a crucial lesson about storytelling, namely that tiny details, if acutely enough observed, can be as telling as big, melodramatic set-pieces. In one scene, in which Viola is spending the evening with Mimi Nelson, as the duo sit together getting drunk, Mimi lights Viola's cigarette and then holds the match for a moment by her face. We then see a big close-up of the two actresses' faces. Their attraction towards one another is evident. The scene ends in bathetic fashion, presumably as a result of the interference of the censors. Viola pushes the other woman away in disgust and flees as if she is being chased by a zombie in a horror movie. Nonetheless, the quiet moment between the two women registers far more strongly than their contrived and melodramatic parting. Viola's suicide is hinted at in a similarly oblique fashion. We don't see her plunge in the water. We just hear a splash off-screen.

As in his later film *The Silence*, Bergman uses a train journey through a foreign country to convey a Kafkaesque mood of unease. Out of the windows at night, the passengers can see the husks of bombed-out buildings left in the aftermath of the war. In one jarring scene, we see Bertil, Ruth and other passengers feeding a swarm of refugees by passing food and money through the carriage windows as they stand on the station platform. As the citizen of a neutral country, Bergman may have been at once removed from the chaos and horror of the Second World War, but again and again in his work, echoes of the upheavals elsewhere are heard.

In his next film, *To Joy* (1950), Bergman looked inward, not outward. He later called the film 'hopelessly uneven' and an 'impossible melodrama',[21] but *To Joy* is intriguing as an early example of the filmmaker's ability to create cinema out of the rawest moments of his personal life. The film begins with Stig (Stig Olin), a violinist, learning that his wife Marta (Maj-Britt Nilsson) has been killed and his daughter injured in a freak accident with a paraffin lamp. The scene is led extra morbidity by the presence of a kid in the background, munching on an apple and playing with a teddy bear, as news of Marta's death is relayed. Then, we are whisked back seven years in time to the early days of Stig and Marta's marriage. Stig and Marta have just joined the Helsingborg Orchestra. Their conductor is Sonderby (Victor Sjostrom).

At the time he was making *To Joy* (the title is taken from Beethoven's Ninth Symphony but used here in a barbed and ironic way), Bergman's own domestic life was in upheaval. As he puts it in *Images: My Life in Film*, 'My second marriage had hit rock bottom'.[22] The film is about the decline and break-up of a marriage. Stig – the character with whom Bergman clearly identified – is feckless, undisciplined and with an overweening belief in his own ability. If this is a self-portrait, it is hardly a flattering one. Stig is a feckless mediocrity posing as an artist, full of self-pity and forever throwing childlike tantrums to ensure that he is the centre of attention. Bergman noted acidly that Stig played 'Mendelssohn's Violin Concerto with about the same lacklustre skill as I exhibited in *Crisis*'.

Marta, by contrast, is talented but has also lost her way. 'Almost all I have done has been a cheat. My whole life', she laments to Stig, insisting that if they are to have a relationship, they must be honest with one another. As young lovers trying to combine their domestic and professional lives – and not to compromise too far in either – they resemble closely the couple played by Lena Endre and her divorced lover (Krister Henriksson) in *Faithless* (2000), the film that Bergman scripted for Liv Ullmann.

Bergman frankly acknowledged the autobiographical undertow to the storytelling. He drew heavily on his own marriage to Ellen Lundstrom as the background: 'It was about me, about the conditions imposed by art, about fidelity and infidelity.'[23]

One critic accused the director of 'spewing himself out'[24] in the character of Stig. However, the filmmaker surely deserves credit for his self-lacerating honesty and for his ability to expose his characters' motivations even when they are at their lowest. In one uncomfortable scene that takes place before their marriage, Stig learns that Marta is pregnant. 'If you had an abortion before you can do it again. It's all disgusting', he also tells her with an absolute lack of sympathy. He also tells her that he is not certain the child is his and then warns her that they have no space in their tiny apartment for a baby, with 'nappies and pee and child care'. It is as if the director – notorious for his lack of interest in his children – is poking fun at himself and caricaturing his least attractive traits.

In later years, Bergman wrote with dismay about his younger self. 'I do not recognize the person I was back then (in the 1940s) … I trusted no one, loved no one, missed no one. Obsessed with a sexuality that forced me into constant infidelity, I was tormented by desire, fear, anguish, and a guilty conscience ... I wanted so very much to be Prospero, and I mostly behaved like Caliban', he confessed.[25] What makes *To Joy* moving and fascinating is the way that even back then, Bergman was trying to make sense of his own behaviour. There are clear overlaps between *To Joy* and later Bergman works such as *Scenes from a Marriage* and *Faithless*. The scenes between Stig and Marta prefigure many equally fraught encounters between couples in Bergman's future films. He is alert to the many sudden changes in mood – the mix of tenderness and loathing, affection and contempt, with which the bickering lovers treat one another. Stig starts by telling Marta to have an abortion, but by the end of the sequence, he is trying to convince her that he is more desperate than she is that they have the child. Bergman captures what Sjostrom's character in the film calls 'this complicated, secret language that two lovers develop and talk unhindered to conceal their most secret and delicate emotions'.

To Joy is cumbersome and uneven. The attempt to combine a closely focused marital drama with a story about a provincial orchestra doesn't always work. Nonetheless, amid the melodramatic posturing, there are many resonant moments. For example, when Stig is given the chance to play Mendelssohn's Violin Concerto as the soloist, he does so in a flashy and meretricious way. He is striving after cheap effects. The camera shows the conductor (Sjostrom) looking more and more agitated at his performance. Stig leaves the concert hall crestfallen, only too aware of how ordinary his playing has been. The next morning, the newspaper drops through the letter box. The review – like so many of those of Bergman's early films – is brutal. 'It is possible that Ericsson is talented', the critic sneers. 'According to the programme, he's been to the best schools.' The performance, though, is referred to as 'an unnecessary suicide'. The inference is clear – Stig should never have been allowed to play. He could be a good orchestra musician. It is just his vanity that drives him to want to become a soloist.

The years pass. Marta has a daughter. She and Stig seem happy together. We see them sitting in the countryside, enjoying the summer sun, seemingly at ease with the world. Almost inevitably, Stig ruins this cosy menage by being unfaithful. Soon, they start behaving as viciously towards one another as George and Martha in *Who's Afraid of Virginia Woolf*. They are reconciled. All seems idyllic again, but then comes the accident with the lamp. With Stig overcome by grief, Bergman ends the

A fleeting moment of happiness in *Summer Interlude*, the first film in which Bergman felt he had mastered his medium.

movie in bathetic fashion. As he plays his part in a rousing rendition of *To Joy*, he thinks of his children and of the happy moments he enjoyed with Marta. The music – once the vehicle of his ambition – is now his consolation. The trite finale notwithstanding, *To Joy* has a maturity and depth of characterisation that many of his earlier films had lacked.

Bergman's next effort as director, *Summer Interlude* (1950), marked the end of his cinema apprenticeship. It was his first fully realised film – one for which none of his habitual apologies were necessary. At last, he felt fully confident in the medium. He had realised that film was like music. 'Both film and music bypass the intellect and assail the emotions. Both film and music are rhythm.'[26]

The ambitious young director had complained about his inability to depict youth convincingly on screen. Most of his early films had been about young people, but as he later acknowledged, he had never felt part of their world. Like many Swedish filmmakers and writers of his era, he tried to create stories conveying 'the happiness of youth' as well as its perils and transitory nature, but he had felt at a remove from the characters he was writing about.

Even later in his career, Bergman used to joke that he had always felt like a perpetual adolescent, not a fully formed adult. He also said that he never felt young, 'only immature'.[27] In *Summer Interlude*, he found a way of dealing with youth that was neither glib and superficial nor portentous. The story is rooted in one of his own adolescent love affairs. The film is also heavy with a sense of foreboding and gloom about the transience of relationships. This must have been at least partly induced by Bergman's own domestic mishaps. At the time he made the film, his life was in upheaval. His second marriage was over. He had left his wife Ellen and his children to run off with his lover, Gun Hagberg, whom he subsequently married.

The guilt he felt about walking out on his family and his memory of the strength of his romantic obsession with Hagberg would feed into his work again and again. 'I was in love with her but I had four kids and a wife in Gothenburg', he recalled in an interview late in his life. 'And then Gun was to go to Paris. And then I – it's really horrible – the day before I was to go to Paris, I went down to Gothenburg. I remember that Ellen was so happy that I had come home sooner than expected. And then ... I didn't even remove my coat. I sat down on the bed and told her all about Gun and myself ... It still feels terrible to think that I could have been so incredibly cruel ... But ... I was.'[28]

Summer Interlude is the story of a 28-year-old ballet dancer. Marie (Maj-Britt Nilsson) is a beautiful but forlorn figure, tormented by the memory of an old love affair. Her looks are beginning to fade. She is slowly being worn down by the rigours of her job. (As her friend jokes to her, ballet dancing takes its toll on both 'your toes and your immortal soul'.) In the dressing room after a stressful rehearsal, she begins to look at an old diary and is reminded of a tragic love affair from her youth.

Bergman relishes showing the mundane backstage world of the dancers. They may be artists on stage, but behind the scenes, they're prey to the gossiping of stage hands. In one scene, we see two old men from the theatre muttering about how thick Marie's legs are becoming and asking why she never married. Marie has a boyfriend – a sinister, wisecracking journalist who could have escaped from some American B gangster movie.

Incident after incident keeps on triggering memories of the love affair. On a whim, she revisits the island on which she spent her happiest times. In winter, it looks grey and desolate. She has barely set foot on the island when she sees a ghoulish old woman dressed all in black, carrying a black bag and a black umbrella and looking like a cross between the Grim Reaper and a nineteenth-century matriarch, wandering across the barren island landscape. The wind is howling. She sits in a deserted summer house, full of discarded bric-a-brac and thinks back in time.

Bergman shoots the sequence beautifully, setting up the flashback with a long, slow camera movement. As Marie's face comes to dominate the frame, we are whisked back 13 years to the ballet school spring show. Marie remembers her first meeting with Henrik (Birger Malmsten). Suddenly, light pours in. We are in the summer house again, but this time, it is high summer. We see Marie waking up, pulling on her swimsuit and going off to fish in her little rowing boat. Swimming nearby is Henrik, accompanied by his faithful dog.

'Summer Interlude has a long history. Its origin, I see now, lies in a rather touching love affair that I had one summer when my family resided on Orno Island. I was sixteen years old and, as usual, was stuck with extra studies during my summer vacation and could only occasionally participate in activities with people my own age. Besides, I did not dress as they did; I was skinny, had acne, and stammered whenever I broke my silence and looked up reading from Nietzsche', Bergman later recalled.[29] During this summer, the gawky adolescent met a shy young girl as lonely as he was. Their love barely lasted the season, tapering out by the beginning of autumn. In Summer Interlude, the love affair ends in a far more abrupt and brutal way.

Yet again, Birger Malmsten plays a character with many of the traits of the adolescent Bergman: a dreamy, solitary figure with a fatalistic streak who has no friends other than his shaggy dog, Gruffman. What is striking is the way that Bergman throws in little hints of the misfortunes to befall the couple even in the most idyllic scenes. As they lie sunbathing together, Marie is suddenly shown in close-up, declaring that she is 'never going to die'. This is not an assertion that Henrik is ready to echo. He has a prophetic dread of tipping 'over the edge into something black, something unknown'.

We are always aware that the events depicted are being recounted to us in flashback and that we are being shown a world that Marie has long since lost.

Maj-Britt Nilsson was a formidable actress. In To Joy, as Bergman enthused in The Magic Lantern, she had succeeded in 'making the desperately idealised wife almost believable, which was as good evidence as any of her brilliance'.[30] In Summer Interlude, she is equally effective, conveying both the skittishness and the naivete of the young Marie and the disappointed, melancholic woman she becomes.

In a famous essay on the film, Jean-Luc Godard posited the idea that Bergman was 'the last great romantic'. Godard noted that Bergman's technique was often derivative and could even be heavy handed (with more flashbacks than decency permits), but added that the director's sensibility shone through his work and made his use of hackneyed old devices appear fresh and original.

'In the Bergman aesthetic, those shots of lakes, forests, grass, clouds, the deliberately unusual camera angles, the elaborately careful back-lighting, are no longer mere showing-off or technical trickery: on the contrary, they are integrated into the psychology of the characters at the precise instant when Bergman wants to evoke an equally precise feeling',[31] Godard wrote.

On the one hand, *Summer Interlude* shares all the hallmarks of other Swedish *One Summer of Happiness*-style yarns about doomed young lovers. Bergman isn't above flights of purple prose. Marie's voice-over recalls 'days like pearls, round and lustrous, threaded on a golden string' and 'days filled with fun and careeses' as well as 'nights of waking dreams'. Even so, the effect never seems mawkish or enervating. There is an edge to the storytelling. The flashbacks are introduced with more guile than in Bergman's earlier films, with their sometimes cumbersome narrative structure and clumsy use of voice-over.

The symbolism is present without being over-stated. In almost every scene, there is some reference, however oblique, to death and mortality. There is even a moment prefiguring the famous sequence with the knight and the Grim Reaper on the beach at the start of *The Seventh Seal*. This time, instead of the knight, it's the old lady – Henrik's guardian – playing chess with the parson. 'According to the experts, I should have died three months ago', the Miss Havisham-like old lady jokes morbidly. She refers to herself as 'the corpse'. The parson, meanwhile, talks of his feeling of sitting 'next to Death himself'. A scene that starts in light, playful fashion takes on an ominous hue. Bergman includes a strange animation sequence, reminiscent of old Fleischer brothers Pop-eye cartoons. The lovers doodle on a record sleeve, and their drawings spring to life, but even here, a playful sequence is undermined by threat-ening images of ghosts and stabbings. Marie somehow knows what lies ahead.

The tragedy, when it does occur, is random and cruel. Henrik dives into shallow water and breaks his back. His death is inevitable. Marie is perplexed and utterly grief-stricken. She wants to spit in the face of God. She throws herself into her work and blots Henrik out of her mind.

Summer Interlude was completed not long before a strike, which brought the Swedish film industry to a halt. This delayed its release for over a year. Nonetheless, when it finally appeared, critics were aware – as Harry Schein put it – that they were seeing the work of a 'new Bergman', a filmmaker who had at last found his own voice. 'This was my first film in which I felt I was functioning independently, with a style of my own, making a film all my own, with a particular appearance of its own, which no one could ape', Bergman later wrote. 'It was like no other film.'[32]

One might have expected that *Summer Interlude* would have launched Bergman on a bold new phase of his career. In fact, it was the prelude to one of the more frustrating moments in his filmmaking life. With a film industry strike about to begin in Sweden, he rushed to complete another film, the political thriller *High Tension* (*This Can't Happen Here*) (1950). It was a project about which he later felt profound shame. The experience of making it induced him to declare 'politics never again'.

Bergman took his art very seriously. However, with ex-wives and children to support, he was put in an awkward situation by the Swedish film strike. It was at this point that he embarked on one of the most uncharacteristic endeavours of his career – the series of commercials he made for soap manufacturer Bris. Bergman may have made the soap ads out of desperation (he needed the money), but he approached the work with the same commitment he brought to his most cherished feature projects. His unlikely foray into the world of commercials gave him licence to experiment. In one Bris advert, he spoofs 3-D films like *Bwana Devil* and Vincent Price shocker *House of Wax*. There is another whose theme is the lack of hygiene in the court of Charles III. The fledgling auteur reached to the indignity of making commercials both by throwing in plenty of irony and in-jokes, as if to distance himself from his material, and by testing out new effects he could later use in his feature work.

'Bergman had the chance to experiment. He had final cut, he had free hands, he could do whatever he wanted',[32] Anders Ronnqvist – co-director of Bergman's *Commercials Preceding the Play* (a documentary about the commercials) – suggested. To his mind, these were one-minute mini-masterpieces that anticipate ideas found in later Bergman pictures.

The ads were all shot on 35 mm and made for the cinema. The soap – originally known as Sunlight – was considered a wholesome but dreary brand. The manufacturers decided to re-market it as Bris (or, in English, 'Breeze'), and that's where Bergman came in. His sophisticated and ingenious ads clearly worked. Proctor & Gamble ended up buying the brand. In one of the commercials, Bibi Andersson had her very first speaking role. (She played a pretty princess who fell in love with a handsome young hog farmer, rewarding him with 100 kisses in exchange for a cake of Breeze.)

Although they still exist, the Bris commercials were rarely shown in Bergman's lifetime. He clearly didn't want to see them included in even the most exhaustive retrospectives of his work. The soap commercials have therefore been largely washed out of film history. In his autobiography, Bergman makes only the most fleeting reference to them. However, they testify to both his pragmatism and his sense of adventure. He accepted the commission to make them for purely monetary reasons, but once he embarked on shooting the commercials, he relished the chance – as he puts in *Images* – to 'make miniature films in the style of Georges Melies'.[33] Whatever else, they were the work of a professional. Now, it was clear, Bergman's apprenticeship was over.

3

The 'Middle Period': 1953–60

IN 1956, BERGMAN was sitting on the lavatory when he learned that his film *Smiles of a Summer Night* (1955) had won a major prize in Cannes. It was an anecdote he would repeat often in later years, as if relishing the incongruity and indignity of it all. The film represented his first major international breakthrough – and he discovered his success while on the shitter.

'I remember sitting on the toilet that morning reading *Svenska Dagbladet*. I suddenly saw the headline "Swedish success in Cannes". Then I saw it was *Smiles of a Summer Night*. They (the Swedish authorities) had sent it there without asking me. They never asked you in those days', he told interviewer Marie Nyrerod late in his life.[1]

There is a certain irony in the fact that *Smiles of a Summer Night*, one of Bergman's lightest films, begat *The Seventh Seal* (1957), the work that would fix his name forever as a purveyor of gloomy Scandinavian dramas pondering faith, love and death. No sooner had he read the newspaper cutting about his triumph in Cannes than Bergman, with his then girl-friend Bibi Andersson in tow, rushed to the Riviera in person to confront Carl-Anders Dymling, the head of Svensk. Bergman thrust his screenplay for *The Seventh Seal* into Dymling's hands and demanded an immediate response. Dymling had already turned the project down. Now, aware that international critics and distributors were full of excitement about *Smiles of a Summer Night*, he changed his mind and agreed to support the film. It was a symbolic moment. After a dozen years of toil and constant battles with collaborators and bosses, Bergman, at one fell swoop, achieved the artistic independence he had been craving for so long.

'Ever since the success of *Smiles of a Summer Night*, nobody has interfered with my work. I have been able to do as I wished', Bergman recalled.[2]

It is worth noting, though, how long it took him to reach this pass and how pragmatic and even mercenary he sometimes had to be to get there. Certain pet themes may have been recognisable in his work from the outset. His films had always had a strongly personal dimension, with actors like Stig Olin and Birger Malmsten playing characters who shared many of his own traits. He may have begun to assemble around his little repertory company of trusted actors and technicians. However, Bergman's films also fitted into pre-existing moulds. They were – at least to a degree – made to order and even derivative. They were summer films, films about troubled youth, dramas about marriages going awry or melodramas about artists and musicians trying to reconcile their personal and professional lives.

Dymling and his colleagues at Svensk had long since realised that Bergman had talent and originality, but they were only prepared to indulge him to a certain extent. Bergman's private life, meanwhile, was so complicated that he was obliged to work, if only to fulfil his financial commitments to his ex-wives and dependants.

At the end of the production standstill in Sweden in the early 1950s, Bergman reluctantly signed a new contract with Svensk. The terms were not at all what he had hoped. He called the contract 'second-rate'. However, Bergman knew that the only way to improve his standing at the studio (and his finances) was to make a hit. As he observed in *Images*, 'a comedy seemed an absolute necessity'.[3]

Waiting Women (1952), made back-to-back with *Summer with Monika* (1953), was the 'comedy' Dymling had demanded. Bergman being Bergman, this wasn't any kind of upbeat romantic farce. The themes were dark and unsettling. Death was again hovering at the edge of the frame. Marriage was portrayed as a battleground – an arena for betrayal and despair.

In the film, a group of wives compare notes on their absent husbands. They are on holiday in the countryside (lovingly shot by Gunnar Fischer). Once the children are in bed, they sit around the table and begin to gossip. Within moments, we learn that their lives are nowhere near as idyllic as they may first appear. An older woman, Annette (Aino Taube), is the first to share some grim revelations about her domestic life. Her marriage to Paul isn't exactly a sham, but there is no warmth or intimacy to it. Only in a Bergman comedy would we hear a wife yearning for her husband to beat her so that at least she knew strong feelings still existed between them.

'You're not as alone as you think … to be deserted, we know the feeling', the younger wives tell her. With this, we're whisked back in time to another summer's day on which Rakel (Anita Bjork), already bored of her husband Eugen (Karl-Arne Homsten), allows herself to be seduced by her old boyfriend Kaj (Jarl Kulle).

Superficially, *Waiting Women* resembles one of those Hollywood romantic comedies from directors like Joseph L. Mankiewicz or George Cukor, looking at faltering relationships in witty and caustic fashion. However, there is a sexual frankness not found in Hollywood films of the era. Bergman, meanwhile, probes away relentlessly at areas far too uncomfortable for mainstream studio directors to explore in any depth: sexual guilt and sexual disgust, suicide, betrayal and cuckoldry. Having cheated on her husband with Kaj, Rakel is in the room with both men. She admits to her infidelity but seems determined to antagonise both men, calling Kaj 'disgusting' and too self-centred to be a good lover.

The comedy often has a very barbed edge. After his failed marriages, Bergman was exploring marital betrayal and misery from a position of strong personal experience. As he shows, the betrayed spouses, at their most distraught, cut inadvertently comic figures. Eugen threatens suicide and runs off to the boathouse with his rifle, yelling self-pitying slogans. In the end, he is talked out of killing himself on the grounds that 'the worst thing is not to be betrayed but to be lonely'. Rakel and Kaj are reconciled.

An even grimmer story is recounted by Marta (Maj-Britt Nilsson), who recalls her relationship with Martin (Birger Malmsten) and subsequent pregnancy. The lovers from *Summer Interlude* are reunited, but they are no happier than they were before.

In one striking sequence rekindling memories of the wizened old lady in *Summer Interlude*, Nilsson is again confronted with a character who seems to be the embodiment of death – a man in a bowler hat seen in blurred outline through the frosted glass of her door. 'I had a horrible feeling of death itself waiting for me outside the door. A poor pedlar or a friend of the family. It could be explained away. Still I was overcome by a paralysing fear of death and my loneliness became the loneliness of death. It was like in a dream where you try to shout but can't utter a sound', she says. As the heavily pregnant Nilsson lies on a hospital bed, just beginning her labour and waiting to give birth, there is an expressionistic flashback to a Paris nightclub. Bergman shows the events leading up to her pregnancy. We see Nilsson in a Paris nightclub

with Bob, an American GI, as escort. The proprietor offers a bottle of
champagne to any guest who can hold a two-franc piece between her
thighs. To Bob's fury, as leering old men look on, Marta performs the feat
and wins the champagne. Then, drunk, she escapes from the GI into the
Paris dawn. In her little hotel room, she is seduced by Martin (Birger
Malmsten).

An idealistic young artist chafing against his bourgeois family background, Martin is yet another of Bergman's Hamlet-like young rebels.
The writer-director's disdain for his own father is echoed here. 'Father
is dead. How fantastic!' Martin exclaims when he learns of his father's
death. Again, this is not a line – or an attitude – that you would expect to encounter in a romantic comedy. The birth sequence, prefiguring Bergman's later drama *Brink of Life* about the experiences of young
women in a maternity ward, is prolonged and does nothing to downplay
the pain the young mother is in. Bergman relishes showing the doctors
and nurses bustling around her as she lies strapped on the hospital bed, in
agony. 'Now push and it'll soon be over', the midwife tells her, seemingly
oblivious to the trauma she is enduring.

Bergman uses some of the flashy techniques he and Gunnar Fischer
had experimented with on their Bris soap commercials: in particular,
flashy dissolves and montage sequences, jarring close-ups, subliminal cuts
and flashbacks within flashbacks. He even allows himself an Alfred
Hitchcock-style cameo (we spot his reflection on the side of a mirror
in which Marta is checking her reflection). Grotesquerie and sentimentality sit side by side as Marta is finally shown to be radiantly happy as a
mother, even if she decided against marrying Martin.

The final section of the film throws up one of the most famous scenes
in Bergman's early work in which the couple gets caught in the lift.
Martin's brother Fredrik (Gunnar Bjornstrand) is married to Karin (Eva
Dahlbeck). Fredrik likes to see himself as a successful businessman, 'a
competent bastard' as he styles himself, who has done well in growing
his father's firm. He is as conceited as he is conventional, convinced that
his children are unusually talented and proud of his beautiful wife. 'It's
as if all the unpleasant things in life go away when I turn up', he boasts
as he and Karin drive home from a party. Karin taunts him, telling him
that he has been standing around all evening speaking to dignitaries, un-
aware that there is shaving foam in his ear. Then comes the celebrated sequence in the lift that gets stuck. All of a sudden, the complacent husband
and wife are stranded in a claustrophobic little space. Their predicament
worsens when the lights go out.

Humiliation was always one of Bergman's favourite themes. With sadistic relish, he enjoys turning the uptight Fredrik into a clown-like figure. He is powerless. His top hat is crushed. It is beneath his dignity to shout for help. His hapless attempts to escape just make his wife laugh uproariously at him. He is the father figure, and Bergman enjoys his humiliation. There is also an erotic undertow to the scene. The couple who've been ignoring one another physically for so long are suddenly trapped in a tiny space. After bickering, discussing their affairs and disappointments during their 13-year-old marriage, they make love.

The sequence is crafted with typical skill by Bergman, who uses shadows, reflections and constant reframing to keep matters dramatic. Like so much else in his work, it was based on an incident in his own life when he and his second wife had been locked out of their apartment on their way home from a dinner party. They had had to sit in the stairwell all night in considerable discomfort. 'But the night was not wasted because we suddenly received an unexpected opportunity to really talk to each other.'[4]

Waiting Women was warmly received by most Swedish critics. 'Ingmar Bergman depicts people like a fish monger skinning a fish: a few swift cuts with the knife reveal what lies underneath. Smiling gleefully he holds up the bare bones, calling the procedure a comedy, or a light embroidery set against a dark background', wrote Karl Ekwall in *Aftontidningen*.[5] Bergman, meanwhile, was gratified by the novelty of having audiences actually laugh at scenes in one of his films. The knockabout humour of the sequence in the lift, which comes close to the end of the film, so delighted them that they seemingly forgot how dark much of the earlier part of the story had been.

Bergman's next film, *Summer with Monika* (1953), was in a very different groove. This was Bergman at his most exuberant and paganistic. It helped that, in his young star Harriet Andersson, Bergman had an actress with the same oomph factor as a Diana Dors or a Brigitte Bardot: someone who combined humour, irreverence and sensuality. Bergman had found her through Gustaf Molander. It was a moot point whether her ability or her appearance attracted him the most. He had only seen her act once – in fishnet stockings in a stage revue.[6] That, combined with what he called her 'elegant décolletage', was enough for him to approach Molander to ask about her.

'I started in a private theatre school when I was 15 years old and I started working in the theatre in 1949', Andersson liked to emphasise her roots as a serious actress lest anyone thought she was simply a sex

Harriet Andersson strikes a Bardot-like pose in *Summer with Monika*.

symbol.[7] Nonetheless, she brought a quality to Bergman's films that they had previously lacked.

Summer with Monika, scripted by Bergman and novelist Per Anders Fogelstrom, is the story of a voluptuous 17-year-old greengrocer's daughter ('mucky Monika' as she is dubbed by the street kids) who elopes by boat with her boyfriend Harry (Larks Ekborg). They spend an idyllic summer together, living like little pagans away from the clutter and chaos of their oppressive family lives. They have a recklessness which chimes perfectly with the similarly unbridled rebelliousness and defiance of the rebels in US teen movies of the period.

Taking his cue from Chekhov, Bergman always liked to anthropomorphise nature: to make the outer world echo his characters' inner feelings. Here, when Monika and Harry are in the first flush of young love, the landscapes seem to respond to the intensity of their emotions. The winds blow; there are frequent cutaways to dark, oppressive skies and the countryside has an Edenic rawness. At one stage, Monika strips off and splashes around in the water as if she is doing an impression of Heddy Lamarr in Czech director Gustav Machaty's succeś de scandale *Ecstasy*. This was a film that Bergman had watched and admired, not just for its celebration of nature (and, notoriously, naturism) but because of its visual power. 'I saw *Ecstasy* when I was eighteen years old, and it deeply affected me', Bergman recalled. 'This was partly a natural reaction because, for once, one was allowed to see a nude woman on scene, but more important, because the movie told nearly everything through images alone.'[8]

Inevitably, the lovers' joyous existence in the wilds, totally apart from the rest of the world, can't last. The seasons change. Soon, they are obliged to head back into the city and face up to their responsibilities as young parents. In Stockholm, they are just another bickering couple who married too young, trying to make a living and to tend to their young daughter. Eventually, their love, which had seemed unbreakable, crumbles.

'Harriet Andersson is one of cinema's true geniuses. You meet only a few of these rare, shimmering individuals on your travels along the twisting road of the movie industry jungle', Bergman sententiously remarked of his leading lady with whom – to complicate his own private life further – he had begun an affair.[9]

Summer with Monika had been shot quickly, using real locations. It had a freshness and spontaneity which strongly appealed to the young French filmmakers of the Nouvelle Vague, fighting their own battles with Le Cinema du Papa.

The freewheeling filmmaking style matches the irreverence of Andersson's performance. Chewing gum, smoking cigarettes, sunbathing on the prow of the boat and stealing the roast meat from the table of a bourgeois family, Monika is endlessly defiant. At times, Bergman films her as if she is an animal in the wild. We see her prowling through the undergrowth, hiding beneath bridges and gnawing on her stolen meat. There are even moments in which the director and the actress conspire, deliberately flouting filmmaking conventions. For example, we see Andersson looking directly at the camera. This is never supposed to happen in a realist film. Andersson lays bare the device, breaking the illusion that we are watching 'real life'. Somehow, though, through sheer strength of personality, she gets away with it. In one famous scene, when she is back in Stockholm, she is shown listening to jazz on a jukebox, utterly unperturbed by her predicament as an impoverished mother. As she lazily smokes a cigarette, she turns her head to the side and the camera slowly moves in towards her face, eventually capturing her in a big close-up, looking back defiantly at the lens, making (as Bergman put it) 'shameless, direct contact with the viewer'.[10] It is perhaps no coincidence that Godard would use similar ways of framing some of his female subjects, for example his use of Brigitte Bardot in the opening of *Le Mepris* (1963). At the time of the film, Bardot was one of the biggest stars of world cinema. Godard relished showing her nearly naked in a long close-up, shot in widescreen. Like Bergman, Godard was playing on the audience's voyeurism. Bardot may not have looked back at the camera (although Godard always liked to lay bare the device), but she also refused to accept the role as a passive pin-up.

To those who know Bergman primarily through later work, whether his autobiographical epic *Fanny and Alexander*, his 'faith' trilogy of the early 1960s (*The Silence, Through a Glass Darkly* and *Winter Light*) or even experimental work like *Persona* and *Hour of the Wolf, Summer with Monika* will come as a surprise. It is rough and exuberant. Its characters come from working-class background. Monika and Lars aren't the precious students, artists, would-be filmmakers or ballet dancers we know from his early work. They're simply a couple of youngsters looking to escape a wretched and oppressive background. Of course, that background draws them back in. By the time they return to Stockholm, Monika is pregnant. Now what awaits is simply the drudgery of life in a tiny, cramped apartment with a baby daughter who cries at night.

Reviews were distinctly mixed. The film was considered too brazen and too scandalous. Certain critics disapproved of Monika, and their annoyance at her behaviour clouded their response to the movie as a whole. In the USA, bizarrely, the film was released as *Monika – The Story of a Bad Girl* and made yet more risqué with some extra nude footage. (Bergman's work had been tampered with in the USA before and would be treated with the same disregard in the future, often being dubbed or cut for American audiences.) The film's US distributor was fined and sent to prison. A US judge made a ruling saying that *Summer with Monika* appealed to 'potential sex murderers'. Ironically, the great auteur Bergman's work was being treated as if it was exploitation fare. It wasn't just in the USA that European 'arthouse' was considered pornography. In the 1970s, Bergman films were shown in Soho cinemas in London alongside X-rated fare and in eclectic repertory cinemas like the Scala in Kings Cross, which also showcased the work of directors like Russ Meyer.

Perhaps some of the resentment the filmmaker felt about being accused of making 'sexploitation' fed into his next film. *Sawdust and Tinsel* (1953), also known as *The Naked Night*, captures brilliantly the loneliness, financial uncertainty and sheer indignity of the travelling performer's life. It is a film about humiliation in almost all its manifestations: sexual, social, political, financial and physical. The contempt sometimes heaped on Bergman, the writer and director, was as nothing with what is endured by the circus owner Albert (Ake Gronberg). It was a measure of Bergman's still uncertain standing within Swedish film culture that he faced such a struggle to get the film financed. In the end, *Sawdust and Tinsel* was made by rival production company Sandrews after having been rejected by Svensk.

Befitting a film that had its origins in a dream, *Sawdust and Tinsel* has a deliberately dreamlike quality. Despite its sombre tone, it reflects its director's love of silent comedy – and in particular of Charlie Chaplin's *The Circus* (1928). This was Chaplin at his most barbed – a tale about a tramp close to starvation who ends up with a stolen wallet and the police on his tail. He runs into a circus mid-performance, leaving a trail of havoc in his wake, getting in the way of the clowns, disturbing and subverting the magician's tricks. The irony is that the audience loves him. The spectators think his bungling is for real and is a planned part of the performance.

Sawdust and Tinsel shares some of the desperation of Chaplin's movie, but there is little redeeming humour here. The story begins with the circus wagons trundling across a grey landscape. The circus performers, en route to their next engagement, are dirty and exhausted. The first

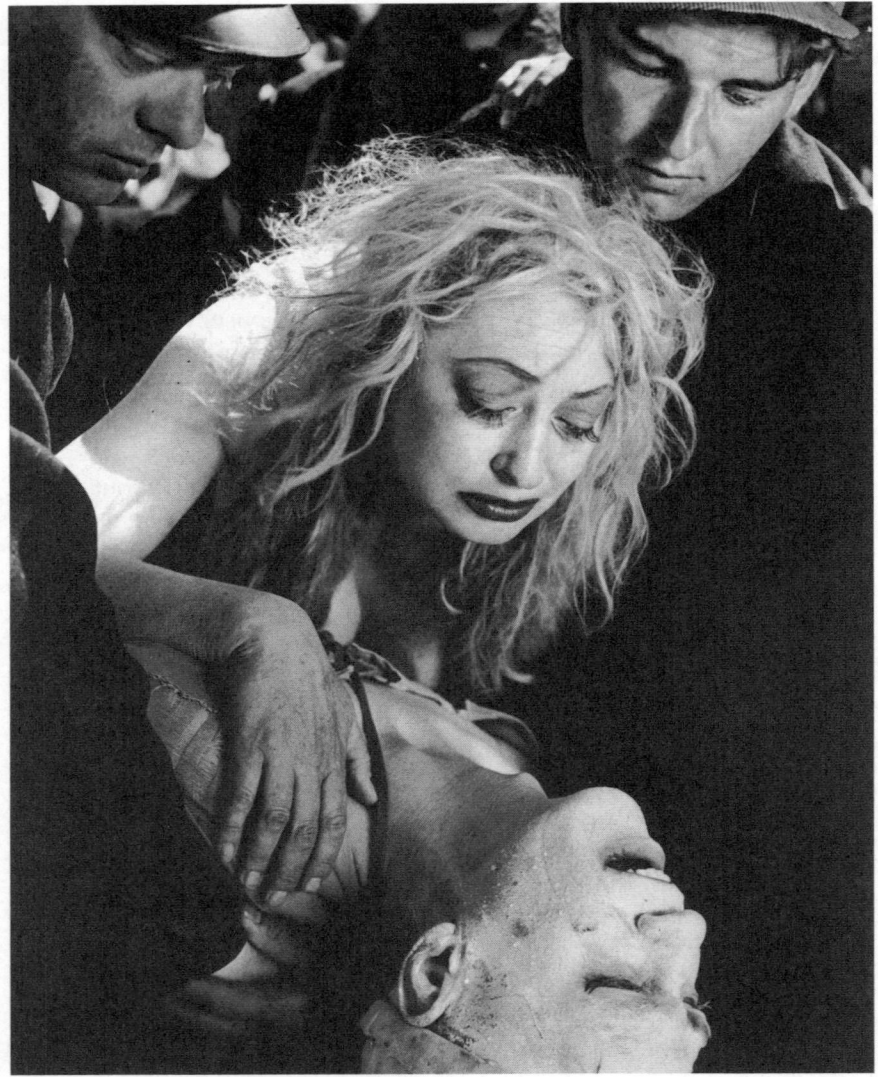

A study in humiliation – Frost (Anders Ek), the clown, and his wife Alma (Gudrun Brost) in *Sawdust and Tinsel*.

we see of Albert, a plump, moustached figure, he is waking from a deep sleep. His girlfriend Anne (Harriet Andersson) is still asleep. He goes to sit upfront with the wagon driver. We learn that he will shortly see his wife and child for the first time in three years. The driver then tells him the story about Frost, the clown, and his wife Alma, prompting a flashback which spells out all the film's themes in microcosm.

The sequence is shot to the accompaniment of music and gunfire. On a sweltering day by the seaside, Alma – evidently very drunk – performs a striptease for a platoon of soldiers who've been holding shooting practice with their cannons. Frost, still in clown's garb, rushes to the scene only to find his wife frolicking in the water with some of the soldiers. The other soldiers are sitting by the shore, watching and guffawing. Frost, in great distress, strips off his own clothes and steps across the jagged rocks. He hauls his naked wife on his back and tries to carry her to safety. She, at last, realises how cruelly she is being mocked. In torment, the clown carries his wife away across the rocks. The soldiers are following close behind him. He keeps losing his footing and in the end has to be carried away by the other circus performers. The clown is utterly mortified by his loss of dignity. In the course of the film, Albert experiences a similar fall from grace.

The clown threatens suicide in *Sawdust and Tinsel*.

Bergman freely acknowledged the autobiographical undertow too. This makes the film feel even more like an exercise in masochism. The Bergman alter ego here isn't some febrile, gimlet-eyed student or artist played by Birger Malmsten or Stig Olin. It is the overweight, buffoonish Albert. 'If a scrawny director aims for a self-portrait, of course he chooses a fat actor to play him', Bergman noted with self-lacerating irony.[11] The sexual jealousy that Albert feels when Anne flirts with Frans (Hasse Ekman), the arrogant actor, was something he had experienced too. He described the film's structure as 'a number of thematic variations on erotics and humiliation in ever-changing combinations'.

There are many moments heavy with symbolism and irony in *Sawdust and Tinsel*. When Albert goes cap in hand to the 'serious' theatre company to ask to borrow costumes, he is treated with withering disdain. A circus ringmaster, like a film director and his entourage, is regarded as a seedy figure, not altogether respectable. The exaggerated politeness with which the theatre manager Sjuberg (Gunnar Bjornstrand) treats Albert and Anna only adds to the sense that he is mocking them. They may be kindred spirits – 'you live in wagons, we in sleazy hotels. We make art, you artifice', Sjuberg tells Albert. Nonetheless, there is a gaping chasm between them. The humblest theatre actor despises the circus performers.

Albert half yearns for a bourgeois stability. In one poignant scene, we see his reunion with the wife he abandoned many years before. He meets his son, who doesn't at first recognise him, and sees that his ex-wife has built herself a stable and contented life away from the circus. She feeds him, gives him beer and fixes his clothes for him. Cravenly, he asks if she will have him back. Of course, she says no.

A film that is a study in humiliation in all its guises ends with Albert being ground into the circus dust. He picks a fight with Frans and tries to horsewhip him. The assumption among the other circus workers is that he will be too big and too strong for the conceited actor, but Frans easily beats him. It's like watching bear-baiting. What makes the scene even more uncomfortable is the sense that just as Anne half relishes being bullied, humiliated and seduced by Frans, Albert welcomes his defeat. It is a confirmation of his own self-loathing.

Formally, *Sawdust and Tinsel* is highly inventive. This was the first film on which Bergman had worked with cinematographer Sven Nykvist, who shot the interiors. Bergman throws in expressionistic sequences, reminiscent of old silent melodramas. He evokes circus life with the same mix of grotesquerie and childlike awe found in Todd Browning's *Freaks*.

On one level, the film is optimistic. Albert and Anne may both be utterly humiliated and left stuck with each other to carry on their precarious lives in the circus. Bergman relishes grinding them down and showing all their illusions being shattered. Albert is so inept he can't even commit suicide properly. Nonetheless, there is still something defiant about the way they stick to their lives on the road. For all the indignities they endure, this – Bergman implies – is a richer, more fulfilling existence than simply staying stuck in a small town, tending a shop – the only alternative that Albert has. Just because it is a shabby, second-rate circus doesn't mean that it can't create magic.

Sawdust and Tinsel now appears as one of the richest, most inventive films of Bergman's middle period. That wasn't how it was regarded on its initial release in Sweden, where the response was decidedly mixed. 'I refuse [...] to perform an ocular inspection of the vomit that Ingmar Bergman has left behind him on this occasion, even though I can well imagine that the original menu was an appetising one. I am of the opinion

Albert (Ake Gronberg) and Anne (Harriet Andersson), the circus couple, at their most wretched in *Sawdust and Tinsel*.

that one should avoid any act of public defilement, even if one has a great deal to flush out of one's system, unless like an August Strindberg one can produce something sublime from one's squalor', wrote the reviewer in *Aftonbladet*.[12] Such an extreme reaction, reminiscent of the revulsion British critics later expressed for Michael Powell's *Peeping Tom*, at least suggests the film was getting under the skin of viewers.

The film had its champions but wasn't the box-office success that Bergman still craved, if only to guarantee his artistic freedom. His status remained that of the talented but unwholesome outsider. His best defence against his critics was his relentless work rate. If one film failed, there would always be another one along soon. He may have been an artist, but he wasn't precious about his work: 'To those who say he has made too many (films), he has several replies', Vilgot Sjoman noted of him in a 1957 article. 'You can't make films the way you make books, by sitting and waiting for a masterpiece to come; film is a product, a beautified everyday object.'[13]

After the soul-baring and messy emotionalism of *Sawdust and Tinsel*, Bergman took a step backward. Working again with Svensk, he began making a series of brittle, sophisticated romantic comedies which he and the studio bosses hoped would prove a little more appealing to the critics so discomfited by his rawer, more personal work. There was a sense with *A Lesson in Love* that Bergman was going against his own instincts. An opening voice-over tells us: 'this comedy might have been a tragedy'. We sense that Bergman might have preferred it had he been allowed to foreground the tragic elements at the expense of the comic rather than vice versa.

A Lesson in Love reunites Bjornstrand and Dahlbeck, the couple so memorably trapped in the elevator in *Waiting Women*. Bjornstrand is cast – a little improbably – as a womanising gynaecologist. ('He that always sees women from odd angles ends up a little peculiar', a disgruntled lover called Mrs Verin tells him.)

Although Bergman recounts audiences responding warmly enough, comedy did not come naturally to him. He risked seeming caustic and flippant. The doleful Bjornstrand is no Cary Grant. The film feels complacent and conventional: a suburban, middle-class romantic drama for mainstream audiences. Disconcertingly, Harriet Andersson, the voluptuous femme fatale of *Sawdust and Tinsel*, has been transformed into a tomboy in a checked shirt.

Dr David Erneman has been married for 15 years but hasn't yet been unfaithful. The lure of the pretty, 21-year-old Suzanne Verin, though, is more than he can resist. When he begins an affair, it gives his wife (Dahlbeck) the licence to do likewise. Bergman tries to capture some of the same spark that had run through Bjornstrand and Dahlbeck's scenes in *Waiting Women*. This time, instead of sharing a broken-down lift, they spend much of the time inside a railway compartment en route to Copenhagen. In the film, Bergman is again anatomising a marriage gone wrong, one of his most familiar themes, but he is under the constraints of his chosen genre to keep matters upbeat. Certain scenes are funny and well observed enough – for example the wife pretending to be a maid and walking in on her husband and his lover as they enjoy a secret tryst in a hotel room. Overall, though, this is thin gruel. Bergman acknowledged that he struggled with farce and that his two lead actors helped him stage the most important set-piece. Confronted with his version of the failed suicide in the screenplay, they told him to 'leave the set, go into town and find something else to do' and then reworked the scene in his absence.

A Lesson in Love isn't a bad film. Dahlbeck brings plenty of anarchic spirit to her role as the wronged wife. Bergman's screenplay engineers some clever plot reversals and is full of pithy one-liners. What is disappointing is how derivative the film feels by comparison with the Howard Hawks and Preston Sturges screwball comedies it tries to emulate.

From Bergman's point of view, the film served its purpose. It proved that he could make comedies and it was a popular success. However, as Bergman's friend and often most trenchant critic Harry Schein pointed out in a review, there was very little substance to the work. 'Ultimately, with the many weeks of full houses for this film, Bergman has demonstrated the art of making something out of nothing: he has managed to conceal at great length the fact that he has nothing to tell.'

Dreams (a.k.a. *Journey into Autumn*) (1955), the comedy that Bergman made next, at least had the emotional rawness that *A Lesson in Love* had lacked. It is one of his most neglected films, but is revealing and personal. Bergman acknowledged that Susanne (Eva Dahlbeck's character), the fashion director hoping for a reunion with her married lover, was based on Gun Hagberg – the journalist for whom he had left his second wife.

Love, betrayal and fear of mortality are among the familiar themes in Bergman's drama about two women whose romantic illusions are shattered. There is a tremendously powerful scene in which Susanne is caught with her lover by her lover's wife. She quickly realises that she has no chance of holding onto her lover. Equally poignant and pathetic is the scene in which the young model (Harriet Andersson) is humiliated by

Susanne (Eva Dahlbeck), the fashion director clinging to the phone in *Dreams*, was based on Gun Hagberg — the journalist for whom Bergman had left his second wife.

the daughter of the elderly diplomat (Gunnar Bjornstrand) who has been courting her. This may be one of Bergman's lesser known works, but it boasts the same emotional intensity and acute eye for observation of the vanities and foibles of its characters as his more familiar films. What is intriguing is Bergman's determination to take the women's perspective. The men come out badly. They are too wrapped up in their own vanity and quest for self-gratification to appreciate the suffering they are causing to the women they toy with.

Dreams was made just as Bergman's own relationship with Harriet Andersson was beginning to fray. The director had begun to see such upheavals as an inevitable consequence of his profession. Creative and sexual tensions were intertwined. Relationships were begun quickly in the mood of heightened anxiety and exhilaration that actors and director felt on set or in the rehearsal room. These relationships often burned out as quickly as they had begun. In *Dreams*, the mood is bleak throughout.

Gunnar Bjornstrand as the old roué trying to seduce the naive model (Harriet Andersson) in *Dreams*.

Dahlbeck's character simply won't accept the end of her affair with a married man. Bergman frequently shows her face in big close-ups, looking as pained as the martyred Joan of Arc. We see her peering in at her ex-lover's happy family home and trudging the streets disconsolately. Dahlbeck conveys brilliantly the character's anguish and desperation as she tries to engineer a meeting with the man who has spurned her. She is a successful career woman, but in her desperation, she behaves like a hysterical teenager.

Equally grim is the story of Doris (Andersson), the young model preyed on by the diplomat who accosts her in the street and offers to buy her a dress she has been gazing at with longing. He lusts after her. It is also clear she reminds him of his estranged daughter. He is trying to start a relationship with her because he knows his daughter despises him. The scene in the jeweller's shop echoes Andersson's seduction by the actor in *Sawdust and Tinsel*. There, the actor's arrogance and youth seduced her into a decision that she hated herself for. Here, it is the promise of pearls that pushes her into a decision she hates herself for. She spends so long being pampered by the old diplomat that she misses her modelling assignment and is summarily sacked by Dahlbeck. The irony is that in her self-pity, she is even more susceptible to the courting of the old diplomat, who now bribes her with pastry and chocolate and fairground rides. They make a grotesque couple, drinking champagne and listening to music together. Then his daughter Marianne (Kerstin Hedeby) turns up, asking for money, and sees Doris in her newly bought gown and necklace and the family jewellery that should by rights belong to Marianne. Doris is called a 'little whore', slapped and utterly humiliated by the daughter. Then, to compound her misery, the diplomat also turns on her and yells at her to get out. These are the kind of scenes that Bergman always excelled in staging: scenes in which characters' illusions about themselves are exposed in the cruellest and most painful fashion.

Doris suffers because she is young and vain. Susanne has no such excuses, but her encounter with her married lover Henrik (Ulf Palme) is just as much an exercise in self-abasement. They meet clandestinely and make love. Susanne is so sick with hatred and jealousy that she wishes his wife and children dead. They hatch plans for further meetings, but as they lie in their hotel room, they are caught out by Henrik's wife. It is a replay of the scene in *A Lesson in Love*, but this time, there is nothing funny about the lovers being caught out. Susanne finally accepts that Henrik will never leave his cosy domestic life for her sake. She has to accept that she has been utterly routed by Henrik's wife. It is a raw, very uncomfortable scene that would be echoed again and again in Bergman's later work, right through to *Faithless* (2002), which again had lovers caught in flagrante by a wronged spouse. At the end of *Dreams*, it is left to Dahlbeck and Andersson to console one another. Andersson is reconciled with her old boyfriend. Dahlbeck finally finds the strength to cut her ties with her married lover, who – in spite of everything – is still trying to lure her into another seedy, clandestine tryst.

At this point – in the mid-1950s – Bergman did not cut a happy figure. Katinka Farago, who was recruited as a teenager to work as a script editor on *Dreams* and went on to collaborate with Bergman for more than 25 years, paints a surprisingly bleak picture of life on a Bergman set.

'They need a script girl – continuity as it is called – and no-one else wanted to work with him', Farago recalled of her first encounter with Bergman. The director had a reputation as being 'not so nice to work with'. It was a reputation that he soon lived up to. 'He was screaming and hollering and very nervous. He wasn't very happy at that time and not very well. He weighed nothing. He was very thin. He had all these stomach problems and so on.'[14]

Farago describes working with Bergman at this stage of his career as 'terrifying'. The director liked his young assistant because she didn't speak too much. 'I was scared to speak', she says.[15] Bergman would frequently dress down his crew members, sometimes in a way that humiliated them in front of their colleagues. Farago testifies that he usually apologised (at least to her), but always in private. He was invariably kind to his actors, who responded with great warmth to him. The technicians were less fortunate. Even his relations with his revered cinematographers Gunnar Fischer and Sven Nykvist sometimes threatened to fray. Bergman would grow suspicious about their experimentalism.

One of Farago's tasks was to go to the post office to mail maintenance cheques to his various dependants – the ex-wives and children. 'It was a lot of money for that time. He was quite poor!'[16]

Dreams – as Bergman bluntly put it – went 'to hell'. It was yet another in his long line of box-office disappointments. His private life was in turmoil. His relationship to Harriet Andersson was now in its death throes. The couple had a little dachshund puppy, but if they shared a doting affection for the dog, it was not enough to keep them together. Bergman had promised Carl-Anders Dymling, his old patron at Svensk Filmindustri, that his next film would be a comedy. Dymling was ready to indulge Bergman, but only so far. He made it very clear to his temperamental director that he wanted a film to please audiences, not another of Bergman's angst-ridden exercises in soul searching.

During this period, Dymling later recalled, Bergman invariably received hostile reviews. 'He was considered difficult, bizarre, incomprehensible, pretentious.'[17] Farago confirms this, saying that Swedish critics were always tough on Bergman, calling him 'a student filmmaker'. Farago recalls that her mother refused to see a Bergman film on the grounds that he was 'a student all his life'.[18] It was only when his reputation began to grow internationally in the wake of the success of *Smiles of a Summer Night*, *The Seventh Seal* and others that the Swedes began to treat the director a little more gently.

Dymling claimed that he had to fight hard to convince his fellow board members to continue backing such an awkward filmmaker. It didn't help that from a financial point of view, a Bergman picture still seemed a 'risky business'. Dymling had enjoyed the scene in *Waiting Women* in which Gunnar Bjornstrand and Eva Dahlbeck had been stuck in the lift. That, he felt, was the way forward for Bergman.

To Dymling's relief, Bergman responded by agreeing to make a romantic comedy. This was *Smiles of a Summer Night* (1955), one of his sharpest and most exquisitely crafted films and (by chance, it seemed) the movie that finally consolidated his international reputation. Bergman later grumbled that he was in poor health when he made the film, losing weight and convinced that he had stomach cancer. None of his anxiety shows on screen. 'I am first and foremost a craftsman and I make fine goods for people's use', he told his friend and sometime producer Jorn Donner late in his life.[19] *Smiles of a Summer Night* may not be his most personal film, but it is as carefully and finely constructed as the mechanical cuckoo clock that features in the film. Svensk had put considerable resources at Bergman's disposal. This was a period piece with extravagantly detailed costume and production design. Hats, feathers, jewellery, glassware and silver are all in conspicuous evidence. *Smiles of a Summer Night* may – as Bergman suggested – pick up on ideas first broached in *A Lesson in Love*, but it is infinitely superior to the earlier film. Bergman didn't have that much time to complete the movie – the shooting schedule was around 40 days – but cast and crew were helped by exceptional weather.

Again, Bergman is exploring one of his favourite paradoxes – namely that people who love one another can't always live together. Again, there is an obvious autobiographical undertow. The writer-director acknowledged that a certain nostalgia had crept into the storytelling and that he was working through in fictional form the 'great confusion and sorrow' of his relationship with his daughter (he doesn't specify which one). This, however, is one of his nakedly confessional efforts. Nor is it a young director's film. Bergman, by now, was on the cusp of middle age, almost 40, and had experienced broken marriages and plenty of career setbacks. There is a gentle irony here which isn't found in his earlier work. Bergman satirises the vanities and self-deceptions of characters he might once have identified with far more closely. The conceited lawyer Fredrik Egerman (Bjornstrand) has a virginal young wife whom he claims to love while still pursuing his ex-mistress, the beautiful but ageing actress Desiree (Eva Dahlbeck). Priests are often older, patriarchal figures in his films, but here the would-be priest Henrik Egerman (Bjorn Bjelvenstam) is young and priggish. Meanwhile, the military officer Count Malcolm (Jarl Kulle) is as conceited as he is jealous, always either showing off or spoiling for a duel. Meanwhile, the voluptuous maid (Harriet Andersson) relishes trying to introduce earnest young Henrik to the sins of the flesh. The tempo is brisk, Gunnar Fischer's cinematography emphasises brightness and light, and the mood is ultimately benign. Nonetheless, Bergman is probing into some very uncomfortable areas. 'Why are young people so dreadfully merciless?' asks Dahlbeck's ancient, Miss Havisham-like mother, who hosts the party that brings the bickering couples together at a beautiful country house. The protagonists here are so narcissistic and self-absorbed that they notice neither how absurd they appear nor how much suffering they are causing one another.

Formally, this is a tour de force. Like Jean Renoir's great country house drama *The Rules of the Game* (1939), it is both a magical, escapist fare and an unsettling psychological drama. Bergman's experience as a stage director is evident in the many long, dialogue-driven scenes set in bedrooms or dining rooms or dressing rooms. At the same time, Fischer's cinematography remains lithe and inventive. The camera is continually moving and reframing. The mise-en-scène is exhaustively detailed. Paintings, photographs and mementoes cram the rooms in which these pampered, affluent characters live. Perhaps the scene that best sums up the film's intentions – and shows how Bergman had matured as a filmmaker – is the failed suicide of the young, would-be priest. The scene is played as high comedy. The priest, full of angst about his romantic desires and how they conflict with his religious beliefs, takes a cord and tries to hang himself. The cord slips. Rather than meeting his maker, he is thrown headfirst onto the hidden lever which sets the bed in the next-door room in motion. The bed slides through the wall, and he finds lying in front of him his father's wife – the woman he loves. Rather than kill himself, he embraces her instead. His next step is to elope with her. This is the first 'smile' of the summer night. The other smiles soon follow. First, Count Malcolm, sure that he has been cuckolded, challenges Egerman to a game of Russian roulette in the summer house. The gun, though, is full of soot. This is the count's little ruse. What it reveals is that for all his philandering, he really loves his wife. The soot-covered Egerman, meanwhile, is consoled by Desiree. Each character has found the right lover. While their romantic conspiracies take place against the backdrop of the country house, Harriet Andersson's maid is busy making love in the hay with a fellow servant.

The same events shown here could easily be reworked into *Miss Julie*-like tragedy, with misery and sexual jealousy foregrounded. Instead, as the birds twitter and the dawn rises, the mood is one of celebration. Still, Bergman can't resist a morbid joke. As one clock chimes, we see not a cuckoo but a skeleton with a scythe – another of Bergman's Grim Reapers and a premonition of his next, far darker film, *The Seventh Seal*.

Strangely, *Smiles of a Summer Night* did not meet with such universal approval from Swedish critics as might have been anticipated. 'The
poor imagination of a spotty youth, the insolent dreams of an immature heart and a boundless contempt for artistic and human truth are
the forces which have created this "comedy". I am ashamed to have seen
it', wrote Olof Lagercrantz, a critic Bergman had formerly admired, in
Dagens Nyheter.[20] It was hard to see what prompted this contempt. Perhaps, critics who thought they knew Bergman and considered him one of
their own were frustrated to see him growing away from them, making
costume dramas rather than telling stories reflecting the lives of young
Swedes. While certain Swedes really accepted Bergman only after he
had been validated by his international success, it was clear that others
resented the popularity he was beginning to enjoy abroad. Bergman, surprisingly thin-skinned, was clearly hurt by the review. More than two
decades later, he quoted it, word for word, in *The Magic Lantern*.

With the passage of time, he acknowledged that the review looked
like a comic curiosity. At the time, though, Lagercrantz's 'poisoned pill'
had caused him much anguish. One wonders if the stomach ailment that
brought him low in the wake of *Smiles of a Summer Night* wasn't at least
partly prompted by Lagercrantz's bilious criticism. Bergman's delicate
digestion can't have been helped either by Svensk's equivocal response
to the film which (Bergman later claimed) they thought too long and too
stilted to make much impression at the box-office.

Given Bergman's obsessive interest in his digestion, it was fitting that
he was 'sitting in the shithouse' when he read of the success of *Smiles of a
Summer Night*. As we have noted, he promptly hurried down to Cannes
to persuade Svensk to back *The Seventh Seal*. Now that the director had
won international approval, the Swedish critics and audiences were at
last willing to treat him with at least a grudging acceptance.

We are so used to the idea of Bergman as the great artist that it is
easy to overlook his opportunism. Bergman's genius lay in his pragmatism as well as his artistry. 'As early as I can remember, the key issue
for me was: What does it take to be a filmmaker in Hollywood?' Martin
Scorsese wrote in his book *A Personal Journey Through American
Movies*.

> Even today, I still wonder what it takes to be a professional or even an artist
> in Hollywood. How do you survive the constant tug of war between personal
> expression and commercial imperatives? What is the price you pay to work
> in Hollywood? Do you end up with a split personality? Do you make one
> movie for them, one for yourself?[21]

On a smaller scale, the same dilemma had always existed for Bergman too. The question was how to keep working: how to appease his paymasters while smuggling his own cherished ideas and themes into his films. Bergman was outspoken with his bosses, freely saying what he thought. 'He wasn't afraid of them (the studio bosses)', Farago recalls. 'They sometimes had problems with him. One, they didn't understand him. Two, they thought he was too self-indulgent.'[22] When Svensk spurned or criticised him, he could turn to his old friend Lorens Marmstedt, whose faith in his talent didn't waver despite the hiccups in his career. However, he needed money. When Svensk demanded comedies, that was what he gave them.

Depending on your point of view, his rate of production was either mind-boggling or heroic. Bergman may have told his friend Vilgot Sjoman that he regarded film as 'product', but he remained fiercely protective of his work and was rarely willing to compromise. As his career progressed, his behaviour on sets mellowed, but this may have had as much to do with conserving his energy as with letting his collaborators off the hook. 'These big scenes made him so tired. I saw it in his eyes when he got angry but he stopped screaming and ordering so much', Farago recalls.[23]

For all his continuing fits of temper, his long years before his international breakthrough had taught him pragmatism and self-reliance. His colleagues grew accustomed to his volatile moods and could even begin to understand why he was so mercurial. 'He (Bergman) gave everything in every movie and every scene. He wanted the people around him also to give everything', Farago says. The anger came as much from humility as from arrogance. It was the frustration of the craftsman unable to complete his job as he had hoped. Bergman seldom made lofty claims on his own behalf. 'He was a humble man toward his own profession', Farago says. She also calls him a down-to-earth and 'practical man' and bemoans the Bergman admirers who have 'blown him up in the sky so he doesn't become human any more'.[24]

The Seventh Seal began as a short play, *Wood Painting*, written by Bergman for his students when he was teaching at the drama school in Malmo. This was also broadcast as a radio play in the autumn of 1954, with Bergman as a narrator. Its imagery – of the dance of death, of the chess match – was inspired by the director's long meditations on religious symbolism and by his childhood visits to churches with his father.

It was not just the Albertus Pictor allegory of Death playing chess with a knight that inspired *Wood Painting*. Bergman also wrote of a mural

Death on the march – Ingmar Bergman's *The Seventh Seal*.

by an unknown artist that he spotted in a little church in southern Smaland. This, painted at the end of the fourteenth century, depicted scenes from a deadly plague that had ravaged the area.

Bergman has talked at length of his religious doubts in the 1950s.

> For me, in those days, the great question was: does God exist? Or doesn't God exist ...what I believed in those days – and believed in for a long time – was the existence of a virulent evil, in no way dependent or environmental or hereditary factors.[25]

These eschatological musings formed the backdrop to *The Seventh Seal* (1956). It is also worth remembering the period in which it was made. Although the film is about a lean-jawed fourteenth-century knight (Max Von Sydow) on his way home from war, *The Seventh Seal* was also at least partly shaped by Bergman's fears about the Cold War.

The play *Wood Painting* took the form of a series of tableaux. Death, the 'stern lord', successively leads away such archetypal figures as the crusader, the common man, the killer, the cuckold and the artist. Death is portrayed in impersonal fashion. The 'stern lord' isn't good or bad. His only important characteristic is that he is relentless.

Bergman's film was eccentric and very personal. It was an essay about his own mortality. He later claimed that writing and directing *The Seventh Seal* was 'excellent therapy' for his morbid obsessions. Svensk had allowed a relatively modest budget for the film, with just three days of location shooting in a total schedule of 35 days. There was no great expectation among the filmmakers or their backers that their film would have much commercial currency. It was considered perverse that Bergman should embark on a film set in the Middle Ages when every other major European filmmaker of the era was preoccupied with contemporary life. Some questioned whether Bergman's ruminations about religion and the loss of faith would have resonance for anybody other than himself.

In the event, Bergman's pet obsessions were far more widely shared than Bergman or Dymling could ever have imagined. Something about *The Seventh Seal* crystallised feelings widely held in Europe and the USA about how precarious life was in the wake of the Second World War and in the middle of the Cold War arms race. That was one explanation why the film had such a strong resonance for international audiences. On another, less exalted level, *The Seventh Seal* was a well-made genre film with a rough naturalism that perhaps appealed to audiences tired of the ersatz world depicted in Hollywood movies of the times. The idea of the lone warrior/survivor roaming through the land blighted by illness and misfortune had long been a staple of sci-fi and adventure movies.

Bergman had a romantic idea of the world of the travelling theatre troupe. As he showed in such works as *Sawdust and Tinsel* and *The Magician*, travelling actors led insecure existences and were constantly prey to humiliation, but there was a purity about their lives too. They had both innocence and a visionary quality.

In his early films, Bergman's alter ego tended to be a delinquent: a tortured artist with a self-destructive personality who would normally be played by Birger Malmsten or Stig Olin. In *The Seventh Seal*, the knight Antonius Blok (Max Von Sydow) presents a very different point of identification for the director. He has an ascetic quality. His torments are not about art or love, but about the nature of faith itself.

Seen today, *The Seventh Seal* suffers from its over-familiarity and the merciless way that it has so often been imitated and caricatured. It demands a suspension of belief that contemporary audiences are not always prepared to give it.

'I have great affection for *Wild Strawberries*, an influence on my own work', observes one leading young US director, voicing an opinion which many others share. 'But have you seen *The Seventh Seal* lately – the film we all thought was so cool in university? It's fucking unwatchable and laughable now. Interesting how that works.'

The symbolism seems portentous and even absurd – the gloomy clouds with a bird of prey hovering over the world, the black-caped reaper and the use of choral music as the Virgin Mary hoves into view with a naked baby at her feet. Nonetheless, the film is still frequently chilling. When the knight's squire (Gunnar Bjornstrand out of evening dress and playing a rough-hewn everyman) turns over what he thinks is a sleeping body and discovers he has disturbed a corpse, the sudden cut and use of a sharp sound remain as disorienting as ever. Bergman's recreation of the Middle Ages is down-to-earth. Despite the apocalyptic events, the characterisation and dialogue are matter-of-fact. When the squire interrupts the artist working on his mural of *The Dance of Death* and asks 'why paint such daubings?', the painter (who looks more like an artisan than an aesthete) replies, 'to remind people they will die', as if he is doing the most natural job in the world.

The director doesn't resort to blurry, phantasmagoric imagery. In a 1971 interview with the critic John Simon, Bergman pointed out that *The Seventh Seal* was 'very, very concrete, like a medieval play. Everything is there, you can touch everything. The Virgin Mary is real, with the child. When they are dancing, they are concrete: they are. It is not fantasies or dreams or imaginations. It is always my intention to be exact ... to be very simple.'[26]

The artist has made a discovery that matches Bergman's own insight into what drove his spectators. 'A skull is more interesting than a naked wench.' In the mid-1950s, as the huge international success of *The Seventh Seal* attests, there was a sizable section of the cinema-going audience that shared his obsession with questions of faith and death.

Another reason that the film appealed to metropolitan audiences was that it could be read on one level as a psychoanalytic case study. When Antonius goes to confession and admits that his heart is empty and that when he sees himself he is 'seized by disgust and fear', his self-questioning begins to sound like the medieval equivalent to what a patient might confess on the couch. His quest for meaning, knowledge and faith clearly had a resonance for 1950s audiences. In an era when existentialism was considered fashionable and *L'Étranger* by Albert Camus (an author Bergman admired and once tried to work with) was a cult book, *The Seventh Seal* had a strong contemporary appeal.

The rough-hewn austerity of the film comes as a complete contrast to the extravagance of *Smiles of a Summer Night*, with its luxurious production design. Just occasionally, we hear distant echoes of Bergman's earlier romantic comedies. For example, Jens cheerfully remarks at one stage, 'I am married but I have hope my wife will be dead by now.'

It would be absurd to call *The Seventh Seal* a 'summer movie', but as in *Summer Interlude* or *Summer with Monika*, Bergman and his cinematographer Fischer make the landscapes as important as any of the characters. Still, the budget didn't allow for much location work. The majority of *The Seventh Seal* was shot at Svensk's Rasunda Film Studios where Bergman had laboured for so long as script slave and jobbing director. Like so many other of Bergman's films, this was an over-determined affair. The influences Bergman cited in interviews and in his writing included everything from Carl Orff's choral work *Carmina Burana* to works by Picasso and Durer. Historians have noted nods in the direction of Carl Dreyer's *Day of Wrath*, Arthur Miller's *The Crucible*, plays by Strindberg and even some of Bergman's earlier plays and films. (The scene of the performer humiliated in the tavern and forced to imitate a bear has obvious overlaps with scenes in *Sawdust and Tinsel*.) In its weakest moments, with its sometimes stilted crowd scenes and chanting, the film can seem like a cut-price Swedish version of a Hollywood epic. Nonetheless, when *The Seventh Seal* was screened in Cannes, it won the Jury Prize. It also yielded a series of images which would become instantly recognisable and would be referred to again and again in discussions of the director by both his admirers and his detractors – the chess game on the beach, the final sequence in which we see the silhouettes of the film's characters in a dance of death on the brow of the hill, under a storm-filled sky, being led away by the Reaper with his scythe and hourglass. Ironically, given the way that film historians have tended to genuflect in the presence of a Bergman film and to have attributed everything in it to the director's genius, the famous last shot was completed, thanks to cinematographer Gunnar Fischer. He saw the cloud coming. By then, late in the day, the actors had gone home, but their costumes were still there. Crew members were recruited to dress up and perform the dance of death at a few moments' notice.

In Sweden, spectators were not always enthusiastic. 'They didn't understand a word', Farago says.[27] Only with *The Silence*, which was treated by the media as if it was a sex film and generated plenty of scandal as a result, did he have a real popular success.

Bergman's most forgiving film: Victor Sjostrom in *Wild Strawberries*.

Bergman followed *The Seventh Seal* with one of his most forgiving films, *Wild Strawberries*. The nightmare sequence that opens the film – the old professor Isak Borg (Victor Sjostrom) adrift in a city with empty, sinister streets and clocks without arms – is like a de Chirico painting sprung to life. Borg is preparing for death. His life, despite his distinguished career, has had its share of bitterness and disappointment. However, rather than the dread which runs through *The Seventh Seal*, *Wild Strawberries* is steeped in gentle nostalgia. The morning after his dream, the professor embarks on a long journey with his daughter-in-law Marianne (Ingrid Thulin) to pick up an award. During the journey, he discovers just how much his son resents him. Through flashbacks, we discover how his wife, now deceased, betrayed him. In one Proustian scene, we are cast back to his early adulthood and see how he lost his first love to his brother.

The director had written the screenplay for *Wild Strawberries* in Karolinska Hospital. (It is striking how often creativity and illness seem to go hand in hand in his work.) His relentless work schedule, making *The Seventh Seal* and then going straight on to mount three major productions at the theatre in Malmo, had exhausted him. As ever, his personal life was in upheaval. (This time, it was his relationship with Bibi

Andersson that was beginning to founder.) Like Isak Borg, whose initials he shared, he had grown apart from his family and colleagues.

When Bergman looked back on his work, he wasn't above a certain vanity. 'I was then thirty-seven, cut off from all human relations', he confides in *Images*, for some reason shaving two years off his real age. 'It was I who had done the cutting off, presumably as an act of self-affirmation. I was a loner, a failure, I mean a complete failure. Though successful. And clever. And orderly. And disciplined.'[28]

As he made clear, Bergman identified closely with the 78-year-old Isak Borg. This itself is a strange departure. In his earlier work, his alter ego had invariably been the delinquent anti-hero or, in *The Seventh Seal*, the crusading outsider. Now, it was someone from an even older generation than that of his father, with whom he had such an ambivalent relationship. There is an Oedipal undercurrent to this identification with the father figure too. Borg's late wife, we learn at the very beginning of the film, is called Karin. This, of course, was the name of the director's mother. 'I B equals Ice and Borg (the Swedish word for fortress). Simple and facile. I had created a character who, on the outside, looked like my father, but was me, through and through', the director later explained.[29]

At the same time, he liked to boast that he was 'forever living in [his] ... childhood'. In many later interviews, he would talk about his uncanny ability to remember the sights, sounds and smells of his childhood. He idealised his childhood even though he spent much of his career exploring in fictional form the misery and betrayals of his earliest years. This is one of the central paradoxes about his work. The inference was obvious. It was precisely because of the terror that his childhood seemed so vivid to him. Fear animated his memory. Had he simply led a contented life as a young boy and been doted on by his relatives, those years would have appeared far more blurred in retrospect. The unhappiness and yearning ensured these memories never lost their focus.

There is a Chekhovian feel to the storytelling – a sense that Bergman is borrowing from stories like Chekhov's *The Bishop* (1902), in which an elderly and distinguished bishop is prompted by a visit from his mother, whom he hasn't seen in many years, to plunge into his childhood memories.

> When he had prayed he lay down, and as soon as he found himself in the dark there rose before his eyes the vision of his dead father, his mother, and Lyesopolye, his native village. The creaking of wagon-wheels, the bleating of sheep, the sound of church-bells on a clear summer morning, ah, how pleasant it was to think of these things![30]

Victor Sjostrom, his former mentor and the director all those years before the release of his beloved *The Phantom Carriage*, proved an awkward and insecure collaborator. Playing Isak Borg, his main obsession at the beginning of every day's work was that he would be finished by 4.30 pm in time for his constitutional whisky. If Bergman called on him for overtime, he could become querulous and impatient. However, just as Isak Borg in the film is coaxed out of his isolation by the people he encounters during his journey, Sjostrom gradually responded to Bergman and his team. In particular, he was charmed by Bergman's actresses.

Katinka Farago tells a story about Sjostrom on the first day of shooting. The old-timer, who had a reputation for sometimes behaving like an ogre himself on his own sets, looked on in amazement as he heard Bergman railing at his colleagues. The old man looked at him with his mild eyes and said, 'Ingmar, what language you are using!'[31] Bergman responded by keeping his temper in check thereafter, at least until after Sjostrom had gone home for the day. Then, he was able to rage in freedom at his technicians. Bergman found it therapeutic to get angry at someone.

It is hard to tell whether there is admiration or exasperation in Bergman's remarks that Sjostrom put an indelible imprint on the film. 'He took my text, made it his own, invested it with his own experiences ... loneliness, coldness, warmth, harshness, and ennui', Bergman later commented of his elderly leading actor.

> Borrowing my father's form, he occupied my soul and made it all his own – there wasn't even a crumb left over for me! He did so with the sovereign power of a gargantuan personality. I had nothing to add, not even a sensible or irrational comment. *Wild Strawberries* was no longer my film; it was Victor Sjöström's![32]

Perhaps Bergman simply wanted to distance himself from a film which carried so many strong personal elements. At the time he was making the film, his relations with his father were especially strained. Nonetheless, Erik Bergman turned out to be a firm admirer of the film, writing a fan letter to its star, which suggested he either was unconscious of its references to his own life or chose to overlook them. He – it should also be remembered – was the one who had introduced Sjostrom to Ingmar all those years before by arranging the screening of *The Phantom Carriage* in the church hall.

> Dear Victor Sjöström!
> Permit me, Ingmar's father, to send you my respectful greetings and my heartfelt thanks for your brilliant performance in Ingmar's latest film. And

thank you for all you have given to Ingmar and to me, and to countless others through your noble artistry and the spiritual inspiration of your entire work. I will always remember with gratitude the friendly, encouraging words you spoke to me about Ingmar when he was still very young, and I stood before you in doubt and uncertainty.
My wife joins me in expressing our warm thanks.
Respectfully yours
Erik Bergman[33]

For those Bergman detractors who accuse the director of making well-crafted bourgeois entertainments, *Wild Strawberries* is often a starting point. Like its two predecessors, *Smiles of a Summer Night* and *The Seventh Seal*, the film won a prize at a major festival (a Golden Bear in Berlin) which helped catapult it into public consciousness. Bizarrely, the film is included on the Vatican Best Films List, recommended for its portrayal of a man's 'interior journey from pangs of regret and anxiety to a refreshing sense of peace and reconciliation'. It has been referred to and imitated by countless other filmmakers. Like Dickens' *A Christmas Carol*, with its famous (and sometimes maudlin) scenes in which Scrooge is taken back in time and allowed to look in at events from his past, *Wild Strawberries* confronts his curmudgeonly hero with some of the key scenes from his childhood. There is something Dickensian about the way Borg learns tolerance, patience and forgiveness by looking back. Sjostrom, whatever his health problems or occasional fits of temper, plays him beautifully, conveying the character's regret but also his courage in the face of his old age. It's a subtle performance in which a flicker of a smile as he watches scenes from his childhood or simply a wistful expression conveys every bit as much as the dialogue.

If *Wild Strawberries* was a gentle meditation on the subject of death from the perspective of an old man, Bergman's next film, *Brink of Life* (1958), was preoccupied with the trauma of birth. This is one of the few Bergman films which has somehow slipped off the radar. The initial impression was favourable enough. Eva Dahlbeck, Bibi Andersson and Ingrid Thulin shared the Best Actress award at the Cannes Festival, while Bergman also received a prize. However, *Brink of Life* was not a film which passed into international consciousness in the same way as *Smiles of a Summer Night* and *The Seventh Seal*.

A claustrophobic hospital drama, *Brink of Life* is about three women in a maternity ward. They are all different ages. They all have very different experiences. What they have in common is that they suffer.

Bergman had fathered five children by the time he came to make *Brink of Life*, but hadn't been present during any of the births. 'Instead,

I got drunk or played with my miniature electric trains or went to the movies or rehearsed or worked on a movie or, inappropriately, paid attention to other women', he recalled with typical frankness in *Images*, justifying his behaviour by saying 'that's how things were back then'.[34] When his son Daniel was born by Caesarian section in the early 1960s, he wasn't even in the hospital but was busy discussing the score of *The Magic Flute* with his wife's piano teacher.

Whatever his own squeamishness or lack of interest about childbirth, he probed into the experience with forensic relish in *Brink of Life*. He even arranged at last to be present during a birth at the Karolinska Hospital, an experience he described as both 'traumatic and edifying'.[35] This is a film full of close-ups of anguished women's faces. We expect that from Bergman, but whereas the anguish in, for example, *Persona* was rooted in a crisis of self, memory and identity, the pain here has much more primal roots. The film has barely started when we hear the distraught Cecilia Ellius (Ingrid Thulin) bemoaning the loss of her baby through a miscarriage. She knows that her husband didn't want the child and believes that she is therefore being punished. 'Its mother was not strong enough to love it on her own', she chides herself. 'Therefore, it could not be born, merely flushed away in the drain.'

Thulin's anguished monologue lasts a small eternity. Her misery is contrasted with the cheeriness (at least initially) of the heavily pregnant Stina Andersson (Eva Dahlbeck). The third main character is Hjordis Petersson (Bibi Andersson), a much younger unmarried woman who regrets her pregnancy and wants an abortion.

It was little wonder that after the film's release, reports soon began to be published of spectators – especially men – fainting. (At a single screening in Norway, eight different audience members were reported to have passed out.) It was as if Bergman had taken Samuel Beckett's famous remark, 'we are born astride the grave', to heart.

The film was based around two short stories from a collection by his friend Ulla Isaksson. As Bergman showed (perhaps drawing on personal experience), the prospect of childbirth and parenthood can have a seismic effect on a couple's relationship.

Bergman isn't often seen as a crusading social campaigner, but in certain, well-observed sequences in *Brink of Life*, he shows how callously women who have had miscarriages are treated. In one scene, a bored young doctor haughtily asks Thulin if she has ever had venereal disease or whether she had induced the miscarriage herself. At the same time as he lays bare such callous attitudes, he also pays tribute to the Swedish healthcare system which won't let anyone slip through the cracks – even unmarried mothers. The plotting is melodramatic and a little contrived. The plot reversals are very easy to predict. Nonetheless, this was one of the boldest films that Bergman had made. Formally, it presented considerable challenges. (Almost the entire film takes place in one small hospital ward.) Bergman places great pressure on the three leads. He deals sensitively with the women's experiences, especially those of Thulin and Dahlbeck, who also lose their babies. The threat of death is never far away, and one mother's joy is contrasted with another's wretchedness. In the most poignant sequence in the film, Dahlbeck forlornly asks the surgeon why the baby she was so looking forward to having had died. The surgeon is helpless to answer her question. All he can tell her is that there was nothing wrong with her and seemingly nothing wrong with the baby either. 'But ... it wasn't meant to be.' Suddenly, in a film set in a gleaming ward in a 1950s Swedish hospital with all the best facilities, we are confronted with the same morbid fatalism that ran through *The Phantom Carriage*.

Not that all the Swedish critics were more charitable than usual. One or two were appreciative, calling *Brink of Life* Bergman's best film. However, there was also the usual sniping. 'Artistically the film is a miscarriage. Dramatically it is abortive and the psychological foundation is surprisingly emaciated', wrote Staffan Tjerneld in *Expressen*.[36]

At least, the criticism wasn't just aimed at him. Isaksson had provided the source material and written the screenplay – and so she too was attacked. 'As this is Ulla Isaksson's first effort in the cinema, one cannot expect any genuine cinematic verve', complained one reviewer.[37]

Bergman himself was a late convert to his own film. As he testified in *Images*, the story may have been long-winded and let down by patchy cinematography and too many literary references, but it was also 'nicely behaved and accurately done and in all likelihood very useful'.

Brink of Life quickly slipped from view. It was rarely revived as part of Bergman seasons. At the time of writing, it is one of the few major Bergman films not available on video or DVD in the UK. However, it is well worth rediscovering. During his years of slaving in the Svensk script department and studying Hollywood melodramas under the eye of Stina Bergman, Bergman had steeped himself in the work of George Cukor and other US directors who excelled at making 'women's pictures'. This was one of the first of Bergman's own women's pictures. It paved the way for such later and far more experimental efforts as *Persona* and *Cries and Whispers* in which, again, all the main protagonists were women.

Bergman returned to more familiar terrain with his next feature, *The Magician* (1958). This was another study of the artist as travelling player. Yet again, this time through the character of Albert Vogler (Max Von Sydow), a magician in mid-nineteenth-century Sweden, Bergman was exploring the thin line between magic and quackery. Yet again, the artist seems both privileged and damned.

Vogler is Von Sydow at his most feline and unsettling. His very presence stirs up unholy erotic passions in the wife of the consul at whose home they are performing. There is an air of mystery and exoticism about him, which intimidates the police chief and the supercilious doctor who treat him so harshly.

Vogler pretends to be mute. He wears a long black wig, dyed eyebrows, false beard, black coat and cravat – an outfit which makes him appear like a cross between Rasputin and Fu Manchu. Like the knight in *The Seventh Seal*, he is obsessed by death. As he and his colleagues drive through the woods, a coachman claims to have seen a ghost. Vogler investigates and is confronted with a drunk, mortally ill actor, who demands vodka. The drunkard can see at once that Vogler is in disguise. Vogler takes him aboard the coach, keen to witness the very moment of his death. 'Look carefully sire, I will keep my eyes open for your curiosity', the actor whispers as the life seeps out of him.

Bergman clearly identified with the magician and his troupe. They are both cherished and despised by the audiences for whom they perform. 'The film is a metaphor for the artist and all the parts the audience projects onto the artist', Von Sydow suggested. 'It is – or rather was – Bergman's own situation, for the audience projected all their fantasies onto him, and he became an extremely interesting and fascinating individual.'[38]

Vogler is an expert in the 'science of animal magnetism'. Bergman shows us constant close-ups of the mesmerist staring forlornly ahead as the authorities taunt him. Though he doesn't speak in public, he is never a neutral presence. We are always aware of his antagonism towards his petty bourgeois tormentors. In one key scene, after he has again been taunted by the doctors, he pulls off his disguise, lies beside his wife (Ingrid Thulin) and at last gives vent to his feelings. 'I hate their voices, their bodies, their movements, their voices', he hisses.

In *The Magician*, one feels Bergman expressing his antipathy towards the critics who lined up to pass judgement on his work: to sniff at his pretentiousness and to mock him. The film, he confessed, mirrored some of his experiences staging plays at the Malmo City Theatre, where he worked throughout the 1950s. It was a period when he and his colleagues were so absorbed in their work that they paid little attention to the world around them.

'The intensive work collaboration made for a closeness, the likes of which I have not experienced before or after', he wrote. 'We all still speak of this time as the best in our lives.' Such remarks take on a certain ironic resonance when one recalls contemporaries' descriptions of him during the 1950s as an unhappy, neurotic figure, prey to tantrums and fretting about money. His work clearly anchored his life at the time. As he wrote, 'a furious work pace and good professional collaboration can construct a fine corset against the onset of neuroses, threatening breakdowns and disintegrations.'[39] What he might have added was that the threat of disintegration was itself a strong creative stimulus.

The harder Bergman and his colleagues worked, the more they were shielded from the scrutiny of those around them. The work was their mask.

> The public believes that it loves us when it sees us in the light of our work and our public persona. But if we are seen without our masks (or, even worse, we are asking for money), we are instantly transformed into less than nothing.[40]

Generally, if Bergman did use his work for settling scores with rivals or tormentors, it was in a subtle and oblique way. In *The Magician*, though, the digs were easier to spot – and he was readier to identify them. He freely admitted that the sneering and sceptical, monocle-wearing health official Vergerus (Gunnar Bjornstrand) was based on the critic Harry Schein (married to Ingrid Thulin). Schein (1924–2006) and Bergman later became friends and collaborators. The Austrian-born Schein was the founder and first managing director of the Swedish Film Institute. He had immense influence on Swedish film culture. Schein was behind the 1963 Swedish Film Reform Act, which paved the way for the creation of the Swedish Film Institute and offered support to 'artistic' filmmaking. However, he had also worked as a critic. Bergman was intimidated and a little offended by his reviews. He therefore caricatured him as the haughty health official Vergerus who is immediately suspicious of anything outside his experience. 'You represent what I hate most of all; that which cannot be explained', Vergerus declares to Vogler in the kind of high-minded and censorious language used by Schein in his film criticism.

Bergman later suggested that the film had turned out crueller, blacker and more brutal than he had intended. Nonetheless, *The Magician* was again warmly received abroad, this time winning the Special Jury Prize at the Venice Festival.

The growing international appeal of the Swedish director was underlined when he won his first Oscar, for his next feature *The Virgin Spring* (1960). Ironically, this now seems one of his least personal and characteristic films. Based on the fourteenth-century ballad *Tore's Daughter in Wange*, it was scripted by Ulla Isaksson (with whom he had worked so successfully on *Brink of Life*). There was a dispiriting sense that he was, for once, trying to live up to his new-found reputation as an international master. As if to rekindle memories of his success with *The Seventh Seal*, he again revisited the Middle Ages. Bergman was a confirmed fan of Akira Kurosawa's samurai movies and wanted to emulate the great Japanese master. (He later called the film 'a lousy imitation of Kurosawa'.) There was a self-consciousness about the way he broached his weighty themes.

The Virgin Spring was a film about death, rape and revenge. Max Von Sydow plays a farmer whose virginal daughter is raped and murdered. Von Sydow, shortly to be recruited by Hollywood director George Stevens to play Jesus in *The Greatest Story Ever Told*, conveys his character's grief and rage in a typically febrile and intelligent way. The closing scenes, when he has just massacred the herders who killed his daughter, provide the rawest, most powerful moments in the film. Rather than catharsis, the slaughter brings him only torment. He prays, but his prayer is a rant against the God who allowed these deaths to happen and did nothing. As atonement for his own sins, he vows to build a church on the site of the massacre.

There was an ambiguity at the heart of *The Virgin Spring* which opened it to many different interpretations. Wes Craven was to remake it as horror film *The Last House on the Left* – an indication, at least, that Bergman's audience extended beyond the arthouse. The film shared elements of the typical exploitation pic in which a vigilante seeks vengeance against those who've hurt his family. Its plotline was as ancient as the ballad that inspired it and was open to being recycled again and again, whether in horror movies or cop dramas or even westerns.

Some audiences picked up on the religious symbolism and chose to regard the film as Bergman's stab at an Old Testament parable. On one level, this was after all a film about a man searching for belief. Others commented on the psychoanalytical aspect. Like Ethan Edwards in John Ford's *The Searchers*, Von Sydow's character has a morbid obsession with the young woman who has been raped and killed. As certain critics noted, his relationship with his daughter had 'Freudian undertones'.[41] Her death released strange and sadistic feelings in him.

The parallels with John Ford's *The Searchers* stretch further than the lust for vengeance shared by Tore and Ethan Edwards. *The Virgin Spring* is full of what have come to be called 'Ford moments' – scenes in which the natural world is filmed in transcendent fashion. Bergman didn't have Ford's Monument Valley, but cinematographer Sven Nykvist fashions many beautifully rendered shots of forests and turbulent skies. Whatever reservations Bergman later expressed about *The Virgin Spring*, its formal qualities were self-evident. Bergman – as Katinka Farago said about him – was down-to-earth and surprisingly practical. With relatively limited resources and a budget that was extremely modest by Hollywood standards, he had managed to recreate the medieval world in an utterly convincing fashion.

Swedish critics, as ever, equivocated about the latest Bergman. 'It hits home like a fist between the eyes, like a dagger to the heart', wrote *Svenska Dagbladet*.[42] Others grumbled that Isaksson's screenplay was clumsy and too literary.

'Ulla Isaksson is more of a literary author than a poet of the screen. Accordingly, she has a weakness for words', wrote *Stockholms-Tidningen*. 'One has the feeling that Bergman has set about the task with cheer, but rather like a director commissioned with staging someone else's ready-made "play".'[43]

'*The Virgin Spring* will not go down in history as one of his best efforts, nor is it one that triggers our most colourful superlatives', was the underwhelming response from *Aftonbladet*. 'The film is – paradoxically enough when one considers the density of the material – somewhat loose in execution, slightly shaky in its composition and somewhat split and circumspect in its attitude to the emotions it purports to advance.'[44]

Nonetheless, it was now evident that critics thought it politic to sugar their more hostile reviews of Bergman films with some sweet thoughts about the director's talents. 'It is as a masterpiece of film direction that one savours *The Virgin Spring*', *Stockholms-Tidningen* said of the film, making it clear that the screenwriter (for once not Bergman) was guilty for any shortcomings in *The Virgin Spring*.[45]

Moreover, internationally the film conformed exactly to what audiences expected of Bergman. It had dark and weighty themes, wondrous landscapes and sterling performances from Bergman's actors. It was the kind of film that presented a welcome challenge to cinemagoers in search of an alternative to Hollywood escapism. When *Playboy* Magazine described the director as 'the acknowledged guru of the art-film avant-garde', *The Virgin Spring* was one of the titles it cited for such an assertion.[46]

Audiences expected his films to wrestle with life and death issues, to ponder God and the devil. Somehow, the transformation was now complete. The gauche and neurotic young rebel of Swedish cinema who had exasperated the studio bosses and who had been considered wilfully and wildly self-indulgent was now accepted as a great European auteur. That acceptance came first abroad and then filtered through to Sweden too. The front-office accountants from Svensk who complained that Bergman's films made them no money were grudgingly forced to accept that a Bergman movie was now a viable commercial proposition.

'In all fairness, even the studio management could no longer deny that I was successful', he wrote with deadpan humour.

> They had denied it as long as they possibly could. It had become a standing ritual for the head accountant, Juberg, at the start of every one of my films, to step into the executive office with his accounting ledgers and show what serious losses my latest movies had inflicted on the company.[47]

Now, the roles were reversed. Bergman was grumbling to Svensk about how they mishandled his films and thereby took money away from him. The studio, he noted, had no experience when it came to foreign sales. Svensk had therefore allowed Bergman movies to be distributed abroad by almost any carpetbagger. 'There was total confusion, which often resulted in my films falling into the hands of robbers', Bergman later lamented.[48]

The Hollywood studio bosses had already begun to take note of Bergman as had big-name international producers like Dino de Laurentiis. The question they asked was how they could package Bergman and capitalise on his burgeoning reputation.

4

Bergman and Hollywood

IN A REVEALING 1959 lecture entitled 'What It Takes to Make a Film', Bergman told a group of students at the University of Lund that film-makers were like conjurers, but that their ability to create magic was dependent on their films being able to find an audience and make money. The moment films lost their audience, 'the conjurer would be deprived of his magic wand'.[1]

Audiences are so accustomed to the notion of Bergman as an artist, expressing personal feelings without compromise in his work, that it is easy to forget that – like every other film director – he faced a constant struggle to finance his films.

'To produce a 2500 metres long tapeworm which sucks life and spirit out of actors, producers and directors. That is what making a film involves', he gloomily explained. 'That and many other things, much more and much worse.'[2]

During the 1950s, critics were often so hostile towards him that Svensk Filmindustri – his principal backer – questioned whether it was worth underwriting his work.

'I can remember when Bergman got very bad reviews, when he was considered difficult, bizarre, incomprehensible, pretentious', the Svensk Filmindustri President Carl-Anders Dymling – with whom Bergman had such a vexed relationship – wrote in the *Saturday Review* in 1960, a time when the temperamental director was at last becoming a viable commercial prospect whose films made money.[3]

Bergman clearly found the 'business' of filmmaking sapping and sometimes soul destroying. 'It would be of interest', he suggested, 'if a scientist could one day invent a scale or measure which could tell how much talent, initiative, genius and creative ability have been destroyed by the industry in its ruthless effective sausage machine'.[4]

His script editor and later production manager Katinka Farago testifies to his fearlessness in dealing with his front-office bosses. She suggests

Bergman's relationship with Svensk was often 'shaky' because Bergman always 'said his meaning. He wasn't afraid of the people over him. They (the bosses) had problems with Ingmar because, one, they didn't understand him and two, they thought he was too self-indulgent.'[5]

Part of Bergman's achievement rests in his uncompromising approach to his work – his refusal to be sucked into the sausage machine. Nonetheless, even Bergman had to choose his battles wisely. With an ever-increasing circle of dependents, he needed money. Between directorial assignments, he had worked as a script doctor for Svensk. When Dymling made it obvious that Bergman had a better chance of finding finance if he made comedies, the director listened.

Given his struggles during the 1950s, it is understandable that he was ready at least to pay attention when Hollywood agents and big-name producers came courting him after his first big international successes towards the end of the decade.

By the late 1950s, he was signed up with the American agents, William Morris. His correspondence with William Morris reveals how many temptations were laid in front of him and how close he – like almost every other major European director before him – came to working with Hollywood.

Bergman had become a major force in the USA. Not only had *The Virgin Spring* (1960) won an Oscar, but his other films had also been distributed on the arthouse circuit, and he was sufficiently well known to be the subject of lengthy interviews in broadsheet newspapers and prestigious magazines.

In the summer of 1959, his agent, Bernie Wilens, was trying hard to talk him into making a biopic about the Russian poet Pushkin, with US crooner and actor Harry Belafonte in the leading role. This was not an idea that Bergman took seriously. 'I think that B. is not the actor who shall create the genius Pushkin', he wrote to Wilens.[6] Belafonte was ready to travel to Stockholm to lobby Bergman. Plans were made to screen Belafonte's latest film *Odds Against Tomorrow* for the Swedish director, but it quickly became apparent even to the thick-skinned Hollywood agents that Bergman wasn't going to be swayed.

'My success depends on my making films, which I have written and directed all by myself', Bergman told William Morris. With either naivete or cheek, he asked if Hollywood could 'order a film by me, in exactly the same way you order a picture of a painter, without first telling him what it is going to be like. I think that would be the best of all the ideas'.

Bergman boasted that any potential US patron would find him versatile. 'Good God! I can paint any kind of pictures, happy pictures, sorry pictures, light pictures and dark pictures and pictures which have everything in the same time.'[7]

The idea that a Hollywood studio would simply commission a movie from Bergman and then leave him to his own devices was a pipe dream. The whole point about the Hollywood system was that filmmakers became part of the machine. They were pampered, flattered and paid outrageous amounts of money, but they were obliged to sacrifice their independence. That was the nature of the Faustian pact. As Bergman's agent wrote back to him: 'At the present time I do not think that the major companies, and they are the only ones able to finance important pictures will simply order a film made by you as one orders a painting.'[8]

Still, the agents continued to suggest new projects that could present Bergman 'to the American audience in your first American effort'. Soon, they were proposing that Bergman should direct a film called *Jean Christophe*, to star Hope Lange and to be produced by her husband Don Murray.

'Hope Lange has starred in quite a few pictures here. Undoubtedly, you must have seen *The Best of Everything* and *Peyton Place*', Bernie Wilens wrote to Bergman in a fit of misplaced confidence.[9] One film that Bergman was highly unlikely to have seen was a Hollywood melodrama like *Peyton Place*. This project also quickly stalled.

David O. Selznick (one of the most famous producers in Hollywood history) invited Bergman to spend a week with him in Nassau to discuss potential collaborations. Selznick was keen for Bergman to direct an adaptation of Joseph Conrad's *Victory* or a project called *The Wall* to star Jennifer Jones. Bergman was quick to dismiss such proposals. After all, he had worked with Selznick once before.

'At that time I was very young and wrote a script on Ibsen's *A Dollhouse* [sic]', Bergman recalled. 'Mr Selznick ows [sic] me still 2000 dollars, that I had the right, after our contract, to get. When I applied to the agreement Mr Selznick's representative answered: "You have to be thankful for what you get. If you want to bring an action you have to do that in USA and I assure you, that Mr Selznick has the economical possibilities to find the best lawyers".'[10]

Bergman was furious when the US trade press announced prematurely that he had struck a deal with Paramount Pictures. Nor was he impressed when the studio bosses came courting him in person. 'I often cogitate over these American producers', he wrote. 'When they meet an artist the whole time they talk about how artistic they are themselves. They talk about their lives, their married complications, their practical jokes and their pictures. They uninterruptedly weigh and measure the artist they talk with.... They believe, that their power and their money make them interesting and they unconsciously expose their amazing lack of spiritual quality.'[11]

The Swedish director admitted that his encounters with studio moguls invariably made him think about the famous encounter between Samuel Goldwyn and playwright George Bernard Shaw. 'Dear Mr Goldwyn, after our long conversations I now understand that you are interested in the art and I am interested in the money', Shaw is reported to have told the studio boss.[12]

Nonetheless, there was one US project that really did tantalise Bergman – a possible adaptation of Albert Camus' *The Fall* (French title *La Chute*). The rights were in the hands of the producer Walter Wanger (a Hollywood veteran who had worked with Alfred Hitchcock and Fritz Lang and who had recently produced *Invasion of the Body Snatchers* and *I Want to Live*). At the stage the project was first mooted in the late 1950s, Camus was still alive and Bergman was keen to work with him. The early signs were promising. The Swedish director was clearly fascinated by Camus' book (about a lawyer who falls from grace) and was determined to make the film 'without compromise and with real ruthlessness'.[13]

There was no chance of that. The agents were already busy tinkering. United Artists, the potential financiers, wanted Cary Grant and Robert Ryan in the leading roles. Bergman immediately balked at such an idea. 'It is a matter, of course, that I am choosing the actors myself', he protested. 'Cary Grant is a very good comedy actor but has no qualifications at all to play the lawyer in *La Chute*.'

It was even suggested that Grant (a fervent admirer of Bergman) should meet Bergman face to face in London to try to talk him round. The Swedish director was having none of it. Nor was he any more receptive when Laurence Olivier was suggested instead of Grant. After Camus' death in 1960, Bergman abandoned any idea of making *The Fall*.

There was talk of the legendary producer Darryl Zanuck backing a film to be made by Bergman in Israel, entitled *The Ballad of Red Rock*. Another project discussed as a potential vehicle for him was Eugene Vale's play *Of the Shadows Cast by Men*.

Meanwhile, various celebrated writers were reported as eager to see Bergman adapt their work for the screen. Italian novelist Italo Calvino wanted him to film his 1952 fantasy novel, *The Cloven Viscount*, about a Christian aristocrat in the Turkish wars of the seventeenth century who miraculously survives being blown into half by a cannonball. Tennessee Williams was keen for Bergman to make a film on *Night of the Iguana* (in the event, John Huston took on directorial duties on this project).

Bergman had expressed an interest in making a film in English, but what Hollywood failed to realise was that he was determined to make it in Sweden, with his regular crew and with actors he had handpicked. He wanted creative control, a producer he could trust, and no hint of interference in the background. He was being offered over $100,000 to write and direct a movie and suspected he might have been able to get more. Such money was not to be scoffed at. However, Bergman made it very clear that his independence was not for sale. If he was to make an English-language movie, it would have to be on his own terms.

American projects continued to be floated in front of Bergman, but now even the agents grudgingly accepted that he was not just another director-for-hire, ready to be made part of the latest Hollywood star-driven 'package'. He did eventually make films in English (*The Touch* and *The Serpent's Egg*) and work with American actors (Elliott Gould and David Carradine). However, the idea – which seemed a possibility in the early 1960s – that he might follow in the example of his fellow Swedes Victor Sjostrom and Maurice Stiller and have a stab at working in Hollywood was soon abandoned.

Bergman remained extremely curious about how his films performed in the USA and the circumstances in which they were distributed. He struck up a close working alliance with American arthouse specialists, Janus Films. The company, founded in 1956 by Byrant Haliday and Cyrus Harvey Jr., operated as much more than just a distribution company. For Bergman, Janus combined the roles of agent, spokesperson, advisor and revenue collector. In the early 1960s, Harvey visited Bergman in Sweden, to meet Svensk executives and discuss US release plans for Bergman's movies in exhaustive detail.

When Paramount Pictures announced it was striking a two-picture deal with Bergman in the summer of 1960, the Swedish director turned to Janus to scotch a story that was false. Harvey told the press that the so-called deal consisted simply of an inquiry from Paramount as to whether Bergman might be 'interested in doing a couple of films for them'.

Janus attempted to stagger the flow of Bergman's films in the US market to ensure there was not a glut. If they were handled with care, these films were potentially very lucrative. Speaking to trade magazine *Variety* in July 1960, Harvey predicted that *Wild Strawberries* would gross '$375,000 to $400,000 on between 1000 and 1500 dates in the US'[14] and suggested that *The Magician* – which was being released in a dubbed as well as a subtitled version – would do even better. (Figures are hard to come by, but it would appear that this was an overestimation of the films' prospects.) Following Harvey's visit to Sweden, Janus also took over the Canadian distribution of Bergman's films.

Harvey and Haliday were prepared to do some extraordinary favours for Bergman. This was an age before video or DVD, and Bergman had turned into an enthusiastic film collector. The Janus bosses provided him with prints of various classics for his collection, including Vittorio de Sica's *Umberto D*, D.W. Griffith's *Intolerance* and Fritz Lang's *Metropolis*. They even approached the rights holder in order to get permission to make a print of Griffith's *Birth of a Nation* for Bergman's personal use. It's a sign of how closely they worked together that when Bergman was looking for an English title for what became known as *Winter Light* (1963), he was ready to listen to them. His original idea was 'The Communicants'. They suggested 'Light in Winter'.

At first, Bergman was delighted with the success that Janus had with his work in the North American market, but there was tension and anxiety in his relationship with the distributors too. He implored Janus not to release *Dreams*, *Waiting Women* or *A Lesson in Love* on the grounds that they were inferior to the work that had so enraptured American audiences (*The Seventh Seal*, *Smiles of a Summer Night* and *Wild Strawberries*). Fretful about his reputation, he wrote to the distributors telling them that it was risky and even wrong to release the movies. Janus argued that even these lesser works were a cut above almost every other European arthouse film being released in the USA and pointed out that they would generate yet more revenue for Bergman.

It soon became apparent the Swedish director was unhappy that his films were being dubbed for some American audiences. The Janus bosses argued that certain cinemas outside the metropolitan centres of New York and Los Angeles simply wouldn't show subtitled movies and that dubbing was therefore the only way to get Bergman's films seen. This, though, wasn't an argument that seems to have impressed the Swedish director.

Money was also much on Bergman's mind. His screenplays were being published in the USA. He was keen to receive payment as promptly as possible and turned to Janus to keep track of the money promised to him. The tone of his correspondence with Janus was joshing, but his remarks invariably had a serious edge. 'When do you think the money from Simon and Schuster will arrive? My wife wants a new lipstick and my secretary needs a fountain pen', he writes in one letter. 'I don't think I can manage to sign 1000 books. I am an old man, my secretary is also an old man and he only forges my signature, when he can really earn something on it', he remarks in another.[15]

Janus had helped create huge US media interest in Bergman, but the company bosses were beginning to wonder if they had overdone the hoopla. 'In a sense, a monster has been created and perhaps you do not recognise yourself in all the mountains of newsprint', Janus wrote to Bergman at the end of 1959. 'I'm sure you realise that this is all simply a way of getting people into the doors of theatres to see your films. I have never had a high regard for the accuracy or sensibility of journalists. At your press conference in Paris I was vastly amused at the stupidity of many of the questions that you were asked. If I had been in your place I would have exploded.'[16]

Nonetheless, this publicity was definitely helping. When *The Seventh Seal* was first released in the USA in 1958, it made little impact. As Bergman's reputation grew, though, so did interest in the film. Janus capitalised on this, re-releasing the film for new runs two or even three times. Meanwhile, *Wild Strawberries* played and played. In LA cinemas, its run lasted over 32 weeks.

Bergman was angry when Janus was obliged to make some small cuts (presumably because of sex and violence) to *The Virgin Spring*. Harvey and Haliday kept him informed of their struggles to get his work into cinemas in its original state but grew exasperated with the heavy demands he placed on them.

Eventually, Bergman would turn to other distributors (including such unlikely figures as B-movie maestro Roger Corman) to distribute his work in the USA. In the mid-1960s, Janus was taken over by new owners. Still, the New York distributor had played a vital role in establishing Bergman as an international name.

Another key event which consolidated Bergman's reputation was the first important retrospective of his work in Paris in the late 1950s. At this point, as critic Cyril Neyrat wrote, 'the critics of Les Cahiers du Cinema thrusted him to the forefront of the struggle of Auteur politics'.[17]

The impact he had on budding cinephiles and would-be directors like Jean-Luc Godard, François Truffaut and Eric Rohmer was enormous. 'For the French, 1958 will have been the year of Bergman as 1953, let's say, was the year of Cinemascope', wrote Rohmer in the pages of *Cahiers*.[18] Godard, meanwhile, wrote his famous essay, 'Bergmanorama', in which he posited his idea of Bergman as 'the last great romantic'.

With the Nouvelle Vague proselytising on his behalf in Europe and
Janus Films busy drumming up publicity in North America, it was little
wonder that Bergman's stature in world cinema suddenly began to grow.
In the UK, Kenneth Rive's Gala Films – a distributor with the same pas-
sion for auteur cinema as Janus – was likewise championing the work of
Bergman.

Just as the Janus bosses had found, Bergman's UK distributor soon
discovered the Swede was an awkward collaborator. 'Bergman was always
difficult', Rive told the *Guardian* in a 2001 interview. 'He refused to make
any cuts to his films. Tremendously talented guy, but always peculiar. He
always said he'd come to the premiere of his films but he never did. At
the last minute he'd always disappear. He had terrible trouble with his
bowels, though – perhaps that's why. He was always being taken short
somewhere.'[19] Nonetheless, Rive stuck by Bergman.

The Swedish director's critical reputation was already established.
However, for all the success Janus had enjoyed with his films on the arthouse circuit in the USA, he was yet to have a substantial box-office hit at
home. That changed in surprising fashion in 1963 with *The Silence*. The
film (which is discussed elsewhere in the book) was one of Bergman's
more formally adventurous and experimental efforts. Its commercial
prospects didn't look especially bright. However, through one of those
strange transformations in public perception largely caused by critics
and protesters, *The Silence* became known as Bergman's 'sex film'. It
was condemned by right-wing Swedish politicians as pornography. The
furore around it turned the film into a succès de scandale. A member of
the Swedish parliament complained about young people rushing to see
the film to enjoy 'the blatant sex scenes, elements of perversion and sick
depravity'.[20] Three clergymen reported the censors to the ombudsman
for passing the film uncut. Meanwhile, Svensk was accused of hoodwink-
ing the censors by submitting *The Silence* for classification in the summer,
when the head censor was on holiday. Bergman came under fire on all
sides. Feminists accused him of degrading women. Radicals complained
that the film lacked social consciousness.

News of the controversy over *The Silence* even reached the British
regional press. The *Birmingham Post* carried a spread on the scandal. As
the paper noted, the film was even pulled into an ongoing debate about
the use of contraception in Sweden. 'Secondary-school students, agitat-
ing for instruction in sexual technique and the use of contraceptives are
angry: "we are not interested," said one of them, "in the kind of eroticism
supplied by Bergman" '.[21]

The more the film was attacked, the quicker the box-office receipts mounted. More than a million Swedes saw *The Silence*. International distributors also did exceptional business on *The Silence*. *Playboy* celebrated 'the most explicitly erotic movie scenes on view this side of a stag smoker',[22] even after the snipping of more than a minute's film for the toned-down US version.

There was nothing unusual in Bergman being fiercely criticised on all sides. The press had come after him often enough before. What was different now was that the criticism was helping to turn *The Silence* into one of his biggest ever box-office hits. The director had mixed feelings, expressing dismay that the film was attracting the wrong kind of spectators, but also clearly relishing its notoriety and its profitability. As his interview with *Playboy* attested, he wasn't at all apologetic about the sexual frankness of the film. 'For many years I was timid and conventional in the expression of sex in my films', he told his interviewer. 'But the manifestation of sex is very important, and particularly to me, for above all, I don't want to make merely intellectual films.'[23] He certainly didn't intend to create a scandal, but there was still something calculating about the way he took advantage of the furore that blew up around him.

Now, it was no longer a case of Bergman having to implore Svensk or others to back his films. Financiers came to him. Bizarrely, in 1963, at the time of *The Silence*, the maverick Italian producer Dino de Laurentiis was assiduously courting Bergman, trying to persuade him to direct part of his portmanteau film, *The Bible*.

'If I may make a suggestion I would like to draw your attention to the figure of Abraham, whose historical, spiritual and dramatic greatness requires the inspiration of a great director', de Laurentiis wrote to Bergman, adding that he had already received 'verbal acceptance' from Robert Bresson, Luchino Visconti, Federico Fellini and Orson Welles that they would also contribute to the project.[24]

De Laurentiis' *The Bible* project never came to fruition, but Bergman did eventually work with the Italian producer, on *The Serpent's Egg* (1976.) Meanwhile, he was often linked with big international productions, few of which were made. These range from a planned film about Jesus, to be shot on the island of Faro, to an erotic portmanteau film to which Federico Fellini and Akira Kurosawa were also due to contribute. (This project fizzled out primarily, it seemed, because Fellini and Kurosawa were not as committed to the project or as diligent about finishing their screenplay as their Swedish collaborator.)

Bergman had become such a venerated figure that private financiers and public funders alike were eager to work with him. Sir Lew Grade, the British impresario and movie producer behind such films as *Raise the Titanic* (he famously quipped it would have been cheaper to 'lower the Atlantic') and *Sophie's Choice*, backed his late film *Autumn Sonata* and would have co-financed *Fanny and Alexander* too if Bergman had committed to keeping its length down. When Grade pulled out, Bergman's friend Jorn Donner, head of the Swedish Film Institute, pumped a huge amount of public money into the film, thereby provoking the wrath and jealousy of other Swedish filmmakers.

In the 1950s, as he struggled to pay maintenance to his ex-wives, Bergman was far from rich. However, by the 1970s, he was a wealthy man. When he needed to find financing quickly for *Scenes from a Marriage* (1973), he invested in it himself through his production company Cinematograph. He and some of his collaborators, including Erland Josephson and Sven Nykvist, put their own money into the film (which was made as a TV series and as a feature). Its success bolstered his personal resources yet further. When Bergman died in the summer of 2007, he was a millionaire who owned a string of houses.

Not that he had ever paid undue attention to money. In his youth, he was thin, he claimed, because he could not afford to eat. As an artist, his focus was on his work. As a filmmaker, he knew the importance of fiscal responsibility. As a craftsman, he knew what his services were worth. To be able to carry on directing, he needed to keep to budgets and ensure that his films recouped their costs. He lived simply. In return, he expected to be paid properly. Politics and money weren't major preoccupations. That is what made the events of the 1970s, when the tax authorities came after him, so hugely unsettling.

5

Tax and Politics

Politics ... never again!

(INGMAR BERGMAN in *The Magic Lantern* expressing his
feelings when he belatedly discovered the truth about
the Nazi concentration camps)[1]

IN DISCUSSIONS OF BERGMAN, the director's 'insane fear of death' (as he
called it) is often analysed in religious and philosophical terms. Bergman
and his critics also acknowledge that films like *The Seventh Seal* (1956)
and *Winter Light* (1962) were made during the Cold War, at a time
of a real threat of atomic aggression. Only very occasionally, though, is
Bergman's obsession with death discussed in terms of what he
witnessed – or at least found out about – during the Second World War.

Sweden may have been neutral during the Second World War,
but Bergman couldn't have been oblivious to happenings elsewhere in
Europe. As is well chronicled, he spent a summer holiday in Germany
in the mid-1930s as an exchange student with a Nazi-supporting family
in Thuringen. He heard Hitler speak at a big rally in Weimar. His brother
Dag was one of the founders of the Swedish National Socialist Party and
his father voted for them.

As with every other episode of his life, Bergman was utterly candid
about his teenage flirtation with Nazism. There is no sense that he tried
to conceal this episode.

'For many years, I was on Hitler's side, delighted by his successes and
saddened by his defeats', he writes with his usual, self-searing honesty in
The Magic Lantern.[2]

Bergman was even franker when speaking with American students
at the Southern Methodist University in Dallas in the early 1980s. 'You
know, when the war started I was nineteen years old', he told the
students.

I was in the military service – with interruptions – more than four years. You must know that Sweden at the time was very influenced culturally, economically and emotionally by the Germans. It's a tradition in Sweden that much more than from Great Britain or from France, we have our cultural influences from Germany. Norway was occupied and Denmark was also occupied. We lived in the "Festung Europa," (Fortress Europe) ...we were supposed to be neutral, but in schools, in the military service, we were all influenced by the Nazis'.[3]

It has been commonplace for detractors to try to out the Swedish director as a closet Nazi. As his former wife, the concert pianist Kabi Laretei, points out, ' "people who want to drag him (Bergman) down" write that "he was a Nazi or almost became one" '. They criticise him because he said openly he admired Hitler in the 1930s. 'Who didn't, of the youth?' Laretei asks. 'So many in Sweden especially admired him (Hitler).' She added that Bergman quickly realised that 'It (Nazism) was a fairy tale.'[4]

For a young writer and filmmaker in 1940s' Europe, it was impossible to regard death just as an abstract idea, to use in symbolic fashion. As Eric Hobsbawm points out in *Age of Extremes*, his short history of the twentieth century, the losses during the Second World War were 'literally incalculable' and have been estimated at 'between 10 and 20 per cent of the total population in the USSR, Poland and Yugoslavia; and between 4 and 6 per cent of Germany, Italy, Austria, Hungary, Japan and China'.[5]

Bergman claimed that he didn't know anything about what was happening in Germany regarding the death camps and the Holocaust. There is no need to doubt him. It is, perhaps, surprising that the sceptical, highly intelligent Bergman – who was in his early 20s by the time the Second World War started – seemingly took quite so long to see through the Nazis. After all, their influence could be felt even in the idyllic Swedish countryside of his youth. As a young man, he later revealed to academic Maria-Pia Boethius for her book *Heder Och Samvete* (*Honour and Conscience*) about Sweden during the Second World War, he had stood by as thugs painted swastikas on the summer house of a Jewish director who lived close to his family. 'And I, cowardly shit, didn't say a word about it.'[6] In *Frenzy* (1944), the film he wrote for Alf Sjoberg, the bullying teacher is explicitly endowed with Nazi traits. Bergman had also staged a version of *Macbeth* in 1944 that was regarded by many as an anti-Nazi parable and had directed a pro-Semitic student version of Shakespeare's *The Merchant of Venice* in the late 1930s. (Erland Josephson had played Antonio.)

You have to take Bergman's confessions of his own flirtation with Nazism with a little scepticism. He dramatises his own life, sometimes contradicts himself and always seems ready to accept blame and guilt, even when it is far from clear that he has done anything to be ashamed of. He behaved exactly as most other Swedes of his generation and class did.

The director suggests he refused initially to accept the evidence of the concentration camps. 'Like so many others, I said the pictures were prearranged propaganda lies', he writes in *The Magic Lantern*. Then, he fell prey to self-contempt and despair. But Bergman was eventually able to exonerate himself. 'I did not realise until long afterwards that I was guilty by association only ... the surface lustre blinded me and I did not see the darkness.'[7]

In the wake of the revelations about the war, he decided: 'Politics ... never again!'

This wasn't a resolution that he fully kept. In 1950, he made a film called *This Can't Happen Here* (a.k.a. *High Tension*), an anti-Soviet political allegory about an eastern European kidnapped in Stockholm. Kabi Laretei, an Estonian refugee herself, says that some Estonian refugees worked on the film as extras. Bergman felt so ashamed that he was trivialising their experience and making an escapist Cold War thriller that he later forbade any public screenings. 'Few of my films do I feel ashamed of or detest for various reasons. *This Can't Happen Here* was the first one', he later wrote.[8] Ironically, the Estonian refugees in Sweden had admired the film. 'They all thought it was marvellous that Ingmar made this film. They were all grateful that the occupation of Estonia would be known about. Nobody in Sweden cared very much. It was a neutral, neutral country. For us, it was terrible. He was very sensitive that he did this film and got it through', Laretei says.[9]

Bergman's reason for turning away from politics was, perhaps, not simply disgust at what he had learned about the Hitler-era genocide, but the realisation that fiction simply could not cope with the reality of what people had suffered during the traumatic years of the 1940s. He therefore retreated into the realm of the personal and the symbolic.

The key themes in Bergman's work are readily identified. Death is a constant in all Bergman's writing and filmmaking. His morbidity long predates the war years. His accounts of his childhood are full of images of relatives and family servants dying painful and squalid deaths. Bergman writes about their demises with curiosity and fascination.

When Bergman directly addressed the origins of the Nazi Party in his 1977 feature, *The Serpent's Egg*, it was striking how closely the film's themes chimed with those he had been exploring in his earlier seemingly much more personal and autobiographical work.

The Serpent's Egg is often dismissed as a failure, but is fascinating on many different levels: as one of the biggest-budget films he ever made, as one of his rare forays into English-language filmmaking, as one of the only Bergman films in which the protagonist is Jewish, for its analysis of the roots of Nazism and for its evocation of Weimar-era Berlin in all its grim decadence.

The film is set over a single week in 1923, between the 3rd and 10th November. 'To buy a dollar it costed you about four and a half billion marks. I think it was a very, very strange and a very, very bad situation – and we have made a picture about this week – what happens to some people in this week', Bergman explained to the unit photographer.

> Everybody had the feeling that next week or perhaps already tomorrow there would be a revolution, and everything will be a catastrophe in blood and fire. So why don't spend your last money, why don't (sic) dance and sing and love, and make love, and drink, and just try to forget everything.[10]

The Serpent's Egg (his 40th film) was made at a pivotal point in Bergman's career, just after his bitter spat with the Swedish tax authorities had led him to go to live in exile in Munich. He had been partly inspired to write it by Joachim Fest's biography, *Hitler*. The film was produced by Dino de Laurentiis, the flamboyant Italian mogul who had been courting Bergman since the early 1960s. They had discussed working on various earlier projects together.

In the build-up to shooting, big-name stars were linked with *The Serpent's Egg*. Dustin Hoffman had been in the frame to play the Jewish acrobat Abel Rosenberg. When he dropped out, Robert Redford (a little improbably) and Peter Falk were mooted as replacements. Richard Harris was eventually offered the role. 'I said that before I commenced filming with him, I'd like to have 8 days with him in Munich to get to know what he expects from the part and from me', Harris informed the Swedish press. 'When I said that, Bergman took me in his arms and kissed me and said: "it's wonderful to meet an actor who takes such responsibility for what he is about to portray".'[11]

In the event, Harris (who had been in Malta filming *Orca Killer Whale* for de Laurentiis) contracted pneumonia and had to pull out. At the last minute, he was replaced by David Carradine. Bergman initially had his doubts about the American, whom he had seen play folk singer Woody Guthrie in *Bound for Glory*. 'He seemed absent-minded and a bit strange ...he was a night owl and kept falling asleep on the set. He was found just about everywhere, sound asleep', Bergman writes in *Images*. 'At the same time, he was hard-working, punctual and well-prepared.'[12]

At the outset, Bergman was convinced that *The Serpent's Egg* would be his masterpiece. He had a formidable production crew. Along with his regular cinematographer Sven Nykvist, he was working with several of the technicians from Bob Fosse's *Cabaret*, including the Oscar-winning production designer Rolf Zehetbauer and the costume designer Charlotte Flemming. The Berlin they evoke is very different from that found in Fosse's film. It is a brooding, nightmarish city, full of beggars, cripples and oppressed, and automaton-like citizens, numbed by their suffering. The music in the cabaret sequences sounds discordant. The performers and the prostitutes are grotesque figures, all with a sense of desperation about them. Certain scenes are horrifically violent. There is the man decapitated by the lift and the utterly brutal sequence in which the soldier pounds the cabaret owner's head into a bloody pulp.

Bergman's workbook for *The Serpent's Egg* testifies to his perfectionism and his obsession with even the minutest details. Pasted at the end of the workbook is an image of Hitler wearing a dark suit, with his hands folded. There is one scene – which plays a very minor part in the finished film – that he revised again and again. It is a description of a horse dying, its intestines coming out on the street. People are beating and tearing the horse to pieces. A woman is coming towards Abel with a piece of meat, screaming 'do you want it'. In a later revision, he writes, 'The horse's blood steams in the chill night air: its entrails steam. A woman carrying a bloody knife stuck into her pail full of horseflesh walks toward Abel. He stares at her ...and runs'.

The screenplay is prefaced by a quote from Georg Buchner: 'Man is an abyss and I turn giddy when I look down into it.' At first, the material seems like a radical departure for Bergman. It is on a bigger scale than his Swedish films; it has an international cast; it deals directly with political and historical issues. The story begins darkly and gradually gets more grim. Abel Rosenberg (David Carradine), an alcoholic trapeze artist, returns to his lodgings and discovers that his brother Max has shot himself. Abel is thrown together with Max's widow, Manuela (Liv Ullmann), who works as a cabaret performer. They are both eventually employed by the mysterious, Mengele-like Vergerus, a scientist Abel remembers from his childhood who has been engaged in sadistic experiments on humans (including, it turns out, Abel's brother).

It is the period of Hitler's failed Beer Hall Putsch, the early 1920s when the German society is torn between left and right, inflation is spiralling and a sense of impending doom is ever-present.

'Our world will go down in blood and fire. In ten years, not more, those people will create a new society, unequalled in world history', Vergerus predicts in the monologue which gives the film its title. 'It's like a serpent's egg. Through the thin membrane, you can clearly discern the already perfect reptile.'

What is fascinating are the many echoes of and overlaps with Bergman's earlier films. That childhood relish for cruelty and death is there. Abel tells a story about a childhood encounter with Hans Vergerus: 'Once we caught a cat and tied it down. Hans cut it open – it was still alive – and showed me how its heart beat, fast, fast. Then he poked one of its eyes out with a sharp little knife and showed me how the pupil continued to react.' Vergerus's archive has its predecessor in the photographs collected by the architect in *The Passion of Anna* (1970): of people eating, asleep or in the grips of violent emotion – or of acts of violence. The slaughtered horse with its steaming entrails has its predecessors too. Bergman has long been fascinated by the slaughter of animals. In both his documentaries about Faro, *Faro Dokument 1969* and *Faro Dokument 1979*, we see farmers killing livestock in grisly, close-up detail. Abel and Manuela adrift in a violent world that has lost its moral bearings aren't so different from the couple played in *The Shame* (1967) by Max Von Sydow and Liv Ullmann, whose relationship and behaviour are utterly transformed in the wake of a devastating war.

It is reductive and simplistic to link Bergman's films too crudely with his own life, however autobiographical many of their elements often are. Nonetheless, you can't help but feel that guilt as well as morbid curiosity induced him to revisit the Berlin of the 1920s. The familiar themes are all there: sexual jealousy, death, despair and humiliation. The difference is that they are given a political and historical context. The protagonists are not middle-class Swedes on an island, agonising over the metaphysical monstrosity of existence, but characters struggling for survival in a world where – as the script notes – 'a pack of cigarettes costs thirteen million marks and ordinary people have largely lost faith in both the present and the future'.

In *The Serpent's Egg*, the historical and political subtext can't be escaped. Bergman may be telling a parable about an alcoholic acrobat, but he is also exploring the origins of the Nazi Party and the morbid fascination that its atrocities and predilection for violence exercised on him. The film – which he had thought his masterpiece – was greeted in lukewarm fashion. By the time he made it, Bergman was already living in exile in Germany.

The story of why Bergman left Sweden reads like a mini-Kafka story in which a citizen finds himself pitted against an unforgiving bureaucracy. It also serves as a cautionary tale about the downside of the bold social experiment in Sweden after the war.

Just as Bergman had said 'Politics … never again', the modern Swedish state itself had sought to move beyond politics, at least as understood in any narrow party-political sense.

Sweden had been neutral in the war. It was a country that had long been ruled by the Social Democrats. Swedish citizens – including Bergman – believed in the practical utopianism of the Social Democrats. Swedes paid high taxes and had certain restrictions placed on their freedoms. In return, they enjoyed the benefits of a generous welfare state. Sweden was egalitarian. There was an essential fairness to the social contract the citizens struck with the state. 'I had always been a convinced Social Democrat', Bergman wrote in *The Magic Lantern*. 'I had embraced with sincere enthusiasm this grey ideology of compromises. I thought my country was the best in the world.'[13]

Bergman accepted the status quo. He wasn't much interested in material possessions. His main preoccupation was his work. After his chastening experience of discovering the truth about the Nazi death camps, he wanted to leave politics alone. He felt that as long as he abided by the rules, the state would leave him alone too. His ex-wife Kabi Laretei testifies to his old-fashioned patriotism. Although he might grumble about Sweden, if she did so, he reacted as if she were maligning one of his close relatives.

Of course, when Bergman vowed 'Politics … never again!', it was inevitable that he would lose the challenge he had set himself almost immediately. Bergman's early post-war films may not have dealt overtly with politics. However, simply by dint of portraying young Swedes, whether the working-class heroine of *Summer with Monika* or his gallery of pampered and tormented young artists, and telling contemporary stories, he was giving his work a political dimension. His later works, whether *The Seventh Seal* or *Winter Light* or – much more overtly – *The Shame*, were all open to political interpretation. As his friend Jorn Donner pointed out, his work was giving a dramatic form to feelings and anxieties that many of his fellow Swedes felt. Films that seemed to many critics out-side Sweden to be a very personal reflection of the director's idiosyncratic and tormented world view were – Donner contended – articulating a foreboding that Bergman's fellow Swedes felt all too acutely as well.

'The sense of crisis, approaching and full of threat, present and over-whelming, is never distant from Bergman's pictures, even the most idyl-lic ones', Donner observed in the mid-1970s. 'This feeling corresponds to the spiritual unrest that has troubled Swedish society during the last 30 years.'[14]

Seen in this light, all Bergman's films were topical and full of politi-cal relevance. They captured the lingering feeling among many Swedes that their much vaunted social experiment wasn't working as well as had initially been thought. This was why Bergman's bitter battle with the Swedish tax authorities in the mid-1970s so quickly became a matter of national and international debate.

On the face of it, this was a case of the tax authorities coming after a rich and successful man who had not been paying his taxes. If this had been the full story, though, one doubts that Bergman would have been treated by the media and public with as much sympathy as he eventu-ally was.

The US magazine *Time* picked up on the malaise in Swedish soci-ety that the Bergman case highlighted. In an article called 'Cries and Whimpers in Socialism's Showcase', *Time* pointed out that bureaucracy in Sweden had grown oppressive. The state, in the shape of the tax authorities and the judiciary, interfered with individual liberties in an often heavy-handed way. Despite the outer sheen of prosperity and social justice, it was self-evident that many within Swedish society were desperately unhappy. As Bergman put it with his usual sardonic wit, 'when all the problems seem to be solved, then all the difficulties come'.[15]

There was evidence of alcoholism. The suicide rate seemed to have shot up. Divorce was on the increase. (Bergman's 1973 film *Scenes from a Marriage* was credited with encouraging a new frankness in discussions between couples. Couples may have been able to talk more openly to one another than before, but the downside was that many relationships ended in the wake of this new emotional glasnost.) Some suggested that young Swedes, living in the brave new world created for them by the Social Democrats, had lost ambition and any sense of direction. *Time* reported Kafkaesque examples of the state interfering in a misguided attempt to improve the living conditions of its citizens.

'A Government agency has even recommended that Swedes achieve a balanced diet at a reasonable cost by eating six to eight slices of bread daily', reported the magazine. 'A man who wants to repaint his house must use officially approved colours (chiefly, various shades of tan). A man who owns a forest cannot forbid others to walk in it. If he builds a fence, he can be forced to take it down again.'[16]

Celebrated children's author Astrid Lindgren, the creator of *Pippi Longstocking*, had (like Bergman) supported the Social Democrats as a matter of course. However, in the mid-1970s, she realised that she was being taxed at a rate of 102 per cent, an absurdity which inspired her satirical fairy tale *Pomperipossa in the World of Money*. Like Bergman, Lindgren was beginning to question whether or not Sweden really was the best society in the world.

What is fascinating about Bergman's own crisis with the tax authorities is that it was a catastrophe foretold. It turned into a story of humiliation and nervous breakdown that the director himself might have written.

The tax scandal is at the centre of his autobiography. By comparison, his embattled relationship with his father and his childhood humiliations pale almost into insignificance. This was the most traumatic episode in a life that was full of trauma. As a rebellious child, he had expected difficulties with authority figures. What he had never anticipated was that the state itself would turn against him.

It all started so innocently. At the beginning of 1976, Bergman had been busy rehearsing a stage production of Strindberg's *A Dance of Death* and preparing Gunnel Lindblom's film, *Paradise Place*, which was to be made through his production company, Cinematograph, which he had formed in the late 1960s. He was beginning to think of the challenges that lay ahead in making a big international production *The Serpent's Egg*, to be produced by Dino de Laurentiis, and was even contemplating working in America. In *The Magic Lantern*, he recalls a visit by two quiet and courteous gentlemen from the tax authorities who wanted to go through the company books. Bergman thought nothing of this. Then, a few weeks later, the police turned up at the Royal Dramatic Theatre during morning rehearsals for *A Dance of Death* to arrest him. He was accused of having made false declarations about his income. Bergman was utterly flabbergasted.

'In the whole of this miserable episode – which lasted several years and caused me and mine considerable pain, which cost a fortune in legal fees, which sent me abroad for nine years and finally led to a tax demand for 180,000 kronor – I was guilty of only one thing – that I had signed papers I had not read or had not understood', he later wrote in *The Magic Lantern*.[17]

His account of his own trials at the hands of the tax authorities is written in language that is often reminiscent of that used in his 1969 film, *The Rite*, about three actors being questioned by a judge about a production that may have broken censorship rules. The actors are full of contempt for the man who presumes to stand in judgement over them. They are intelligent, artistic and glamorous. By contrast, the judge, Mr Abrahamson, is – at least in their eyes – a small-minded voyeur and dullard. 'Christ, you're ridiculous with your bloody self-esteem, your lower-class curiosity and tactlessness, your lack of education and sympathy', they taunt him as his questions grow more intrusive. They accuse him of a lack of hygiene. They point out – inevitably – the dirt under his fingernails. They notice the way he sweats when he is nervous. To them, his small-minded officiousness seems utterly absurd. They spot his vanity – his desire to hog some of their limelight. 'Your picture in the paper next to us. It feels good to pester us with humiliating questions under pretence of decency and discretion. Pulling down our trousers and giving us a spanking.'

The actors' disdain for the judge in *The Rite* anticipates the disgust and incomprehension Bergman felt towards his tormentors during the tax crisis. In his description of the tax detectives who came after him, Bergman can't resist highlighting their repulsive physical characteristics – the dirty fingernails, flowered shirts and grubby complexions. The government's intent was clear – to make an example of a rich and famous personality and thereby both to demonstrate its power and to terrify other citizens into abiding by the law. Bergman was having his trousers pulled down and being given a symbolic spanking. There was a widespread assumption that he must have been guilty of something. If not, why was the state making such a fuss? This was an assumption shared even by some of his children. They were on the left politically: to them, he was not only an establishment figure getting his much deserved come-uppance but also a negligent father who had shown scant interest in their lives.

In Bergman's biography, the drama is invariably in the private sphere. He wasn't a war hero or a politician or a teacher. He didn't make public interventions. His life was in his work and in his relationships. Thanks to the tax authorities, though, he was prised out into the open. It wasn't a sensation he relished at all.

At the same time, Bergman couldn't resist dramatising his own predicament. Both in his response at the time and in what he later wrote about the crisis, Bergman portrays himself as a King Lear-like figure, battered on all sides, self-pitying and his sanity fraying. He had frequently depicted such characters in his films. Think, for example, of the hypersensitive artist Johan Borg played in such febrile fashion by Max Von Sydow in *Hour of the Wolf* (1968). Under the goading of his aristocratic tormentors, he slowly loses his mind.

At first, the Swedish authorities were utterly unapologetic about swooping down to arrest the country's most famous film and theatre director during morning rehearsal for a production at Stockholm's most prestigious theatre. Gunnar Bjoerne, chief of the Department for Individual Taxation in the Finance Ministry, told the press that Bergman had been given permission in 1967 to start a film production company in Switzerland and had transferred funds there to pay start-up costs. However, Bjoerne contended, the Swiss company had never made a film. Instead, it had been used to collect the profits from the foreign sales of his films.

'It was a clear tax-evading arrangement. Bergman says he is quite innocent: he knew nothing. But if you look at how he set up his companies, he cannot be quite so innocent', Bjoerne told *Time*.[18] Whatever Bjoerne's opinion, the Bergman case became a cause celebre.

An open letter was printed in his support with signatures from some of the most famous figures in Swedish society. 'We, your friends and admirers of your exquisite art in theatre and film, are appalled by the deeply offensive act done in a democratic society by rule of law and we want to express our sincere sympathy in view of what has happened. We still hope you will find it possible even in the future to continue your work of art beyond our country's border', the letter stated. Signatories included Tore Browaldh, Alf Henriksen (writer and historian) and many others, including the King (or at least someone signing in his name).

Meanwhile, Bergman went on the offensive, sending his own 'open letter' to the press. 'By theft and extortion, they (the tax authorities) are trying to get me to admit that they were right in the beginning but I refuse to be part of this game', he declared.

He had now decided on a course of action. He was going to quit Sweden but would leave his money in a closed account so the tax authorities can take whatever money they feel he owes them. He was going to close his company Cinematograph and to abandon plans to build a film studio on Faro, but he would, of course, make sure that all staff were compensated.

In the letter, he talks about how he had always thought of Sweden as the best of all countries, but now he experienced a shock and humiliation that were almost unbearable. He felt that the tax authorities were like a cancer that could attack anyone at any moment.

The media hadn't been sympathetic towards him, but he chose not to attack the newspapers because he felt it was 'pointless'. The newspaper in the front line of the attacks against him was *Aftonbladet*, whose political views closely aligned to those of the Social Democrats. This depressed and dismayed him.

Bergman concluded his open letter by saying he would not seek to sue the tax authorities. 'This is also meaningless.' One day, though, he threatened that he might write a small farce on the subject of his trial by tax inspectors. He ended the letter by quoting Strindberg: 'Be careful you son of a bitch. I'll see you in my next play.'[19]

It was a huge emotional wrench for Bergman to leave Sweden and go into voluntary exile, as he did in April 1976. Nonetheless, there had been at least one or two unlikely benefits from the tax trauma. Bergman had had a nervous breakdown in the wake of the attack on him by the tax authorities. He ended up sectioned in the psychiatric clinic at the Karolinska Hospital – an experience he later looked back on as bizarrely rewarding.

'I tell you, the time at the clinic was very fascinating', he said in a television interview, enthusing about the ten days he spent drugged up to his eyeballs with 12 other patients, all with mental problems.[20]

Bergman was always a man of routine, even when he was locked up in an asylum as a 'drugged zombie' living on a diet of Valium and Mogadon. He'd be up at 5.30 am every day to ensure he could be the first to use the bathroom. He spent his days reading, watching movies or making small talk with his fellow inmates. In the evening, they all watched the world ice-skating championship on a fuzzy TV screen. Under the influence of the drugs, he slept well and suffered from no bad dreams. In the hospital, he achieved a contentment that he had seldom ever experienced before. His demons vanished. There was no anger or anxiety, just a series of pleasant, uneventful and identical days running into one another. Again, the image he gives of himself evokes memories of *King Lear* when his madness seems to have run its course. 'Come, let's away to prison; we two alone will sing like birds i' th' cage.' (Fittingly enough, *King Lear* was the first play he directed when he returned to Sweden in 1984 after almost nine years of exile.)

Bergman recreated his sinister idyll in the asylum in his remarkable late film *From the Life of the Marionettes* (1980). Here, the inmate isn't incarcerated because he failed to pay his taxes but because he murdered a prostitute and then had sex with her corpse. 'The emotional avalanche has now been set free', the doctor says of his patient, who now spends his days quietly playing chess – not with the Grim Reaper, but with a computer. The patient is polite to staff but very reserved. He obsessively tidies his room and cleans himself. He keeps the outer world at bay, never reading newspapers or listening to the radio or watching TV.

What Bergman discovered during his time in the hospital was that he needed his demons. Everything that tormented him – the impatience, the tendency towards explosive anger, the cowardice, the fetish for order and the vindictive strain in his personality – also fired his creativity. The challenge, as he often confessed, was to keep the demons in order: to reach a point of equilibrium which would enable him to continue working.

Many countries were keen to play host to Bergman in exile. In the end, he chose to go to Germany. It was there that his 40th film, *The Serpent's Egg*, was set. Munich appeared to offer him a home away from home. Not only would he be able to direct plays at the Residenztheater – Germany's equivalent of the Royal Dramatic Theatre in Stockholm – but he also had the Bavaria Film Studios at his disposal and access to some of the world's top film technicians.

Bergman's resolution – 'Politics ... never again' – could no longer be sustained. Following his battles with the tax authorities, he had surely come to accept that 'politics' were involved in every decision about his career he made. Thanks to the tax scandal, Bergman had even emerged as a political spokesperson. With his contacts and his fame, he was able to fight back against the state in a way that would have been impossible for normal Swedes. He was also in a position to find refuge elsewhere.

'It is good that I can leave Sweden', he told *Time* magazine. 'But thousands are staying, held down, silent. They cannot leave. They don't have the connections. They have family here. They love the country. And besides, where in the world can you have a summer house with such a magnificent view?'[21]

The irony about the whole tax debacle was that Bergman was the quintessential modern Swede. The state preached the doctrine of efficiency, discipline and order. This was a doctrine that Bergman himself – the most rigorous of craftsmen – adhered to absolutely. He too believed in regulation and routine. In forcing him into exile, the Swedish authorities were guilty of a public relations disaster. Instead of being praised for taking stern action against a tax dodger, they were reviled for forcing one of their most prominent citizens to leave his homeland. Olaf Palme, the leader of the Social Democrats and a so-called revolutionary reformist, was ostensibly Bergman's friend, but the director despised him for his failure to intervene on his behalf. In the wake of its handling of the Bergman tax scandal, the government's popularity plummeted. Newspapers compared his departure from Sweden to that of Solzhenitsyn from Russia.

Bergman's arrest took place on 30 January 1976. On 23 March, less than two months later, the charges against him were dropped. Nonetheless, the damage was done. Bergman's sense of outrage at the way he had been treated would never leave him. He had 'a memory like an elephant and never forgot grudges'.

The filmmaker freely admitted that his work was 'strongly linked with ... [his] environment and ... [his] language' and that working elsewhere, he might well be a diminished figure. Nonetheless, he was determined to leave. On 22 April, he began his exile.

Many Swedes were shocked by the savagery with which Bergman had been treated and feared that they too could be persecuted equally viciously if they fell foul of the state.

'There is something evil in the atmosphere that nurtures us, our politicians and our bureaucrats. Bergman's case is part of the same pattern of oppression', suggested the author Kjeli Sundberg in the wake of Bergman's exile. 'The way society treated Bergman is the way ordinary people are treated daily by the tax system, by the judicial system, by the penal system, by schools, by regional development policies and so on. The only difference is that most of us are insignificant and patient.'[22]

In his impatience, Bergman – the apolitical filmmaker – had undergone an unlikely transformation: he had turned into a political figurehead.

6

Bergman's Actresses

You can't dissociate them (the actresses) from his own life, his own relationship with the actresses he has filmed. There's this huge autobiographical element in his films that makes it deeper and even more disturbing in many ways.

(OLIVIER ASSAYAS)[1]

THE ACTRESS AND later filmmaker Mai Zetterling made a very revealing remark about why she felt uncomfortable working with Ingmar Bergman. Zetterling had co-starred in Alf Sjoberg's *Frenzy* (1944) (Bergman's first feature script) and had also appeared in Bergman's 1947 feature. 'I think I was intimidated by him (Bergman)', she commented. 'He wanted to be extraordinarily close to his actors – too close for comfort. I didn't want to be one of his puppets.'[2]

Her choice of metaphor is instructive. A puppetmaster was precisely how Bergman himself often liked to describe his role as director. (As a child, he presided over his own self-assembled puppet theatre, complete with sophisticated lighting and costumes, putting on shows for friends and relatives.) He also often likened himself to a musician or a musical conductor. The actors were like the soloists in the orchestra. He wanted them to play their parts with the same fluency and virtuosity as a great violinist or pianist interpreting a piece of music.

'He (Bergman) often said that as musicians start when they are children, they have to have work severely', his ex-wife Kabi Laretei recalls. 'Actors become actors when they are grown up and there is no precision in what they do.'[3]

Another metaphor Bergman frequently used was that of the director as violinist and of his favourite actresses as the instrument on which he played. When the collaboration worked, there was a magic about it.

One of his favourite metaphors was of himself as a skilful violinist playing a Stradivarius. He called Max Von Sydow 'the first and best Stradivarius that I have ever had in my hands'.[4] The implication was clear – to play such an instrument required a musician of uncommon discipline and touch. As the director, he was the one coaxing the performance into life.

Bergman's actresses, while acknowledging that they did much of their best work for him, have sometimes questioned the direction in which he pushed them. 'I am not that dark. I really am not. Maybe I would have liked to do more life-affirming stuff', Liv Ullmann said in a 2001 interview. 'The parts other people would give me were very often the same kind of thing. They thought this was my speciality.'[5]

She suggested that Bergman understood women but also found them mysterious. Sometimes, he would write roles for actresses whom he wanted to work with, but those roles would be based on his own experience.

It is striking that in his very first feature as a director, *Crisis* (1945), the main protagonist was a woman. Many of his subsequent films also had women as their leading characters. Underlining Zetterling's remarks about wanting to get close to his actresses, Bergman was prepared to delve far more deeply into the lives of his women characters than any other major (male) director of his era.

There are plenty of cod psychological explanations for this fascination with women in his work. You can root it in his childhood and his obsessive love for a mother who was embarrassed and even repelled by his puppyish displays of affection. His professional life and his love life invariably went hand in hand. 'Drama and film are incontrovertibly two professions that are immensely erotically charged', he acknowledged late in his career and talked of the 'incredibly pleasurable tensions' that the quest for perfection shared by him and his actors could cause.

Bergman's relationship with his leading actresses was often as demanding as that between lovers. He expected a level of commitment that took some of his actresses by surprise. Lena Olin, who appeared in his late film *After the Rehearsal* (1984) and was also an extra in *Face to Face* (1975), was startled by Bergman's intensity and by his curiosity about her.

'At the wrap party for *Face to Face*, Bergman spent the whole night talking to me', Olin recalls.[6] At the time, she was only 20 years old. She was flattered by the attention from this man, who was of her parents' generation and who was also a national celebrity. Her only comparable experience was – she says – when she was much older, had become an established actress and had just appeared in her husband Lasse Hallstrom's film, *Chocolat* (2000). She and Hallstrom were both introduced to the then president of the USA, Bill Clinton, and he likewise took an intent interest in her. 'I had the same feeling – the President of America just talking to me and Lasse for hours!'

Olin had intended to go to medical school to study to become a doctor. Bergman encouraged her to go to drama school instead, an advice she heeded by enrolling in Sweden's National Academy of Dramatic Art the next year. 'He said you've got to try (to go there.) It's a good school.'

Bergman's flattering attention in her continued. Not only did Bergman cast her in *After the Rehearsal*, but she also played Miss Julie on stage for him and appeared as *Cordelia* in his production of *King Lear*. However, when she became pregnant during rehearsals for a production of Strindberg's *A Dream Play*, his attitude towards her changed completely. When he realised she was no longer available for the play, he lost all interest in her. Worse, he became actively hostile. In *The Magic Lantern*, Bergman writes that he was 'happy for her happiness' and describes Olin as 'lovely and decent'.[7] However, what she recalls is that he was 'very furious' about the pregnancy, 'and very unforgiving as well. He was really mean to [her] ...'.[8]

Years later, when Bergman tried to work with her again and offered her a part in another Strindberg play, she turned him down again. Her kids were in school in New York, and she wasn't prepared to decamp to Stockholm without them. 'I had to call him and say I can't do it. I had been afraid of calling him (Bergman). I knew he could be very, very vengeful, especially when he cares – and I knew he cared', Olin recalls.

The relationship between Bergman and Olin stretched back a long way. She was the daughter of Stig Olin, who had appeared in many of his early films (often as his alter ego). Nonetheless, when he felt that Lena had betrayed him, he dropped her. 'You've got to leave it a few years!' she joked about when they might next be able to speak again without rancour.[9]

As Olin's story attests, Bergman could be as vindictive and unforgiving as a lover scorned to an actress he felt had let him down.

There is a paradox here. Bergman was famous for maintaining cordial and even affectionate relationships with most of the women with whom he had had long-term relationships. Many (whether Harriet Andersson, Bibi Andersson or Liv Ullmann) continued working with him after their relationships ended. His first wife Else Fischer worked as a choreographer on *The Seventh Seal* long after their marriage had ended. Kabi Laretei became close friends with him following their divorce and used to live and work during the summer in one of his houses on the island of Faro.

'I must be able to exchange souls with my partner. The ones I've been with for the other thing – well, I can count them on the fingers of one hand. And deep down I am faithful – though no one will believe it. My being is actually fidelity: All those whom I have grown fond of in some way, I am faithful to afterward', Bergman said.[10]

Bergman may have cited the playwright Strindberg as one of his chief inspirations, but unlike Strindberg, he was no misogynist. 'Strindberg hated women more. Ingmar is much more sympathetic to the women', Liv Ullmann said of him.[11]

Some of his collaborators were baffled by Bergman's reverence for Strindberg and close identification with the tormented playwright. Others realised that what linked Bergman and Strindberg most closely was the way both looked inward for inspiration. 'Many of Ingmar's ways of thinking were similar to those of Strindberg's. It is said of Strindberg that he lived his life so as to be able to have something to write about', comments Barbro Hiort af Ornas, an actress who first worked with Bergman in the 1930s. She was 16 at the time, just starting to act in an amateur youth club in the old town in Stockholm. This was in 1939, just before the war. He was 20. He was 19 when he started his job as the leader of the dramatic section of this youth club.

'He had it all from the start – the personality and gifts and his talents were obvious at an early age', she recalls. 'Of course, he has learned a lot along the way, but the ground for it was all there – even when he was a young boy ... so did Strindberg. That is how it was.'[12]

As actresses who have worked with him make clear, his professional life came first. He was utterly uncompromising about anything that might make one of his films or plays less good than it should be. An actress might be brilliant, but if she was neurotic or unreliable, he would have no qualms about discarding her.

At the same time, Bergman was a surprisingly sympathetic figure. For all his tantrums and neuroses, he wasn't dictatorial. He listened to his collaborators and would pay heed to constructive suggestions. Although he could be brutal with technicians, his method with actors was to make them feel cherished and special. Partly for this reason, actresses were always eager to work with him and to be in his orbit. 'He was attractive because he was so talented and made life so interesting. That is all I can say about it. He wasn't extremely good-looking. And he was absolutely not the flirtatious type. He was very severe, very dark-minded.

He was a deeper thinking character than the rest of us youngsters – and we admired him for that', adds Hiort af Ornas.[13]

For many, 'Bergman's women' became as identifiable as his films themselves. He helped make international stars of, among others, Bibi Andersson, Harriet Andersson, Ingrid Thulin and Liv Ullmann.

Bergman had a knack for spotting talent in unlikely quarters. Harriet Andersson, for example, had left school at the age of 15 and taken a job as elevator operator in a department store in Stockholm. Around this time, she had enrolled in Calle Flygare's stage school. She had worked as a chorus girl and in reviews before being cast in a prominent role in Gustaf Molander's *Defiance* (1952). The legend is that Bergman spotted her in fishnet stockings in a revue. When he cast her in the lead in *Summer with Monika* (1953) and also began a relationship with her, Molander was openly jealous. Bergman seemed to know intuitively which actresses would shine on camera. As he later said of her, 'I think the camera loves the particles that surround Harriet, and that she likes them too.'[14] He was also aware of how stars can help sell films internationally. Some of his reported statements about Andersson sounded as if they had been made for maximum publicity value – or had perhaps been drafted on his behalf by the PR agents. For example, Bergman was reported as saying that 'in the entire history of Swedish cinema no other actress has exercised such a deeply savage and erotic attraction as Harriet. She was ravaging'.[15]

The original Svensk posters for *Summer with Monika* – over which Bergman (one guesses) must have had some influence – were deliberately provocative. In one, there are four separate images of her taken from the film. The main one, in the centre of the poster, is a full-length portrait of her in tight shorts and a see-through blouse, staring out at the horizon. Like Heddy Lamarr in *Ecstasy*, she is portrayed as the earthy, sensuous woman, going back to nature.

Partly thanks to the roles that Bergman gave her, Andersson became one of a new generation of sex symbols who emerged in European cinema in the 1950s. This was the era of Brigitte Bardot in Roger Vadim's *And God Created Women*, of Jeanne Moreau in Louis Malle's *Les Amants* (1958), of Marilyn Monroe's emergence in Hollywood and of Anna Magnani in Italy.

It was a paradoxical period in which prudery and liberation walked hand in hand. In Europe, the 1950s marked the beginning of the Nouvelle Vague, a time when directors and their actors embraced a new, far less inhibited style of filmmaking. Cracks too were beginning to

appear in the patriarchal world of Hollywood. The women were begin-
ning to talk back and to frighten the men. (Witness Jane Russell and
Marilyn Monroe as the gold diggers, terrifying any male they meet, in
Gentlemen Prefer Blondes.)

On-screen, Andersson appeared defiant, open about her sexuality
and unwilling to kowtow to the men. Off-screen, though, she struck a
surprisingly modest and self-deprecating note. Asked about representations of femininity in European and Hollywood films of the 1950s, she
parried the question. 'I didn't think about that. I was working. That was
my life', she said. 'Also, in the 1950s, women didn't talk so much. They
were supposed to look sweet and nice and keep their mouths shut.'[16]

Bibi Andersson, Harriet Andersson's successor both as Bergman's
lover and as his muse, had first met the director as a 15-year-old would-
be actress when she appeared in one of his Bris soap commercials. (She
was the princess who had to give the swineherd 100 kisses to procure a
bar of soap.) They were together as a couple in the mid to late 1950s,
at the time of *Smiles of a Summer Night* and *Wild Strawberries*. She
worked as part of his theatrical troupe in Malmo. Bergman described his
life with Andersson as one filled with kindness and creativity. Nonetheless, by the time of *Wild Strawberries*, their relationship was beginning
to founder.

Bibi Andersson later claimed she felt as if she was walking a tightrope
when she collaborated with Bergman. 'He likes you to come up with
ideas', she told one journalist. 'If you show nothing, he gets very angry
because he says he must have a starting point; you must show that you
have some idea of what the scene is about. But if you are too firm in your
convictions you can have terrible arguments with him.'[17]

As she pointed out to *Time Out New York*, Bergman was nothing if
not paradoxical. 'He was always, as a director, very tender and very nice.
But as a person, he could lose his temper.'[18]

A pert and pretty blonde, she excelled at playing ingenues and young
rebels. She was the young virgin, tantalising and infuriating the Don Juan
sent by Satan to seduce her in Bergman's 1960 comedy *The Devil's Eye*,
Isak Borg's sweetheart in *Wild Strawberries* (1957), a reluctant mother
in *Brink of Life* (1958) and an idealised one in *The Seventh Seal* (1957).

Bergman had first encountered Norwegian actress Liv Ullmann when
she was part of a delegation from Norway that visited the Royal Dramatic
Theatre. He later saw a picture of her sitting next to Bibi Andersson on
the set of the 1962 film *Summer Is Short*, an adaptation of Knut Hamsun's

Pan directed by Bjarne Henning-Jensen. Bergman was struck by how 'like and unlike' each other the actresses were. Their similarity gave him the germ of the idea that would develop into *Persona*.

Actresses who worked with Bergman were invariably given a range of roles. Many were part of his repertory company at the Malmo Municipal Theatre. Malmo was where Bergman and Ingrid Thulin first worked together.

The actresses in Bergman films moved beyond being sex symbols. Those who worked with him regularly were cast in very different roles. Harriet Andersson liked to joke about the wildly contradictory range of characters she played for Bergman – roles which often reflected the os- cillations in her relationship with him. 'First, I was a sumptuous thing in *Summer with Monika*. Then, I became the object of jealousy in *Sawdust and Tinsel*, complete with the wife in the background. After that comes *A Lesson in Love*, where I was a defiant and sad little teenager. Then came *Dreams*, where I was a sad girl again and where neither of us felt well', Andersson recalled on stage during the 2006 'Bergman Week' Festival on Faro (with Bergman in the audience). 'He (Bergman) began writing *Smiles of a Summer Night* before we separated, if I remember correctly. And if you take a look at how things went on to develop between me and Ingmar, then I became the maid in Smiles ..., obviously amiable and funny, but all the same.'[19] In *Through a Glass Darkly*, she played a men- tally disturbed character. In *All These Women*, she was a maid again. She died in *Cries and Whispers* and committed suicide in *The Blessed Ones* (which was made for TV). 'First he made me a maid, then crazy and then he killed me off a couple of times' was how she jokingly liked to sum up their career together.

Ingrid Thulin had an equally varied portfolio of Bergman roles: she was the sympathetic confidante in *Wild Strawberries*, the neurotic and hypochondriacal lesbian in *The Silence*; the mousy teacher whose love the priest repels in *Winter Light* and the androgynous woman with psy- chic powers in *The Magician*.

Tellingly, the two films of which Bergman often appeared most proud, *Persona* (1965) and *Cries and Whispers* (1971), are both 'women's films' – films in which he pushes his actresses to probe away remorselessly at such feelings as grief, jealousy and terror.

'I think I can say without singing my own praises that *Persona* and *Cries and Whispers* are two films in a class by themselves ... I think that in this case I have been able to stretch the medium to somewhere beyond

Alma The Nurse (Bibi Andersson) in *Persona*.

its normal limits', he told Marie Nyrerod in a late interview.[20] The reason that he was able to push the medium so far was the fearless, intense
performances he was able to coax out of his actresses.

Bergman described *Persona* (1966) as a sonata for two instruments –
the instruments were the leads, Liv Ullmann and Bibi Andersson. This
was a film conceived in illness. Bergman began to write the screenplay
when he was convalescing in Sophiahemmet, the royal hospital in
Stockholm, from a bout of double pneumonia and acute penicillin poisoning. He was in a state of nervous exhaustion following his efforts as
head of the Royal Dramatic Theatre. His state of mind in this period
was – he later suggested – most clearly articulated in the essay *The
Snakeskin*, which he wrote when he received the Erasmus Prize in
Amsterdam in 1965. There was a sense that Bergman – the establishment figure who had been running Sweden's most prestigious theatre
company – wanted to reclaim his status as an unruly and rebellious child.
In *Persona*, he was – in a sense – revisiting his adolescence.

'I never, it seemed to me, excited enough interest in my fellow human
beings', he wrote in *The Snakeskin*.

And so, when reality no longer sufficed, I began to make things up, regaling my contemporaries with tremendous stories of my secret exploits. There were embarrassing lies which inevitably foundered on the scepticism of the world around me. In the end I withdrew from fellowship and kept my dreams to myself. A contact-seeking child, beset by fantasies, I was quickly transformed into a hurt, cunning and suspicious daydreamer.[21]

Cinema was the medium that this daydreamer had decided to use to put across his message. At its purest, he argued, cinema used a language that is spoken 'from soul to soul, in terms that avoid control by the intellect in a manner almost voluptuous'. He had spent 20 years making movies, communicating 'dreams, sensual experiences, fantasies, outbursts of madness, the convulsions of faith, and downright lies'. He compared his art to a 'snakeskin full of ants. The snake itself is long since dead, eaten out from within, deprived of its poison; but the skin moves, filled with busy life'. He wanted to keep on making films – to keep that snakeskin moving.

His language was instructive. One might have expected a filmmaker receiving a prestigious international prize to adopt a high-minded and sententious tone. Instead, Bergman was deliberately provocative – self-deprecating and self-mocking. He had started questioning his art more intently than ever before. His unease is reflected in *Persona*.

The film has thematic overlaps with Strindberg's short play *The Stronger* (1890). Set in the corner of a lady's cafe on Christmas Eve, this is about two actresses, one unmarried and one married. In a long monologue, Mme X goads Mlle Y. 'If you wanted to shoot me', X tells Y, 'it wouldn't be so surprising, because I stood in your way – and I know you can never forget that – although I was absolutely innocent. You still believe I intrigued and got you out of the Stora theatre, but I didn't. I didn't do that, although you think so. Well, it doesn't make any difference what I say to you.'[22]

Mlle Y stays silent throughout, reacting to the married woman's monologue with irony, curiosity and laughter, but never speaking.

Mme X uses the same intense and barbed language that is heard in *Persona*, switching from affection to unbridled malice and back again in the space of a few sentences.

'Our acquaintance has been so queer. When I saw you for the first time I was afraid of you, so afraid that I didn't dare let you out of my sight; no matter when or where, I always found myself near you – I didn't dare have you for an enemy, so I became your friend. But there was always discord when you came to our house, because I saw that my husband couldn't endure you, and the whole thing seemed as awry to me as an ill-fitting gown – and I did all I could to make him friendly toward you, but with no success until you became engaged .... Everything, everything came from you to me, even your soul crept into mine, like a worm into an apple, ate and ate, bored and bored, until nothing was left but the rind and a little black dust within. I wanted to get away from you, but I couldn't; you lay like a snake and charmed me with your black eyes; I felt that when I lifted my wings they only dragged me down; I lay in the water with bound feet, and the stronger I strove to keep up the deeper I worked myself down, down, until I sank to the bottom, where you lay like a giant crab to clutch me in your claws – and there I am lying now.'[23]

The end point of the play is the utter hatred that Mme X feels for Mlle Y – a hatred exacerbated by the other woman's provocative silence, by jealousy over some incident in the past, by the memory of the violent friendship they used to enjoy and by the lingering attraction X still feels for her.

There are obvious similarities between *The Stronger* and *Persona*. The latter isn't about two actresses, but is about an actress and a nurse. Elisabet Vogler (Liv Ullmann) suddenly falls silent during a performance of Electra and refuses to speak. Nurse Alma (Bibi Andersson) accompanies her to a seaside retreat and tends her. The nurse does all the talking. She chatters and gossips but eventually reveals more and more intimate details about her own life including a story about having unprotected sex on the beach with a teenage boy and becoming pregnant. Alma is still racked with guilt about ending the pregnancy. She is angered and humiliated by a dismissive letter that Vogler writes to a friend in which the actress mocks the nurse's confessions.

Just as in *The Stronger*, power relations are in a constant state of flux. Mme X may seem like the woman in charge. She does all the talking. However, the more she speaks, the more she betrays her own self-doubt and weakness. The same applies to *Persona*. The mute actress may be the patient, but the nurse is the one whose weaknesses and neuroses are being exposed. The silence is a trap. With Vogler refusing to speak, it is left to Alma to fill it – and one confession sets off another. As their roles are reversed, the personalities of the two women begin to overlap. Vogler's silence is both a sign of defiance and – on one level – an expression of honesty. As the doctor tells her, 'at least, you don't lie'. Alma's role has always been as the listener. She finds it intoxicating to speak and can't help but regard Vogler, her confidante, as friend and sister. She doesn't notice how predatory Vogler seems as she shares her reminiscences about her sexual escapades and subsequent abortion. She has the aloof but curious look of someone studying her subject, looking for tell-tale signs and weaknesses – although we subsequently discover that Alma's experience of an unwanted pregnancy chimes with her own – or, at least, it seems to. The account of her giving birth to a child she detests and rejects comes towards the end of the film when the lines between the two characters have become so indistinct that it is difficult to work out just whose experience is being discussed.

Another self-evident influence on *Persona* was the work of psychologist Carl Jung. He had theorised that the 'persona' was the outer appearance that individuals present to the world. It is their mask – their way of protecting and projecting themselves in their relations with others. The danger is that they use their persona to deceive not just others but themselves.

Persona wouldn't have worked if it hadn't been for Bergman's absolute trust in his actresses. What might have otherwise seemed an awkward, self-conscious piece of experimental cinema takes on a real emotional edge because of Ullmann's and Andersson's virtuosity. This was to become one of Bergman's most famous and often revived features. Critics have made huge claims on its behalf, some even calling it 'one of the greatest films ever made'. It is also one of his most daunting. The montage sequence that opens the film is a provocation to viewers. We see celluloid seeming to burn. There is a shot of an erect penis. (This was taken out of several international cuts of the film although it is so fleeting that you can barely register it.) We see blinding light coming out of the projector, some upside down footage of animated film that suddenly sticks and snippets from the spoof silent movie scene that Bergman had already used in one of his first films, *Prison*. There is a shot of the eye of a dead sheep, which seems intended to evoke memories of the severed eyeball in Bunuel and Dali's surrealist classic *Un chien andalou* (1928). A nail is hammered into a hand. There are mortuary shots of the corpses of an old man and woman. On the soundtrack, there is discordant music, the noise of a drip and the distant echo of a telephone. Finally, a naked boy reading Lermontov slowly turns his head and reaches out as if to touch the camera lens. In the next shot, he is moving his hand over a huge image of what appears to be Liv Ullmann's face.

It is a bravura but baffling sequence, full of subliminal images and bleached-out lighting, that might have been expected to alienate a mainstream audience. Bergman is not only laying bare the device in time-honoured, Brechtian fashion – showing that we are watching a film and inviting us to question all the artifice that goes into making an audience suspend its disbelief. At the same time, he is reminding the audience of the magic lantern aspect of cinema.

> The basic thing in cinematography is the perforated film containing 52 frames per metre, each separated by a thick black line. On closer study we see that these small frames, which at first glance seem to be similar photographs of the same subject, are slightly different to each other due to movement of the subject. By means of projection, when each of these small frames appears on the screen for a twenty-fourth of a second, we are given the illusion of movement.[24]

Bergman contended that 'the road away from the public may lead to sterility or to an ivory tower'.[25] This is just the road that he appears to have embarked on in *Persona*, but Andersson and Ullmann provide points of identification for audiences who otherwise might have been left flailing. Their performances are subtle and nuanced, relying on looks, gestures and the smallest shifts in expressions.

'For the first time I met a director who let me express emotions and thoughts that no one else had previously seen in me', Ullmann said of the film which marked her first collaboration with Bergman. 'A director who listened patiently, finger pressed against his forehead, and understood everything I was trying to express. A genius who created an atmosphere where anything could happen – including things I never believed I was capable of.'[26]

One of the fascinations of *Persona* is that although this is a two-hander and we appear to be locked away from the outside world, there are continual hints of the tumult in that world. Over the opening credits, there is an image of a street protester setting fire to himself. In an early scene, after Elisabet has lost her voice, we see her walking around her hospital room as an English-language news report from the Vietnam War blares out from her television. Again, we see the burning man. This horrifies her. 'Reality is bloody-minded. Your hideout isn't watertight', the doctor goads her about her attempts to cut herself off from the world.

Later, we see her staring at a photograph of Nazis rounding up Jewish women and children. The camera zooms in on the photograph, showing the small boy with his hands up as the Nazi with his gun stands behind him. The camera then zooms in again until the boy's baffled and terrified face is in big close-up. It is an image which must have induced a certain guilt in the filmmaker, given his failure during the war to appreciate the enormity of the Nazi crimes.

Bergman wasn't especially forthcoming about *Persona* to Kenne Fant, who had become head of Svensk two years before in 1963. 'Well, it's about one person who talks and one who doesn't, and they compare hands and get all mingled up in one another.'[27] However, Bergman reassured Fant that the film would not be expensive. On that basis, Fant was happy to finance it, although he asked that Bergman changed the title from 'Cinematograph' (the original name he had given it) to 'Persona'.

The film has been pored over more exhaustively than almost anything else that Bergman made. It doesn't give its meanings away in any glib or simplistic fashion and is therefore open to myriad interpretations. Alma makes a remark which could serve as the film's motto: 'it doesn't make sense. None of it fits together'. Vogler can be seen as the embodiment of the cunning and uncompromising artist and Alma as the woman who has given in to banality and petty domesticity. They have been described as two sides of the same personality – an interpretation to which the shots of the faces merging or of the two women, looking identical in straw hats, comparing hands, lend weight. It is a film acted almost entirely in close-up. Alma even talks about how alike they are. Sven Nykvist's astonishingly lithe camerawork plays continual formal tricks to heighten the sense that the women's identities are beginning to blur, for example zooming in on Andersson's face in profile in order to obscure Ullmann, with whom she is talking.

Whatever else, *Persona* showed Bergman disregarding the lessons he had learned about script development and story construction during his apprenticeship as script doctor at Svensk. 'The gospel according to which one must be comprehensible at all costs, one that had been dinned into me ever since I worked as the lowliest script slave at Svensk Filmindustri, could finally go to hell (which is where it belongs!)', he wrote in *Images*.[28] The film is deliberately and wilfully inchoate. It was conceived in chaos and illness. Although he later claimed that the film was painstakingly planned, Bergman shot constant retakes. He relished his new-found freedom. The challenge he accepted now as a filmmaker – and which would define much of his later work – was how best to reconcile freewheeling and anarchic creativity with the formal rigour required to make movies successfully. The effect was as if a figurative artist had belatedly discovered the joys of dark and messy abstraction.

Predictably, audiences were baffled by the film, but they were intensely curious about it too. Some critics mocked its pretentiousness. Inevitably, at some screenings, projectionists and spectators were convinced that the film actually had caught fire during the opening montage.

In making *Persona*, Bergman had discovered that his anger and his creativity went hand in hand. 'I think an immense rage somewhere forms the basis of *Persona*. There is such anger in the film at times', he reflected to Marie Nyrerod.[29] His actresses helped him to harness that anger.

In *Cries and Whispers* (1972), Bergman was again working with an almost all-female cast, exploring grief and bereavement with an intensity matching that of *Persona*. As he stated again and again, the film had its origins in a single image: a room with red walls full of women dressed all in white. He eventually improvised his screenplay around this image, which had nagged away at him for 'a full year'. The title was borrowed from what a music critic had written about a Mozart concerto: that the music sounded like 'cries and whispers'. The words are also used in a Swedish psalm. The film was to be about three women waiting for a fourth to die.

At the time Bergman began writing *Cries and Whispers* in 1970, he was at a low ebb. He had experienced the deaths of several people close to him, including that of his father and his former wife, Gun Hagberg. His relationship with Liv Ullmann was teetering. It was, he noted in *The Magic Lantern*, 'an unsuccessful production' with two protagonists and the isle of Faro as the setting. One protagonist had moved on. Meanwhile, Bergman remained hypersensitive about his critical reputation. He claimed that he remained 'unaffected' when the critics 'again' started pronouncing that his career might be drawing to an end, but the fact that he was still fretting about what they had written ten years later suggests this wasn't the case. He may have included oblique references to the Vietnam War in *Persona* and *Shame*, but for a younger, radical generation, he still seemed very much the establishment figure. He was openly attacked for the lack of social and political contexts in his movies. To young 1960's radicals, his work could appear smug, too tasteful and too bourgeois. The international respect he had earned only damned him further in their eyes.

Bergman told the media that the film was partly inspired by his ambivalent relationship with his mother, but later disowned his own remark. 'It was a lie. I said it in order to have something to say. It's very hard to say anything about *Cries and Whispers*.'[30]

This 'confession' underlines the pressure that Bergman's status placed on him. His every remark was treated as a Delphic utterance. Interviewers looked to him to provide the key to open up his work.

There is both poignance and irony in the casting in *Cries and Whispers*. Harriet Andersson, the embodiment of youth, vitality and sexuality,

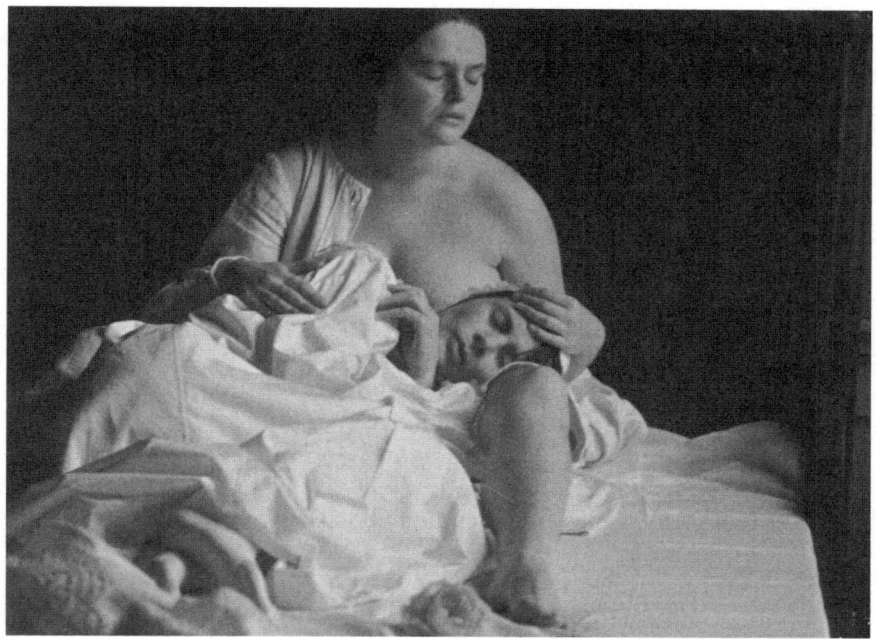

The excruciating scenes that lead up to the death in Cries and Whispers. The dying Agnes (Harriet Andersson) cradled by the maid Anna (Kari Dylwan).

here plays a 37-year-old woman raddled with cancer and on the verge of death. Those who have witnessed close relatives on their deathbeds have testified to the accuracy of Bergman's recreation of such a setting. For example, British director Terence Davies (*Distant Voices, Still Lives*) recalls, as a child, seeing his father dying of a long, painful battle with stomach cancer.

> He was screaming like that virtually all the time. It (*Cries and Whispers*) is very, very hard to watch because it opens up those memories. But there are other elements in it which are equally frightening. There is that mixture of the dread of death and oblivion and of religion, which says that that (oblivion) is not the case. When she is dead, the actual body seems to come to life which is terrifying. My father's body was in the house for 10 days before he was buried. It was horrible – that smell of death which is sweet and unpleasant.[31]

As a meditation on death and grieving, *Cries and Whispers* is very moving. The film opens beautifully. The credits are in white against a red backdrop. The first images, beautifully shot by Sven Nykvist, show the grounds of an old country house on a cold, autumn morning. All we can hear on the soundtrack are gentle chimes. A clock is ticking. We eventually see Harriet Andersson rising on her sick bed, her face contorted with pain. Her sisters are watching over her. The house is full of puppets, dolls, statues and ornaments.

As she prepares for her own death, Agnes thinks constantly of her beloved mother, who has already been dead for more than 20 years. She remembers how she used to follow her mother into the garden and spy on her. As Agnes describes her mother's contradictory traits (at once warm, beautiful and friendly but also cold and rejecting), it is hard not to be reminded of the director's characterisation of his own relationship with his mother. There are flashbacks to her childhood, with the same Christmas parties, slide shows and magic lanterns that Bergman was to use later in the openly autobiographical *Fanny and Alexander*. As a child, Agnes was always the jealous outsider – the one who just couldn't join in the fun. Her mother is played by Ullmann, who also plays her beautiful self-centred sister Maria.

The carpets, wallpaper, furnishings and curtains are all red. The women wear white. (Bergman claimed, a little pretentiously, that he saw the colour red as 'the interior of the soul'.) Dialogue is pared down. As Agnes dies, the characters around her react in very different ways. All the familiar emotions are in play – lust, jealousy, bitterness as well as grief.

Bergman gave his actresses subtle hints as to how they should play their roles. Sometimes, this would be a case of providing an insight into the psychology of the character. For example, in trying to convey how spoilt and self-absorbed Maria was, he is reported to have told Ullmann she was a woman 'who has never closed a door behind herself in her entire life'. Ullmann plays the part brilliantly. She is someone trying to feign a grief that she doesn't feel. When Agnes begins writhing and gasping in what seem to be death-like spasms, she can't help but recoil – she leaves the maid to tend her ailing sister.

Andersson too is exceptional: red-eyed, sallow, wasting away, but still beautiful in a severe way. At times, as she screams in pain, hits herself and tries to vomit; she is like the possessed Linda Blair in *The Exorcist*. It is as if we are watching a Chekhovian horror movie – an impression reinforced by an extraordinary scene in which the dead woman appears to come back to life. The maid sees a tear in the corner of her eye and talks to her. She grabs Maria and tries to kiss her.

Bergman's instructions to Andersson on how to play her role were simple and straightforward – a matter of suggesting how long she should maintain a pose or wait to open her eyes.

The irony is that Agnes, the solitary and ignored child, is now receiving all the attention that was for so long denied to her. The sisters read Charles Dickens' stories to her and comb her hair. This is a film full of close-ups and clock faces. Like the puppets in the dolls' house shown early in the movie, the characters appear trapped. The tone is bleak. There are several traumatic moments – for instance, Karin (Ingrid Thulin) slashing at her own genitalia with a shard of glass and then smearing the blood over her mouth. Throughout, we hear the constant ticking of the clocks, counting down time on the women and their wretched lives. There are strong class tensions. These rich sisters with their cynical and avaricious husbands turn out to care very little for Anna, the maid who tended the dying woman. Maria tosses her a bank note as if that absolves her of any responsibility for the woman's future. They have already forgotten about the trauma of Agnes' death. Nonetheless, the film ends in a dreamlike and very moving way with the sisters at last in harmony and walking together in the park. The scene is illusionary. It is something which Anna seems to have conjured up as she reads an old entry in Agnes' diary in which she describes a rare, idyllic afternoon with her sisters. Their sheer presence alleviated the pain of her illness. 'The people I'm most fond of were with me', she writes. 'I heard them chatting. I felt the presence of their bodies, the warmth of their hands ... I wanted the moment to stay, and I thought: this really is happiness.'

Working with such versatile and expressive actresses – Ingrid Thulin, Harriet Andersson, Bibi Andersson and Liv Ullmann – Bergman was able to achieve an extraordinary psychological depth in certain of his films. The roles he asked them to play, especially in *Persona* and *Cries and Whispers*, showed off their beauty and grace while also conveying vulnerability and viciousness. Despite Bergman's disavowals, it is hard not to see all these women as containing at least elements of the beloved mother with whom he had such a complicated relationship. In *The Magic Lantern*, Bergman writes very movingly of his mother's death and how he spent several hours in the apartment in which she had passed away a few minutes earlier.

> I thought that Mother was breathing, that her breast was heaving and that I could hear a quiet indrawn breath. I thought her eyelids twitched. I thought she was asleep and just about to wake, my habitual illusory game with reality.[32]

She was dead and what he remembered was the band-aid on her finger.

Not every actress was admitted to the Bergman family. One of the most poignant moments during my visit to the Bergman archive was when I was shown a letter written to Bergman by the American actress Jean Seberg. This was kept in a special drawer. You were obliged to wear protective gloves before touching it. The letter was written in January 1979, eight months before her death at the age of 40. Seberg had once been one of the best-known actresses in the world. 'Discovered' by Otto Preminger, she had played the lead (Joan of Arc) in Preminger's 1957 feature, *Saint Joan*. Three years later, she co-starred opposite Jean-Paul Belmondo in Jean-Luc Godard's *A Bout de Souffle* (*Breathless*) (1960), a key film in the emergence of the French Nouvelle Vague. With her close-cropped hair and elfin features, she looked effortlessly chic in Godard's film. She combined defiance and charm.

Seberg's subsequent career rarely matched up to the heights of *Breathless*. In the late 1960s, she became involved in radical politics and fell foul of the FBI. Her life was tinged with tragedy. When she wrote to Bergman, she was clearly desperate for work. In the letter, which was written in Swedish in blue Biro and addressed to Bergman, care of the 'Opera Company in Stockholm', Seberg's tone was apologetic and awed. She told Bergman that she realised he must be very busy and promised not to take up too much of his time. Perhaps, she suggested, Bergman might already know who she was. Seberg dutifully listed one or two of her better-known film credits: *Breathless*, *Joan of Arc* (she mentioned Preminger in parenthesis as if to jog Bergman's memory) and *Bonjour Tristesse*.

> My weight is 47 kilos, my age 40. I look a bit like Bibi Andersson. Funnily enough, I am at the moment learning Swedish with Lennart Olaf, a friend in Paris. Wouldn't it be possible I humbly beg of you to try and make a film together. It would make me extremely happy and pull me out of something that Lennart calls 'basement frost'.

Seberg then added that she had forgotten her best film of all, Robert Rossen's *Lilith*. She didn't mention, though, that she had played a schizophrenic in the movie. Signing off as 'The most devoted friend you have', she added a strange P.S., asking Bergman if he had ever been in psychoanalysis.

It was a letter from a vulnerable, highly sensitive woman who was, perhaps, close to breaking point. Seberg wasn't so different from some of the women that featured in Bergman's films, whether Bibi Andersson's needy and insecure nurse in *Persona* or Harriet Andersson's lost soul in *Through a Glass Darkly*. She was never going to escape from what she called the basement frost. The knowledge that there is no evidence Bergman replied to the letter only adds to the pathos that Seberg's note evokes when read today.

7

Religious Faith – the Trilogy: *Through a Glass Darkly, Winter Light, The Silence*

We shouldn't talk about God but about the holiness within man and that through the musicians, the prophets and the saints, we've been enlightened about other worlds. Particularly through music, of course. We ask: where does this music come from. I've asked so many musicians why we have music and the strange thing is they never had a proper answer.

(INGMAR BERGMAN, speaking to *Marie Nyrerod*)

THE YOUNG SWEDISH director Lukas Moodysson – seen by some as Bergman's heir – makes a point of trying to show his films to priests. He claims to be more interested in their opinions than in those of conventional movie critics. Priests, he points out, deal on a daily basis with life and death.

Moodysson was struck by how quickly, in times of crisis or joy, his fellow Swedes turn to the church. By way of example, he cites what happened when the Estonia Ferry sank in 1994, with the loss of over 800 lives. 'The churches filled up. They were just filled with people. When life is really on the edge, then you go to church.'[1]

Moodysson's remarks are instructive when contemplating Bergman's engagement with religion. As the son of a Lutheran pastor, this was never a subject that he could escape. Religion was a fundamental part of his upbringing. In the same way that as a young man he turned against his father, he also began to question his religious beliefs. Nonetheless, as a filmmaker and storyteller, his preoccupations weren't so different from those of his father.

'The father must have had an artistic charisma when he was preaching. He was something of an artist and an actor too,'[2] Bergman's former wife Kabi Laretei notes of Erik Bergman.

There is one story about his father that Bergman tells in *The Magic Lantern* and that he repeats in interviews and uses in a key scene of his film *Winter Light* (1961). He tells the story with admiration, although it could be seen as yet another example of his father's bullying and inflexibility. During the preparations for *Winter Light*, when his father was 75 years old and in poor health, Bergman accompanied him to a service in a little church in Uppsala. There were only three or four other people in the congregation. The pastor conducting the service was not well. Before he began the service, he came out and told the churchgoers that there would be no communion that day because he was too sick to administer it. Rather than show sympathy, Erik Bergman reacted with fury and contempt. He left his pew and limped into the sacristy to confront the 'creature' who was letting down his congregation. The next thing Bergman saw was his father in white robes. If the local priest wasn't able to do it, Erik Bergman was determined to oversee the communion himself. There was a message here – one that his son took absolutely to heart. 'Irrespective of everything, you will hold your communion. It is important to the churchgoer but even more important to you. We shall have to see if it is important to God. If there is no other god than your hope as such, it is important to that god too.'[3]

Ingmar was full of admiration for his father's unwavering self-discipline. The discipline came before the belief. It was the corollary of that belief. The two went hand in hand, one facilitating the other.

The question of belief could be put to one side. There was something about the mindset and persona of the dedicated priest that Bergman clearly found appealing. Rigour and repetition helped keep the demons at bay. That unwavering routine – the one-hour walk, the three-hour writing period – enabled the work to move forward. The irony, though, was that the priest's routine could also be used as a way of avoiding the question of faith. By paying lip service to the familiar rituals and keeping himself ever busy with the daily tasks, the priest left no time for doubt. This was the paradox at the heart of *Winter Light*.

'A masterpiece but a boring masterpiece' was the reaction of Bergman's then wife, Kabi Laretei, to the film. It was one of his most expensive movies. Svensk had to finance the building of a church, complete with a flat stone floor which gave the right acoustics, for Bergman to use.

His cast and crew were extremely sceptical about the project. Alexander Ahndoril's otherwise eccentric book *The Director*, a biographical novel that attempts to portray Bergman's innermost feelings and doubts at the time he was making *Winter Light*, captures the mix of bafflement and bewilderment that Bergman's collaborators felt about the film.

> It's so goddamned grey and dreary.
> Who actually wants to see the film apart from your father?
> It's all just a load of crap.[4]

These are some of the reactions to *Winter Light* that Ahndoril imagines coming from Bergman's technicians and actors, even as the film was shooting.

Even the film's ostensible star Gunnar Bjornstrand – who plays Pastor Tomas Ericsson, the priest wrestling with his faith (or lack of it) – wasn't especially keen on his role. Bjornstrand was used to playing witty old roués and seducers, fretting husbands stuck in lifts with their wives and errant fathers who hit on women young enough to be their daughters. Tomas, however, was dour and monotone. 'He didn't like his part because he wasn't able to show his charm', Bergman later said of him.

The film made sense to its writer-director, but seemingly had little resonance for anybody else. It didn't help that morale and energy levels were sapped by an outbreak of flu on set. However, the weariness and gloom induced by illness were entirely in keeping with the subject matter. The director reportedly relished the fact that his leading actor was sick. Some say he even tried to trick Bjornstrand into thinking he was far more ill than he actually was. 'Well, of course it is wonderful that Gunnar is so off-color and unwell when he has to play *this sort* of part. Imagine if I'd gotten a sun-tanned, hale-and-hearty guy to play someone worn out and ailing!' he told his friend Vilgot Sjoman.[5]

Bjornstrand and Bergman went back a very long way. They first met when Bjornstrand was a drama student in Stockholm in the mid-1930s and Bergman was beginning to direct his first student productions. Bjornstrand was a Catholic and a committed socialist. His own religious beliefs must have made the task of playing Tomas even more uncomfortable.

Contributing from the audience to a debate at the 2006 'Bergman Week', Bergman freely admitted that there was a strong autobiographical undertow to the story.

> Tomas, the priest, who lives in a kind of desperate, loveless state where he can't reach or connect with people any more – I experienced this strongly, myself, something that was an intrinsic part of me. So it was a self-portrait. And if you draw a self-portrait, then you become very hesitant.[6]

As self-portraits go, this was a lacerating one. Tomas in *Winter Light* is far from sympathetic. 'He exists beyond love, actually beyond all human relations', Bergman writes in *Images*. 'His hell, because he truly lives in hell, is that he recognises his situation. Together with his wife he has maintained a kind of fiction. The fiction is God is love and Love is God.'[7] His wife has died and his faith is beginning to crumble.

When directors are asked about their most cherished films, they often confound expectations by choosing not their most popular or successful efforts but the ones that have caused them the most trouble. 'You tend to love your least successful children', Robert Altman used to say. *Winter Light* was a film which Bergman felt all the more affection for at least partly because of its awkward gestation. 'I like this film very much, because it's always contrary', he said late in his life.[8]

Bergman made *Winter Light* with few concessions to the public. It wouldn't take much to turn the same story into *The Exorcist*-style horror film. Tomas has all the hallmarks of one of those characters who turn against their faith and embrace the devil. Bergman, though, is too austere and serious a filmmaker to trivialise his own themes. His motivation was to address his own spiritual crisis – something which his producers, wringing their hands at the rising cost, felt to be self-indulgent in the extreme.

The director went out of his way to take out anything that was ingratiating or soft. The beautiful actress Ingrid Thulin, who plays the substitute teacher Marta, was deliberately made to look weak and ugly. She is given ungainly spectacles and a coat made of cheap wool. Bergman wanted the film to be as hard as wood. Tomas is a cruel and brutal man. The characterisation of Marta – and the depiction of Tomas's disgust at her afflictions – is at least partly drawn from Bergman's five-year marriage to Ellen Lundstrom, who suffered from eczema. 'All that business about the eczema on her hands and forehead, for example, I'd pinched that straight from my second wife. She used to suffer from it and went about with big pieces of sticking plaster on her forehead and bandaged hands', he later admitted.[9]

Winter Light is a film full of hatred and disdain. Bergman confided to his friend Vilgot Sjoman that Tomas is envious and jealous of Christ. In his diary, Sjoman couldn't resist interpreting this envy in the light of Bergman's childhood. What was it like, Sjoman wondered, 'being a small child in a clergyman's family, with father going off every Sunday to devote his time to someone else, an utter stranger called Jesus Christ?' Nonetheless, international audiences and critics were more receptive

Insanity and religious ecstasy side by side in *Through a Glass Darkly*.

to it than might have been anticipated. After Bergman's death, the *Guardian* called *Winter Light* his greatest work. These audiences had their own questions about faith. One of the excitements and attractions in Bergman's work for them was his readiness to tackle the big themes. They accepted the film's idea that abjection and despair can finally lead to enlightenment.

'In earlier films I have always left the question open – the question of God's existence', Bergman said in an interview not long after the completion of *Winter Light*.

> In *The Virgin Spring*, I let God answer. I resorted to a ballad with the sudden appearance of this spring ... In *Through a Glass Darkly* it is more clearly expressed where the credo is: God is love and love is God. So the proof of God's existence is the reality of love. Love as something real in our world. In *Winter Light* I have dealt with this problem and I have had to destroy the whole concept of God.[10]

Often, a single image or idea provides the kernel from which Bergman grows a screenplay. In *Cries and Whispers* a decade later, he built an entire film around an image of women in white in a red room. Here, the starting point (Bergman stated in his own words) was a visit to an abandoned church to 'converse with God … to finally give up either my resistance to God or my unceasing conflict. Either to bond to the stronger, to the father, to the need for security or to reveal his being as a jeering voice from centuries gone by'. From this beginning, Bergman evolved his downbeat story about the anguished priest. He called it 'a very dark, tragic and sad picture'.[11]

No sunshine intrudes. (Bergman and his cinematographer Sven Nykvist shot only when it was overcast.) The camera is largely static. When Tomas recites the Lord's prayer at the beginning of the film, we see shots of the landscape around the church. The ground is frozen. The slow-flowing river has a sheeting of ice. At the same time, whites are foregrounded. Tomas's congregation consists of only a handful of worshippers, all of them looking as miserable as he is. Even the child with the teddy bear seems utterly bored.

Tomas is visited by the fisherman Jonas (Max Von Sydow) and his wife Karin (Gunnel Lindblom). Jonas is deeply depressed and needs counselling. Tomas tries to fob him off. 'I understand your anguish but life must go on.' Jonas immediately interrupts him, asking 'why do we have to go on living', and Tomas finds he simply doesn't have an answer.

Despite the stark settings and his insistence that this was a chamber play, Bergman uses certain self-reflexive devices. For instance, we hear Marta read her wretched, confessional letter to Tomas in which she talks about the revulsion her skin condition induces in him. The outer world also intrudes in the extraordinary scene in which Jonas comes back to see Tomas. A gaunt, anonymous figure with frizzy hair in a drab mackintosh, Jonas is very unlike the knight Von Sydow played in *The Seventh Seal* or the sleek charlatan he played in *The Magician*. Jonas is not a character in a heroic mould. He is a suicidal depressive with too much of an inferiority complex to look anybody in the eye. As his wife told Tomas, Jonas is 'at his wit's end'. He has been driven to the brink of despair by newspaper stories about China. 'The article said that the Chinese were brought up to hate and it's only a matter of time before the Chinese have atom bombs', the wife explains. Shy, sensitive Jonas can't cope with his feelings of dread. Of course, he is not soothed in the slightest by Tomas's anguished confession that he has been a lousy priest who saw God as something ugly and revolting. Tomas seems to think that by saying how wretched he himself is, he will somehow help Jonas cope. 'If there is no God, would it really make any difference?' he asks the man he is ostensibly trying to help. Repeating Christ's words ('oh, God, why has thou forsaken me?'), he is blind to his own narcissism. Jonas shoots himself only moments after leaving the priest.

The most uncomfortable scene in the film comes after the suicide, when Tomas turns on Marta. She loves him, but he tells her he is sick of her fussing and clucking, her short-sightedness and her clumsy hands, her 'timid ways in bed', her poor digestion, her rash and her periods. It is a devastating critique couched in the very personal language that Bergman uses again and again in his films. (Even in his last film *Saraband*, the bile was still there – witness the equally brutal and humiliating way in which Erland Josephson's father turns on his son.)

Tomas achieves a kind of redemption simply by finding the resolve to carry on with his work – to hold the communion in spite of his own ill-health and the fact that Marta is the only person in the congregation. He is finally able to rise far enough above his self-pity to see the purpose he serves as a priest in helping others deal with their suffering and crises of faith. Whether he answers his own central question – is God in the house? – is another matter altogether.

Winter Light was the second part of Bergman's so-called religious trilogy. It was made in counterpoint to *Through a Glass Darkly* (1960) and preceded *The Silence* (1962). 'When I wrote *The Glass*, I thought I had found a real proof of God's existence: God is love. God is all kinds of love, even perverted forms – and the proof of God's existence gave me a great feeling of security', Bergman told Vilgot Sjoman.[12] He called *Through a Glass Darkly* a romantic film, especially when set against the bleakness of *Winter Light*. Such a characterisation may suggest that the first film is cosy and benign in tone – New Testament Bergman as opposed to the fundamentalism and wrath of the Old Testament Bergman of *Winter Light*. However, *Through a Glass Darkly* is itself a deeply unsettling film, broaching such subjects as schizophrenia, incest and religious hysteria.

With that familiar licence which he granted himself for contradicting his own remarks, Bergman first posited the idea that the three films constituted a trilogy and then rejected it. In his notes for the screenplays of the films, he wrote, 'these three films deal with reduction. *Through a Glass Darkly* – conquered certainty. *Winter Light* – penetrated certainty. *The Silence* – God's silence – the negative imprint. Therefore, they constitute a trilogy'.

Later, Bergman suggested that the idea that these three films constituted a trilogy was a 'Schnapps-Idee'[13] – that is to say, something that

The battle for faith – *Winter Light*. The priest (Gunnar Bjornstrand) struggles to minister to the depressed Jonas (Max Von Sydow) and his wife Karin (Gunnel Lindblom).

sounded impressive when it was contemplated over a glass of alcohol but was revealed as bar-room intellectualism in 'the sober light of day'. By the time he had decided the three films weren't a trilogy, it was already far too late. That was how they were perceived by audiences and reviewers. For better or for worse, the three films were now inextricably linked. They were released in box sets, were revived together and were the subject of academic treatises.

In *Images*, Bergman writes that *Through a Glass Darkly* was connected to his marriage to Kabi Laretei and their lives together. The marriage was Bergman's attempt at his version of bourgeois respectability. Laretei was a brilliant concert pianist: a highly cultured woman with a professional career of her own – someone Bergman could regard as an equal.

When I interviewed her in the summer of 2007, she acknowledged that Bergman's assertion in *Images* that they had 'no common language' was correct. They appeared to complement one another perfectly. However, this seemingly perfect relationship foundered on miscommunication and on the very different expectations each had of the marriage. Both were unwilling to put domestic happiness in front of professional success.

'I was in the middle of my career and so I don't think I made an effort to understand him completely with his needs and so on. I had my interests and he had his', Laretei recalled. 'We had great love to each other but not enough knowledge and patience. I could have been different and more understanding and he also'.[14]

They had first met each other properly when she played a concert in Malmo, where he had his theatre group. The concert was in the same hall where the theatre was. He went to all the rehearsals. After she had played Beethoven's Fourth Piano Concerto, he came forward to meet her. He was very complimentary about the TV programmes on classical music that she then hosted. At the time, she was married to a conductor who was in the midst of planning a performance of Stravinsky's Oedipus Rex. Kabi invited Bergman to attend. First, he accepted. Then he wrote a letter saying he would not be able to attend. However, she and Bergman stayed in touch.

> We started a correspondence which became tighter and tighter – so before we met next time, six months later, we already knew we belonged together. They were personal letters. Afterwards, I divorced. Ingmar followed me to the places where I played. He came to Helsinki and he came to all kinds of places. And I explained the music to him.[15]

They married in 1959.

Quickly, it became evident to Laretei that Bergman had a great longing for security. He was looking for a wife who would take care of him – not one who was going to spend much of her time touring Europe, playing classical concerts.

Bergman may have dedicated *Through a Glass Darkly* to Kabi, but the film hints at the strains that were already beginning to appear in their relationship. Both must have had some affinity for David, the writer played by Gunnar Bjornstrand. He is a widower: someone who lives for and through his work. Like Bergman, he is a man with a stomach complaint. He has been so busy with his novel that he hasn't even realised that his son-in-law Martin (Max Von Sydow) has sent him a letter about his daughter Karin (Harriet Andersson), who is mentally unstable and has recently been through electric shock treatment. David may write bestsellers, but he frets that the critics don't take him seriously enough. The three – father, son-in-law and daughter – are together on an island. Also staying with them is David's 17-year-old son Minus (Lars Passgard).

The film is significant as the first Bergman shot on the isle of Faro. Bergman had come on a token visit to scout for locations. He thought that he would simply declare the place unsuitable and then demand that his producers allow him to make his film in the Orkney Islands, as originally intended. In the event, Bergman fell in love with Faro. Within moments of arriving, he had decided he wanted to live there. Svensk's desire to save money on locations had helped him find his spiritual home.

Through a Glass Darkly was also a departure for Bergman in terms of its intense and narrow focus. This wasn't a historical epic like *The Seventh Seal* or *The Virgin Spring*, the films that had established his reputation. It shared some of the hallmarks of an old-fashioned Swedish summer movie. It's about a family on holiday on an idyllic island. Again, as when she played 'mucky Monika' in *Summer with Monika*, Harriet Andersson plays an anarchic free spirit with a highly sensuous nature, albeit this time the character is unstable. There is a Chekhovian aspect to it too. It was no coincidence that Bergman had been preparing a production of *The Seagull* at around the time he made the film. However, the film also looks forward to such intimate psychodramas as *Persona* or *Cries and Whispers*. Bergman called it his 'first real ensemble drama ... the beginning of something new, perhaps not yet worked out'. Some of the strongest scenes are the most pared down and abstract – for example the sequences of Karin alone at night time or Sven Nykvist's moody cinematography of the rocks and skyscapes. Also very striking is the subtle way Bergman uses classical music by Bach to induce a sense of foreboding and melancholy.

In *Images*, Bergman both praises his own formal and intellectual adventurousness and mocks cruelly what he feels are the film's shortcomings. He squirms at the nakedly confessional dimension to the film, saying that it 'offers a horrendously revealing portrait of the creator and the condition that he was in at the start of the film, both as a man and as an artist'.[16] The film also reveals his continuing penchant for melodramatic plotting. In his earliest films, he often used voice-overs to reveal key narrative information. Here – as in *Persona* five years later – a pivotal moment involves the heroine snooping, reading something which she shouldn't. In *Persona*, Bibi Andersson's nurse is stung when she opens the mute actress's private letter and finds herself mocked in its pages. Here, in an equally contrived piece of plot business, Karin comes in the dead of night to open her father's desk and read his diary. 'Her illness is incurable' are the first words she finds in its pages. Her father also confesses to something that Bergman was prey to – a morbid curiosity about the misfortunes of those who are closest to him and a desire to observe and record how they react in their distress. Like Bergman, David draws on the most painful and intimate parts of his own biography for his art. Karin is crestfallen to discover that he wants to use her.

Given Bergman's remarks about his marriage to Laretei inspiring the film, some of the dialogue takes on a painfully personal ring. Karin has something uncanny about her – a visionary quality. No more than Laretei is she the kind of woman who is ready to stay at home and look after her husband. 'Imagine having a calm woman who gave you children and coffee in bed ... who was big and soft and warm and beautiful', she says to Martin. Karin is a febrile, unstable character but is very creative. She has more of the traits of the true artist than her father, who is timid and detached – and prefers to look in at life rather than to live it. What David and Martin see as her hallucinations could equally well be regarded as ecstatic religious visions. She hears voices, sees shining lights and imagines that God is about to reveal himself to her from behind the wallpaper. Whereas in many other Bergman films questions about faith are couched in abstract and intellectual terms, Karin's perspective is physical and sensual.

'I really succeeded in expressing that mix of religion and sexuality which I have always found so hard – so painfully hard – to sort out', Bergman boasted to Sjoman.[17]

The director was brutally dismissive of the efforts of some of his cast. Bjornstrand had worked with him many, many times and was ostensibly a friend. Even so, Bergman intensely disliked his performance as David. Maybe this was because he saw so many of his own least attractive traits in the character. As played by Bjornstrand, David radiated smugness and self-importance. Even when he accepts blame for his own behaviour, he does so in a way that makes him the focus of attention, not his desperately ill daughter. As Von Sydow sneers at him, he is always on 'the hunt for themes' for his book and is as ready to prey on Karin as on anyone else. He hides behind words and can always justify himself simply because he is quicker and more articulate than his accusers. However, the one phenomenon he 'doesn't have the slightest clue about' is life itself.

It was well known that Bergman drew heavily on his own biography in his work. Here, he was providing a devastating portrait of a novelist who does the same, and he deplores what he has created. David's account of his failed suicide attempt is taken directly from Bergman's own aborted suicide attempt when he was staying in Ascona, a mountainous resort on the Swiss/Italian border, just prior to making *Smiles of a Summer Night*. His plan was simply to drive off the road, plunge to his death and leave the world to think it was an accident. In the event, he was 'saved' by a telegram from Carl-Anders Dymling, the head of Svensk. In *Through a Glass Darkly*, Bjornstrand tells the story of the failed suicide as if it were an epiphany – a moment which changed him and enabled him to rediscover his love for his children. The actor was a recent convert to Catholicism and regarded the scene as being about a lost man finding his faith. That wasn't how Bergman saw it at all, at least in hindsight. 'Out of my own obviously horrible situation in Switzerland came absolutely nothing. It was a dead end', he recalled of the failed suicide attempt.[18]

Bjornstrand's David radiates complacency when he apologises to his daughter and confesses to her that after her mother died, he was more concerned with 'making it' as a writer than with mourning her death. ('I was secretly rejoicing.') Bergman must have been dredging up personal experiences to convey so effectively the way the artist feeds on his own life for material, oblivious to the pain he is causing to those closest to him. If the confession scene feels phoney, that has as much to do with the way it was written as with how it was performed. The same applies to David's philosophising at the end of the movie, when he talks about knowing that love exists for real in the human world. 'I don't know whether love is proof of God's existence or love is God.' Given what has gone before, such words can't help but sound hollow and trite.

Bergman acknowledged his mistake in casting Lars Passgard as Minus, Karin's young brother, for whom she had such incestuous feelings. Passgard was too bland, too clean-cut. He had none of that contrariness and perversity that actors like Stig Olin or Birger Malmsten had brought to their roles as the anti-heroes in Bergman's early films. Harriet Andersson, however, was exceptional. She played Karin with a mix of blazing intensity, intelligence and pathos. In her close-ups, she has the same rapt and ecstatic look as Falconetti in Carl Dreyer's famous silent film, *The Passion of Joan of Arc*. (At times, *Through a Glass Darkly* seems like a modern reworking of the Joan of Arc story.)

Equally assured, albeit in a far less showy and prominent role, was Von Sydow. Bergman wrote of the 'purity and authority' he brought to his roles. A pathologically shy personality off-stage (at least when he was young), Von Sydow's film career had started in earnest when he was 27, with his role as the questing knight Antonius Blok, looking for knowledge and human contact in the face of death, in *The Seventh Seal* (1956).

'We all knew that Max was one of the most talented actors of his generation. In private, he was rather shy and quiet, but on stage he had an absolute command of a part and of his audience', Bergman later told film historian Peter Cowie.[19]

The young actor's background was very different from that of his director. Though he was brought up a Lutheran, he wasn't especially religious. He was born in April 1929 in Lund in southern Sweden. His father, William Von Sydow, was a professor of folklore at the Royal University of Lund. His mother was a former schoolteacher. It was expected that he would pursue a career in academia or, perhaps, become a lawyer. His interest in performing was sparked when he was a teenager and was taken to see a production of *A Midsummer Night's Dream* at a theatre just opened in nearby Malmo.

Bergman knew better than anybody else how to draw the most subtle and intense performances out of Von Sydow. Much of the actor's magnetism on screen lies in his brooding, angular physiognomy. He is a tall, lean, bony presence. See his films with Bergman and you'll notice that his dialogue tends to be sparse but that he is shown in close-up after close-up. At times, Bergman treats him almost as if he is a silent movie actor. What was striking too was how effective he was in supporting roles (as in *Through a Glass Darkly* and several of his other films with Bergman). He was extraordinarily versatile. In *Winter Light*, he is tormented and suicidal – somebody who simply can't cope with what the modern world and politics throw at him. By contrast, in *Through a Glass Darkly*, he plays an anchoring role – he is the one stable character.

The Silence (1963), the third in Bergman's so-called religious trilogy, was very different from its predecessors. It provoked a scandal because of its frank sexual content (lesbianism, masturbation, voyeurism) and became one of his biggest box-office hits largely as a result (see Chapter 4). Bergman's notebooks show he drew on seemingly random ideas and images to develop new screenplays. In this case, the first spark came when he was out scouting locations for *Winter Light* with Sven Nykvist and discussing lighting. He began to think about 'the whole complex of sensations that occurs when our car meets an oncoming car or passes another car'.[20] This prompted him to begin free associating. Images sprang to his mind – four strong young women pushing a wheelchair that carries an ancient and skeletal old man. He pictured the man walking through a hotel. Next, he evoked a child's nursery nightmare of a corpse tumbling out of a toy cupboard. Soon, he was thinking about an old man and a boy travelling together. One of his recurrent ideas is of the outsiders adrift in a foreign city. He thinks of acrobats who've lost their partners (this idea would later feed into *A Serpent's Egg*). He cites a 1907 short story by Sigfrid Siwertz called *The Circle* as responsible for embedding the idea of the huge, foreign city in his youthful

Bergman enjoyed an unlikely box-office success, partly thanks to the scandal
generated by *The Silence*. Sweltering in the carriage are Anna (Gunnel
Lindblom), the boy Johan (Jorgen Lindstrom) and Ester (Ingrid Thulin).

consciousness. The city is linked in his imagination with decadence and
unrest. In one of his radio plays called *The City*, he wrote about a
metropolis built on land that has been mined and where 'abysses open
up; streets rupture'.

As these impressionistic jottings attest, Bergman had romantic and
adolescent ideas about 'the city' which seem rooted in early twentieth
century modernist literature. The city stands for cosmopolitanism, forbidden pleasures, consumerism and display. It also stands for alienation,
impersonal and oppressive bureaucracy and the potential of political upheaval. In cities, there are refugees and homeless people. There is poverty
and inequality.

'New cities arouse too many sensations in me. They give me too
many impressions to experience at the same time: they all crowd in on
me. Being in a new city overwhelms me, unsettles me', Bergman told
Playboy when asked why he didn't leave cold, dark Stockholm in the
winter months to shoot elsewhere – maybe in Rome or in Hollywood.[21]
(He may have been reluctant to leave Sweden – at least until the tax
authorities forced him out – but he was able to recreate the cities of his

imagination at Filmstaden, Svensk's films studios in Rasduna, in the north
of Stockholm.)

Eventually, all the random thoughts and ideas coalesced into a story
about two sisters, Anna (Gunnel Lindblom) and Ester (Ingrid Thulin),
and a 13-year-old boy (Anna's son) in a strange city. Ester is ill and the
three are staying in one of those stately but fast-decaying European hotels found in every city.

Formally, *The Silence* is the antithesis to *Through a Glass Darkly*
and *Winter Light*. 'Ingmar, why don't you move your camera anymore?'
the director had been asked after the rigour and restraint of the first two
films in the trilogy. He and Nykvist reacted by shooting *The Silence* in a
lithe and expressionistic fashion reminiscent of Orson Welles's *The Trial*
(made at around the same time) or – in its most self-conscious moments –
of Alain Resnais' *Last Year in Marienbad* (1962). There are also moments
of grotesquerie that recall the work of Tod Browning, especially his notorious 1932 film *Freaks*.

The Silence also carries echoes of several earlier Bergman movies.
One thinks, for example, of the couple confronted by refugees when returning home by train or the lesbian scene in *Three Strange Loves* (1949)
or of the eerie scenes of Maj-Britt Nilsson adrift in Paris in *Waiting
Women*. Many Bergman films contain train sequences akin to the ones
that open *The Silence*. The circus elements – the travelling dwarves –
echo *Sawdust and Tinsel* and *The Magician*, while the references to the
inexorability of time (the furious ticking over the credits) were fast becoming a leitmotif in his work. Meanwhile, the shots of tanks rumbling
through the streets show Bergman at least acknowledging the political
upheavals of the post-war years (the Prague Spring, The Hungarian Up-
rising, etc.).

One of the key differences between *The Silence* and earlier Bergman
movies is that the director – working with Sven Nykvist – now has the formal mastery to carry off effects that would appear showy or pretentious
if they weren't so sleekly accomplished. The wide-eyed boy looking at
the tanks passing by the train window is yet another variation of the child
enraptured by the magic lantern show. There is the same play of light
and darkness. The train window provides a screen effect. The noise of
the train chugging along is not so dissimilar to the rattle of the projector.

'We had an enormous amount of fun making *The Silence*', Bergman
later wrote in *Images*.[22] He clearly found it liberating to make a film so
full of visual flourishes. Nykvist, however, told a grim story about how he
learned during shooting that his mother was very ill. He wanted to leave

the production to see her in hospital before she died. He interrupted rehearsal to see if this would be possible, and Bergman reacted with utter fury. 'Don't you dare leave now – right in the middle of a shoot! If you go now, you bastard, you can stay at home for good', the director shouted at his cinematographer. The two were quickly reconciled. However, one wonders if Liv Ullmann was thinking of Bergman when I interviewed her at the time of *Faithless* (2000) and she suggested:

> maybe to be a genius, somewhere you have to be completely heartless or whatever. I can remember a director I know who worked with a cinematographer that that person loved. The cinematographer was not well. The person continued to work with him until the end of the movie and then a genius said to that director: 'why didn't you fire the cinematographer?' The person replied: 'he's my friend. How could I do that?' 'Ah, if you think those things, you will never be great.' So you have to have the choice: do you want to be great as an artist or live comfortably with what you believe in. I would say for me that I'd rather live comfortably with what I believe in. There are some who are probably greater artists who want everything to be perfect, even if you have to tread on somebody else's soul.[23]

Bergman, it often appeared, was ready to 'tread on somebody's soul' if it improved the work. During production, he aimed to create a self-contained world in which the artists and crew could function at their best. He claimed that during the shooting of *The Silence*, 'the actresses were talented, well-disciplined, and almost always in a good mood'.

That was not entirely how Gunnel Linblom remembered it. 'It's OK to turn my soul inside out but my clothes stay on', the actress reportedly told Bergman, who is said to have used a body double for any shot requiring Anna to be shown naked.

Bergman placed heavy demands on his two leads. Thulin, for example, is shown early in the film boozing and masturbating on her hotel bed, but then is heard begging God that she be allowed 'to die at home'. The director was determined to depict sex frankly but (he hoped) without prurience. 'There is much in common between a beautiful summer morning and the sexual act; but I feel I've found the cinematic means of expressing only the first, and not the other, as yet', he told *Playboy*. 'What interests me more, however, is the interior anatomy of love. This strikes me as far more meaningful than the depiction of sexual gratification.'

In later years, Bergman didn't exactly disavow *The Silence*, but he did try to distance himself from the scandal it had caused and expressed disapproval of audiences who had been coming to see the film for the 'wrong' reasons. His behaviour wasn't entirely consistent. Both he and

Svensk clearly relished the fact that at last a Bergman film had been a real box-office hit. By giving an interview to *Playboy* in 1964 (even if the magazine did carry heavyweight profiles alongside sex features), he was reaching out to a new audience that was more interested in sex than the metaphysical musings of Lutheran priests.

His interviewer Cynthia Grenier had also written pieces on the likes of William Faulkner and Moshe Dayan and went on to work for *The Washington Times* as well as *Playboy*. Her line of questioning was more Hugh Hefner than *Cahiers du Cinema*. How, she wondered, did Bergman persuade his actresses to perform in such steamy scenes?

'Some people claim that I hypnotise my actors – that I use magic to bring the performances out of them that I get', Bergman replied. 'What nonsense! All I do is try to give them the one thing everyone wants, the one thing actors must have: confidence in himself. That's all any actor wants, you know. To feel sure enough of himself that he'll be able to give everything he is capable of when the director asks for it. So I surround my actors with an aura of confidence and trust … if that's magic, then I am a sorcerer.'[24]

The religious references are far sparser than in *Winter Light* or *Through a Glass Darkly*, but they are there. God's silence isn't unbreakable. Bach music features prominently. When Anna goads her sister with an account of her sexual exploits, she is quick to mention that she went from the cinema, where she had seen a couple make love in front of her, to a church to have sex with a waiter she had met in a bar. 'We had intercourse in a dark corner behind some pillars. It was cooler there.'

Woody Allen and others have suggested that Anna and Ester are 'two warring aspects of one woman'. That is one way to interpret the film. Certain scenes – notably when the sisters' faces are shown together in a close-up as Anna taunts Ester – anticipate ideas about doubling that Bergman explored in even more radical fashion in *Persona*. This, though, wasn't what lured a million or more Swedes to see *The Silence*. The film was accessible and interesting to a mass audience not just because of its sexual content but also because of its dreamlike and enigmatic quality. Spectators could see in it what they wanted: a story about a child confronted by adult behaviour that baffles him, another of Bergman's studies of illness, a near-silent movie with both comic and horrific elements. (The hotel waiter is somewhere between a clown and a ghoul.)

As ever, Bergman was drawing on specific incidents in his autobiography. The scene in which Anna and her lover, overcome by lust, meet in the hotel corridor and he desperately tries to turn a key in an awkward lock so that they can get into a room together was at least partly inspired by the beginning of Bergman's affair with Gun Hagberg. They fled together to Paris in the early autumn of 1949 and booked into a reputable but uncomfortable family hotel near Avenue de l'Opera. Their room was rectangular, 'like a coffin'. Bergman had just walked out on his wife and children. We can't tell whether the hotel was quite as seedy as he suggests or whether his guilt affected the way he experienced and remembered it. He writes in *The Magic Lantern* of the 'musty, cold and damp air' and of the 'windows in the asphalt to let light into the hotel kitchen, where one could see numerous white-clad people moving about like maggots; out of this chasm rose the stench of refuse and cooking smells'.[25]

Anna sees all of this in *The Silence* as she sits on the bed after having sex with the waiter whose language she doesn't understand.

In all three films in the trilogy, there is a redemptive ending of sorts – a final scene which suggests the characters are reconciled. There is forgiveness and self-knowledge. Whether it is the priest going through with the communion in *Winter Light* or the son finally being able to communicate with his father in *Through a Glass Darkly*, the protagonists find their own way of overcoming their sense of despair and carrying on with life.

In making the trilogy, Bergman was able to address his anxieties about religion and to move on from them. 'No one is safe from religious ideas and confessional phenomena', he tells his interviewer in 'Bergman on Bergman'. 'Neither you nor I. We can fall victim to them when we least expect it. It's like Mao flu, or being struck by lightning. You're utterly helpless. Exposed'.[26]

His choice of metaphor is telling: he is talking about his obsession with religion as a fever. In making the three films, he helped shake that fever off.

Religion was an integral and defining part of Bergman's background. He was the child brought up in the parsonage, and that obviously affected the way in which he saw the outside world. 'I come from a world of conservative Christian thought', he said. 'I've absorbed Christianity with my mother's milk.'

After the trilogy, religious themes would still remain in his work, but they would no longer be foregrounded in the same way.

> When my top-heavy religious superstructure collapsed, I also lost my inhibitions as a writer. Above all, my fear of not keeping up with the times. In *Winter Light* I swept my house clean. Since then things have been quiet on that front.[27]

It was often Bergman's habit to wrong-foot his followers by making sudden about-turns in direction. Having finished the trilogy, he embarked on one of his least characteristic and most playful films, *All These Women*. It was a comedy, a ghost story and his first film in colour. (He and Nykvist had always preferred the starkness and contrast that black and white gave them.) Its opening intertitle – 'any resemblance between this film and the so-called real world has to be a misunderstanding' – signalled the director's intentions clearly enough.

'Sometimes considerably more courage is required to put on the brakes than to fire the rocket. I lacked this courage and realised, only too late, what kind of film I should have made', Bergman wrote in *The Magic Lantern*[28]. The obvious problem he faced was that audiences and critics simply weren't going to accept a witty but brittle and superficial comedy from a director whose work was characterised by its depth and intensity. The reception to his earlier comedy, *The Devil's Eye*, had been lukewarm. Reviewers were even cooler about *All These Women*. Bergman was being provocative by making the central character a critic. The smug and unctuous Cornelius sums up his feelings about the breed. We first see Cornelius (Jarl Kulle) in his sunglasses, stiff collar, black tie and white shoes, turning up at the 'Villa Tremolo', home of the famous cellist Felix, whose biography he proposes to write. We know immediately that he is an absurd and conceited figure. He kisses the valet, mistaking him for the maestro. His asides and observations are trite in the extreme.

The film is set in some fantasy world: part jazz age, part art deco wonderland. Bergman's actresses (Bibi Andersson, Harriet Andersson and Eva Dahlbeck are all on display), playing the maestro's lovers, are dressed like flappers. Bergman may have loved Charlie Chaplin, but his attempts at slapstick (the critic knocking over a statue and struggling to put it together again) are strained. When you see Bergman trying to raise laughs through pekinese dogs with purple ribbons in their hair, you can tell something must be amiss. Bergman had co-written the screenplay with Erland Josephson. The jokes about censorship (the screen suddenly goes black and we then cut to a dance sequence when a couple are making love) fall flat.

The maestro is barely seen other than with his back turned or waving from a balcony. We hear his cello playing in the distance as Cornelius runs amok in the Villa Tremolo, being seduced and teased by the maestro's womenfolk. Even the birds shit on him. Whatever happens, he doesn't lose sight of his objective. Any detail about the maestro or his way of life is immediately entered into his notebook.

Bergman was preparing for his first season as head of the Royal Dramatic Theatre and so clearly was not as focused on *About These Women* as he would have been on any of his other films. He later wrote of his desperate shame about having made the film.

'Genius – is to make a critic change his mind' is a motto repeated several times in the movie – presumably a dig at all those reviewers who excoriated Bergman one moment and praised him to the hilt the next. The director enjoys taking a few sideswipes at the critics. At one stage, we see Cornelius writing in the bath, discussing the 'distinction between the subjectively personal and the objectively personal' in the maestro's work and then asking himself what 'the blazes' he actually means. By this stage in his own career, Bergman was clearly used to obscurantist criticism of his own work.

The irony (presumably not intended) is that the critic is an engaging and even sympathetic figure. His conceit is so transparent and he is played with such energy by Kulle that audiences are as likely to root for him as take against him. He may snoop, he may be unscrupulous and self-evidently mediocre, but he provides any of the zest that is going in the movie.

Bergman makes some trenchant points about the way the maestro's followers have their own pet images of him and how they wilfully misunderstand him, how critics toady to him and how women fall at his feet. The film is full of beautiful cello music. In the end, though, Bergman's attempts to keep matters light backfired. *The Silence*, one of his bleakest and seemingly most impenetrable films, had been a huge box-office success. *All These Women*, in theory one of his most accessible works, was 'a dismal failure'. Light-hearted comedy, it seemed, was simply not what anyone expected from Bergman.

8

Bergman the Polymath

IN INTERVIEWS GIVEN at the height of his film career, Ingmar Bergman would often give the impression that cinema was – if not exactly a sideline – a secondary part of his career and that his real affection was for theatre. On the one hand, this was a gambit through which he could wrong-foot the journalists and academics who came in long queues to try to speak to him. Bergman was sometimes exasperated by their deference and enjoyed confounding their expectations of him. It was the same instinct that led him to tell the *New York Times* journalist Michiko Kakutani in the early 1980s that he spent his evenings watching the US soap opera *Dallas*.[1] It is a jarring image – the great sage of European cinema sitting down in his slippers after his dinner to watch J.R. Ewing, Pam, Sue-Ellen, Digger Barnes and all having affairs and breakdowns, stabbing each other in the back and living the high life on the proceeds of their oil fortunes.

At the time Bergman expressed his 'special fondness' for *Dallas*, the series was the focus of scholarly and political debate about US cultural hegemony. Books began to appear with titles like *Television Today and Tomorrow: Wall-to-Wall Dallas?* Wim Wenders had famously remarked that 'the Americans had colonised our unconscious'. During the 1980s, the French government was busy negotiating a 'cultural exception' to world trade laws to protect its own films and TV dramas from being submerged by Hollywood. Bergman was a totemic figure for European cinema, and yet here he was, cheerfully admitting that he spent his evenings watching Hollywood soap operas. It was his way of relaxing, recharging and preparing for the next day's shooting or rehearsals.

However, even if he enjoyed distancing himself from his reputation as the dark, forbidding man of cinema, Bergman's passion for theatre wasn't feigned. 'The strange thing is that the work for which I have received the most recognition internationally is my films and filmmaking but what I consider most important is my work at this theatre', he told journalist Marie Nyrerod in one of his last interviews.[2] The frequency with which he repeated the assertion that he was 'much more attached to theatre than to film' suggests its sincerity.

Between 1938 and 2002, Bergman directed well over 120 theatre productions. The rhythm of theatre appealed to him in a way that that of filmmaking did not. To be on a movie set was to be in a state of constant stress. It was a continual battle against technical, logistical and financial problems; bad weather; interfering producers and erratic actors. Everyone looked to the director. If he showed sign of strain or weakness, the entire project would begin to creak. At the end of any given day, the most that could be hoped for was – if he was lucky – three minutes of finished film 'in the can'. Theatre, by contrast, was a continual evolution.

'To work in the theatre is a way of living. To make a picture is a heavy job', he said to Lise-Lone Marker and Fredrick J. Marker. At the time of their interviews with him, conducted in 1979 and 1980, he was already looking forward to retirement from feature filmmaking but insisted that he would carry on working in theatre 'until they carry me out'.[3]

The often exalted language Bergman used to discuss theatre is instructive. In his descriptions of rehearsals in which he and his ensemble of actors all strive after the same goal, he often sounds as if he is describing a religious experience. It is also an erotic experience. He liked to talk of the 'incredibly pleasurable tensions' that the quest for perfection shared by him and his actors could cause. Moreover, everything about theatre was magical and surprising to him. This applied both to his experiments as a child with puppet theatre (which ran alongside his adventures with magic lanterns) and to the most prestigious productions he staged at the Royal Dramatic Theatre. It also applied to his earliest trips to the theatre to see productions such as Alf Sjoberg's staging of Gustaf af Geijerstam's *Big Clas and Little Clas*. (The young Bergman was so rapt with excitement at the experience of being in a proper theatre that he promptly came down with fever as soon as he returned home.)

Nothing could dampen this wide-eyed enthusiasm. When he became Sweden's youngest theatre director, at the Helsingborg Stadsteater in 1944, he had to cope with a theatre infested by fleas. It didn't put him off in the slightest – nor did the relative poverty in which he and his collaborators had to live. Late in his life, Bergman still maintained that directing plays gave him the same excitement he had felt when, as a boy, he and his brother would visit the nursery after breakfast to open the cupboard that contained all their toys. 'I would throw open the doors and plan what I would play with that day', he told Marie Nyrerod. 'The silly thing is that when I get to the studio or walk out onto the stage or into a rehearsal room, I still get that same feeling. It's very strange.'[4]

Bergman saw the Royal Dramatic Theatre as a spiritual home. He first visited it when still a boy and last saw it not long before his death. When he was head of the theatre, he would spend more time there than at his home. It witnessed many of his biggest triumphs, but it was also the site of one of his worst humiliations – it was here he was arrested by the police on the nod from the tax authorities. It was here that he earned notoriety – as well as admiration – for thumping a critic. In 1969, he was fined 5000 Swedish kroners for knocking down Bengt Jahnsson of the newspaper *Dagens Nyheter* during rehearsals for Georg Buchner's *Woyzeck*. 'It was the first time that they had met', the *Guardian* reported the incident, 'but the incident was the climax of a two year feud'. Bergman, who conducted his own defence, said that the attack was 'a planned act to scandalise and humiliate' Mr Jahnsson. Bergman, who had a knack for making even his courtroom appearances dramatic, continued: 'I am against all forms of violence in principle, but for me this was the last resort of an artist to defend himself and the acting profession against a critic's persecution that has long constituted a serious threat to the Swedish theatre.'[5]

He loved the theatre's history and its smell, and firmly believed it was haunted by the big names who had appeared on its stage and given vent to their emotions. 'If you stand on the stage when it's silent, you feel that there's an enormous charge', he claimed. Harriet Bosse, the Norwegian-Swedish actress known as Strindberg's muse, was the most celebrated of the ghosts in residence. 'She walks around here, in the Upper Circle, and I've seen her', Bergman boasted of his encounter with the spirit of Bosse, an elegant lady in a grey suit who he says he saw disappear behind a marble pillar. Bergman also suggested that he would come back to haunt the theatre himself. Perhaps he was talking tongue-in-cheek, but even if he was gently teasing his interviewer, the anecdote underlined his identification with the theatre and the personalities behind it.[6]

Early experience of directing plays came at Master Olofs Garden, a youth initiative in the old part of Stockholm. He started there with a play called *To Foreign Parts*. His second production was Strindberg's *Lucky Per's Journey*, which was performed in a small chapel.

Theatre was both a refuge from the outside world and an alternative to that world. It gave him a freedom that he didn't always enjoy with his film work. Bergman wrote relatively few of the plays that he staged, whereas he scripted and originated almost all his films. Staging the classics by Shakespeare, Moliere, Ibsen and Strindberg gave him a feeling of freedom. He felt far closer to the music conductors he so admired than when he was trying to bring his own material to life in front of the camera and was assailed by doubt not only about the writing but also about his ability to animate it.

In his theatre work, as in his film work, Bergman was nothing if not pragmatic. When he was appointed head of the Royal Dramatic Theatre in 1963 (having joined the theatre as a director in 1959), he went to great lengths to make the theatre accessible to everyone. Belying his reputation as a director of oppressive productions of the classics, he promoted afternoon plays for teenagers (e.g. *The Diary of Anne Frank* and Thornton Wilder's *Our Town*) and held some open rehearsals. He reduced ticket prices, boosted actors' salaries and proselytised energetically on behalf of the theatre. Quite apart from his artistic achievements, he was an efficient, cost-conscious manager with a flair for marketing. 'The schoolchildren of today will be our audience of tomorrow', he told his staff. 'Why shouldn't we impart to children today a taste for the theatre?'

Strindberg was Bergman's particular favourite. Bergman directed 30 productions of Strindberg's plays for the theatre, TV and radio. He had first read his works as a 14 year old. 'I understood the tone, I understood the aggression, I understood the rage', he said. In his library at Faro, he had a 55-volume annotated edition of Strindberg's collected works. He claimed he liked to lie down on his bed and look at them. 'Through the years since then (his first teenage encounter with Strindberg), the plays have had varying effects on me', he reflected. He would return to *The Dream Play* again and again and even had dreams about encountering the great playwright. Not all his collaborators shared his passion for Strindberg. Some found him misogynistic and pretentious. 'That was one of the failures of our marriage. I didn't like Strindberg so much', Kabi Laretei jokes of the playwright.[7] For Bergman, though, Strindberg ranked as high as Bach and Mozart in his affections. 'I love him as music. His way of treating the Swedish language is unequalled', Bergman said.

Just as Strindberg had his muses, Bergman also found actors who inspired him and with whom he wanted to work again and again. The 'decisive factor' in his decision to mount any particular play was to find the right performers for the parts. With the likes of Pernilla August, Lena Endre and Peter Stormare, he found younger actors in whom he had the same confidence as he did, for example, in a colleague like Erland Josephson, whom he had known since the very beginning of his career.

Younger Swedes may have chafed against Bergman as an oppressive establishment figure, but he always tried to reach out to them. In the mid-1980s, for example, he staged a revisionist version of Hamlet with Stormare in the leading role. *Time* magazine wrote of Fortinbras bursting 'onto the scene like a Che Guevara in black leather, to the sounds of blaring rock music'. The balconies, the magazine noted, were filled with the 'under 20 crowd ... in baggy sweaters and jeans'.[8]

In his 1984 TV film *After the Rehearsal*, about an elderly director staging a Strindberg play, Bergman gives his most confessional account of what theatre meant to him. For all his dewy-eyed enthusiasm about the camaraderie of the work and the magic of the greasepaint and lights, there was little sentimentality with this chamber piece. The elderly director Henrik Vogler (played by Erland Josephson, but with many of Bergman's own traits) remains combative and riven with anxiety, even in his declining years. The young actress Anna (Lena Olin) is the daughter of Rakel, one of his former stars at the theatre. When he speaks nostalgically of Rakel's beauty and talent, Anna reacts with contempt. 'Mum had a lot of kids she didn't like and then died from alcohol poisoning' is her description of her mother's career after leaving the theatre. She hates her mother. Her loathing collides with Vogler's affectionate and even lustful memories of the woman with whom he once had an affair.

The film was shot at the Royal Dramatic Theatre. Bergman attempts to capture the richness and mystery of the building. He relishes the idea that at least traces of the feelings 'real and enacted' and of the laughter, rage and passion generated by the actors can still be felt. That is what makes the theatre both ghostly and magical. Every prop – whether a sofa once used in *Hedda Gabler*, a table from *Tartuffe*, a cupboard or an old chair – has totemic significance. They too link the theatre to its past. Vogler calls them 'old acquaintances'. Ghosts are everywhere and the lines between real life and drama are utterly blurred. At one stage, we see a subliminal shot of Bertil Guve, the young child lead from *Fanny and Alexander* – a character based on Bergman himself as a boy.

In his voice-over, Vogler mocks his own pretensions: the cliches he speaks to the young actress to convince her that she is right for her part.

The project had started as an idea for a drama about the correspondence between an elderly director and a young actress. Bergman appeared to have intended to write a radio drama, but then decided it would be more enjoyable if one could actually see the protagonists.

'While I wrote, I must have hit a sore nerve or, if you like, an underground vein of water. From my watery unconscious, twisted vines and strange weeds shot up; everything grew into a witch's brew', he wrote in *Images*.[9]

There was an element of self-indulgence in *After the Rehearsal*. Bergman admitted he had made the film because he relished an opportunity to work with old friends again. However, his summoning up of old ghosts was not as pleasant as he had anticipated. The mood during shooting was grim. Ingrid Thulin, playing the mother, showed a sentimentality that irritated Bergman. Josephson had trouble remembering his lines. All the familiar demons came back to assail Bergman – stress, anger, cowardice – and he remembered just why it was that he had wanted to give up filmmaking. Still, the attritional mood on set mirrored that of the characters in Bergman's screenplay. The weight of memory was oppressive.

'I love actors. I love them as a phenomenon. I love their profession, their courage, their contempt of death ... their black ruthless honesty', Vogler tells Anna. It's an affection that is also tinged with exasperation and even hostility. Vogler (the director's alter ego) detests 'all things spontaneous, rash and imprecise'. The irony is that it is often precisely the chaos and spontaneity that can animate an actor's performance.

No sooner has Vogler conjured Anna's mother back into existence than she is taunting and accusing him. Rakel is a sick woman – an alcoholic. She lurches from anger to self-pity. Her teeth are falling out. Her old beauty has all but faded although she still makes a pass at her old director. She 'breathes decay'. Bergman, taking his cue from music, often referred to his actors as his instruments. Vogel does likewise. Rakel had been one of the best 'instruments', someone through whom he heard tones he had never heard before. She was a great tragic actress. However, Vogler sees nothing compelling in the mess or misery of her private life. As they spar, they are more like George and Martha in *Who's Afraid of Virginia Woolf*, Edward Albee's drama of marital discord, than two professional collaborators.

If Vogler is discomfited by Rakel, he is equally irritated by Anna. Just like Lena Olin in real life, the actress has become pregnant at precisely the moment her career appears to be taking off. 'Pregnant! I just don't get it', Vogler sneers at her, completely unable to understand how she can put her private life ahead of her profession.

In *After the Rehearsal*, the actors are so steeped in the world of theatre that they have forgotten how to behave naturally or spontaneously. Their every outburst and gesture is calculated with at least half an eye on its dramatic effect. They are like kids playing. The problem is that the world of make-believe spills into their lives. For example, the director might start an affair with his leading actress, 'mostly for fun ... an experiment that has no importance', but the affair will inevitably have repercussions. During rehearsal, the director and the star might have a trivial argument, followed by recriminations.

The shooting style in *After the Rehearsal* is pared down. The action takes place entirely on the stage, after the rehearsal. There are constant close-ups, as if the further the lens approaches towards the actors' faces, the greater the truths it can uncover.

The film is a very uncomfortable excoriation. In *Wild Strawberries* more than a quarter of a century before, Bergman had shown Victor Sjostrom's old man in an idealised way as someone who, for all his petty vanities and regrets, was wise and gentle. When Bergman himself became an old man, his portrayals of old age grew ever harsher. There is much more doubt and bitterness in Erland Josephson's Vogler than there was in Sjostrom's Isak Borg. Vogler is a lonely old man who – at the end of the play – is left on his own.

Critics responded rapturously to *After the Rehearsal*. This, one guesses, was partly because it seemed so confessional and partly because Bergman was well into his 70s when he made it, and like much of his work in the 1980s, it was, perhaps, 'a final word' – a case of the prophet coming down from the mountain top one last time.

'He (Bergman) has attained a sublimity of self-revelation in this masterpiece such as few artists have achieved in any medium', enthused leading US critic Andrew Sarris. Richard Corliss wrote in *Time* that the film was 'as direct, serene and human as any he has made'. Swedish critics were equally enthusiastic.[10]

In this period, Bergman's stage work was also praised to the hilt. If anything, the fact that he was no longer making movies induced critics to treat it with yet more enthusiasm. It is instructive to read John Lahr's review in the *New Yorker* of his 1995 production of Moliere's *The Misanthrope* at the Royal National Theatre in Stockholm. Noting Bergman's method (e.g. his decision to insist his cast wore crinolines, corsets and Moliere-era costumes from the earliest days of rehearsal), Lahr goes to great lengths in his review to highlight the way in which the director probes beneath the surface wit in Moliere's comedy of manners.

'What Bergman engineers in masterly style is both a wonderful comedy of manners and a subtle dissection of the nature of manners themselves', he writes. '*The Misanthrope* is the third in a trio of monumental Bergman productions. The previous two – Shakespeare's *The Winter's*

Tale and Yukio Mishima's *Madame de Sade* – taken together are the finest displays of stagecraft I have ever seen.'[11]

For all his lofty reputation, Bergman was never snobbish about which medium he worked in. Bergman was a prolific writer and director of radio plays. 'He was very interested in radio as a dramatic medium. *Easter* by Strindberg was one of the first plays. We were a young gang, around 30 years old, in the main parts. We were a happy gang and it was happy work. Strindberg and he were sort of soul mates. Many of Ingmar's ways of thinking were similar to those of Strindberg's. It is said of Strindberg that he lived his life so as to be able to have something to write about', recalls Barbro Hiort af Ornäs.[12] She points out that Bergman was fully aware of possibilities radio offered for a different kind of expression to theatre or cinema.

> He was a very clever radio producer because he left things out. He left out all the sounds that you usually hear in radio plays – doors closing, steps on the floor, bells and everything. There was none of that. It was just the voices, just the simple dialogue between two people. It came out very well. You can't do that when you are filming but with radio you can do without all the unnecessary sounds.

The director was also a pioneering figure in Swedish TV drama, relishing the chance to shoot plays 'live', for example his 56-minute TV movie *The Venetian* (1958). Several of his subsequent works, including *The Rite* (1968), *Scenes from a Marriage* (1973) and *Saraband* (2003), were made for TV in Sweden and released theatrically abroad.

Quite apart from his directorial career, Bergman was a writer: a novelist, diarist and playwright. He often gave the impression that writing was a laborious chore. Every morning, at a fixed time, he would sit down and write for precisely three hours – not more and not less. The same compulsion that he felt as a director to organise his actors and technicians was felt in his private life too. He needed to marshal his time. The disciplinarian and stickler for punctuality was terrified of his own will to chaos and sloth. The daily writing stint was one of the most important ways of keeping order in his life. Only towards the very end of his life, when his eyesight was diminishing and his health was failing, did he deviate from his routine. This routine wasn't just about work and self-discipline – it was a way of keeping the prospect of death at bay. When he stopped writing and creating, he had no way of deferring any longer that which he dreaded most. The work was the equivalent of the knight's chess game – an increasingly desperate attempt at postponing the inevitable.

Bergman's early screenplays were created in a novelistic fashion. As we have seen, when he was starting out as a writer-director at Svensk, he would submit his projects as short novels and only later rework them into a screenplay. This approach partially explains why his work always placed so much emphasis on the interior lives of the characters. When you are writing descriptive prose, you can delve deeper into the consciousness of the protagonists than when you are simply relying on dialogue and stage instructions. Take the following passage from his book *Sunday's Child* (which was made into a film by his son Daniel Bergman in 1992).

> Even in those days I had difficulties with reality, its limits unclear and dictated by adult outsiders … and if there were no ghosts, why did Maj talk about the watchmaker from Borlange, who hanged himself down at Berglund's? Or the girl who drowned one winter in the Gimmen and floated up in the spring down by the railway bridge with her stomach full of eels? I saw them myself when they carried up the corpse. She had a black coat on and a winter boot on one foot, the other foot gone and the bone sticking out. She haunted me. I met her in my dreams and sometimes I met her without dreams or darkness.[13]

This passage, like much of his autobiography *The Magic Lantern*, illustrates just how Bergman could go further in his writing than in his films and plays. He was able to give full vent to his confessional urges, his lyricism, his morbidity and his perverse humour on the page.

'I'm so miserable about the fact that it costs so much money to make films', the British director Anthony Minghella (like Bergman, also a writer) told *Screen International*. 'It burdens you with stuff you don't want to deal with.' Bergman sometimes struck a similar sentiment. Writing, though, required little more than a desk and a chair.[14]

Bergman's 'retirement' from directing feature films after *Fanny and Alexander* (1982) was at least partly prompted by a desire to escape the burden Minghella discussed. However, even after this retirement, Bergman still adhered to his old routine, writing the same number of hours every day. He also continued to make films for TV, for example *In the Presence of a Clown* (1997) and *The Image Makers* (2000). In such works, Bergman would recycle and refine ideas that he had been exploring throughout his career. One of the small miracles of Bergman's filmmaking was that he managed to remain so prolific in spite of a lifestyle which – on the surface – contained little in the way of dramatic events. He wasn't a great traveller. He hadn't fought in wars. His solution was to look inward for inspiration and to explore the same themes (childhood, the fraught relationship with the father, the fawning love of the mother, the obsession with death) again and again. He felt little guilty about re-cycling ideas in different formats – creating screenplays out of old stories or novels from films.

In the Presence of a Clown was based on a story he discovered among the papers left by his uncle at his death. 'At a time when you most often have to persuade people to do something, it is refreshing to meet a man who is so creative, who has an enormous urge for action, and who is al-ways so positive at work', his producer Ingrid Dahlberg commented of Bergman's continuing desire to work on the eve of his 80th birthday.[15]

In the Presence of a Clown is the story of Uncle Carl, a figure readers of *The Magic Lantern* will remember well: the dishevelled, comic idiot savant with hairy red ears and an incontinence problem, who helped the young Bergman with his cinematograph. Bergman's mother and grand-mother also feature in it. Carl Ekerblom, a Franz Schubert admirer, is in the midst of a tempestuous affair with Pauline Thibault (Marie Richard-son), of whom the writer-director had 'a blurry recollection'. At 54, he is a patient on the psychiatric ward in Akademiska Hospitalet in Uppsala. He has been sectioned for an alleged attempt to beat his fiancée to death. Another patient is Professor Osvald Vogler (Erland Josephson), and to-gether they start a film project: a living talkie. Before long, they are on tour. This late exercise in autobiographical self-reflexivity was screened in Un Certain Regard at the French Festival. Critics couldn't help but note its modest technical credentials. This was a low-budget TV movie. 'Tech credits are extremely modest', noted US trade paper *Variety*. Nonethe-less, Bergman fans found a project so full of both autobiographical ele-ments and references to the director's earlier work to be both stimulating and rewarding.

With *The Image Makers* (2000), there was a sense of Bergman's ca-reer coming full circle. As a child, he had been overwhelmed by Victor Sjostrom's *The Phantom Carriage*. Now, in his 80s, he was exploring the circumstances behind its creation. *The Image Makers* was Per Olov Enquist's play about Selma Lagerlof and Victor Sjostrom after the shoot-ing of *The Phantom Carriage*. Bergman staged it at the Royal Dramatic Theatre in 1998 and made a TV movie version two years later. Both starred Elin Klinga as the beautiful actress Tora Teje confronted by the formidable Nobel Prize-winning author Lagerlof (Anita Bjork), who wrote the book on which *The Phantom Carriage* is based. The setting is the studio where the film has been shot. Victor Sjostrom (Lennart Hjulstrom) and his cameraman Julius Jaenzon (Carl-Magnus Dellow) are preparing to show some footage to Lagerlof.

Tora is Sjostrom's mistress. She is furious that she wasn't cast in *The Phantom Carriage* and deliberately stays around to meet Lagerlof because she knows that Sjostrom doesn't want her there. When Lagerlof advises her to be careful about interfering in other people's marriages, she reacts with fury, telling the distinguished old lady to 'kiss ... [her] arse'. The more she rages, the more embarrassed Sjostrom becomes. Lagerlof, though, enjoys the novelty of someone prepared to speak frankly and rudely to her – not even the King dares as much.

The Image Makes can be seen as a companion piece to *After the Rehearsal*. It is again a study of an abrasive young actress and a distinguished older figure circling round one another. Tora is an admirer of Lagerlof's work, but demands to be told secrets about it that the author doesn't want to share. As an actress, she demands clarification. Lagerlof, though, isn't inclined to explain just why her characters behave in the way they do.

When footage of *The Phantom Carriage* is shown, Tora complains that she wasn't given the leading role. Lagerlof, to Sjostrom's disappointment, refuses to discuss her response to the footage in any detail.

Tora and Lagerlof stay behind to 'chat a bit'. The actress tells the distinguished writer that the only way to get ahead is to 'kiss arse' and sleep with the director. Her language is deliberately provocative. She mocks Lagerlof for being so far removed from the 'filth' of everyday life. The irony is that Lagerlof is far tougher and more worldly-wise than the actress busy abusing her. She recognises aspects of herself in the younger woman.

Bergman must have felt an affinity for both characters. As a young writer-director, he was as fiery and narcissistic as Tora. As a distinguished director, he had plenty of experience of the deference and sycophancy that Lagerlof has become used to encountering. In a pivotal moment in *The Image Makers*, Tora asks the old writer about her father.

In Lagerlof's Nobel Prize acceptance speech in 1909, she spoke with huge affection of her father and of how she thought of him a few days before, when she was sitting on a train, travelling to Stockholm.

> I felt a deep sorrow that he should no longer be alive, and that I could not go to him and tell him that I had been awarded the Nobel Prize. I knew that no one would have been happier than he to hear this. Never have I met anyone with his love and respect for the written word and its creators, and I wished that he could have known that the Swedish Academy had bestowed on me this great Prize. Yes, it was a deep sorrow to me that I could not tell him.

During her train journey, Lagerlof said, she had begun to daydream about meeting her father in heaven and discussing her prize with him.

In *The Image Makers*, Tora tells Lagerlof that she studied the speech as a schoolgirl and was moved by it. She is therefore startled when the distinguished novelist suddenly tells her that this exalted father was 'a lousy bastard' who drank himself to death and that she hopes he burns in hell for ruining her life. We begin to see just where she dreamed up the central character in *The Phantom Carriage* – the drunkard and vagabond David Holm. In a lengthy monologue, as Lagerlof speaks with disgust of her bloated, corpse-like, drunken father or of her beloved mother, she begins to sound like Bergman discussing his childhood. Lagerlof is obsessed with the memory of her father. One of the reasons she feels such bitterness towards him that is that, even now, she can't stop thinking about him. He dominates her imagination. When she was 21, she had told him to go to hell and had resolved to leave home. He had attempted to beat her but was too drunk and had simply slumped into a chair. She knew he would die without her to tend him. She found the courage to leave but has been tormented by guilt about it ever since.

Just as resonant are the scenes between Tora and Sjostrom. She goads and mocks her older lover too, laying bare his hypocrisy. He won't leave his wife for Tora, but her honesty is what draws him to her. For all her rage and ability to hurt those around her, she is the one pure character.

The Image Makers showed Bergman taking someone else's material – Per Olov Enquist's play – and making it seem utterly personal. To audiences watching it today, the film seems as much about him as it does about Lagerlof. Bergman may have been a polymath, but whichever medium he chose to work in, his imprint was always immediately discernible.

9

The Magus

Johan: This hour is the worst. Do you know what it's called?
Alma: No.
Johan: The old folks called it 'the hour of the wolf'. It's the hour
when most people die, when most children are born. Now is
when nightmares come to us.

(*Hour of the Wolf*)

The sorcerer suffers but he also derives pleasure from his art.

(Film critic LASSE BERGSTROM on *Hour of the Wolf*
in *Expressen*)

DEVILS ABOUND IN Ingmar Bergman's work. The little doodle of the demon with his horn and fork was his pet motif. (The Bergman Foundation
uses it on stationery and pens as if it was the face of a brand – like Mickey
Mouse for Disney.) In his work, the devil was sometimes represented
literally (as in his comedy *The Devil's Eye*). More commonly, the devil
was conjured up in metaphoric fashion. In contemporary-set films, the
demons lurked within the characters themselves, pushing them towards
madness and into destructive behaviour.

In *Hour of the Wolf* (1968), the demon is portrayed as the force of
creativity itself. The film is about a painter Johan Borg (Max Von Sydow).
Some years before, an opening intertitle states, he 'vanished without a
trace from his home on the Frisian Island of Baltrum'. The narrative
conceit is that the film is a case study. The narrator has used Borg's diaries together with interviews with Borg's wife Alma (Liv Ullmann) to
piece together what happened to him. Bergman later said that this device
was borrowed from the stories of E. T. A. Hoffmann. The idea of having
Alma speak directly to camera – which many will have seen as a piece of

self-reflexivity in the manner of Jean-Luc Godard (this was 1968, after all) – was also apparently taken from Hoffmann, who likewise interrupted the flow of his stories with authorial interventions and digressions.

'You do discover – and that's what's so bloody fascinating – that a film is far from suffering if one breaks the illusion, breaks people's expectation of illusion and sends them back to the cinema. It's useful to wake up the audience for a bit only to re-immerse them in the drama', Bergman said in an interview conducted with Stig Bjorkman, Torsten Manns and Jonas Sima not long after the film's release.[1]

The experience of *Persona* had freed the director both to be bolder on a formal level and to adopt a new simplicity. He was confident that he wouldn't lose his audience through experimentalism. In *Images*, Bergman accepts that *Hour of the Wolf* is about 'a deep-seated division within me, both hidden and carefully monitored, visible in both my earlier and later work'. The film has an openly autobiographical element. For example, the story about Borg being locked in a wardrobe as a child was taken directly from Bergman's biography. 'You see, they told me that a little man lived in that wardrobe. And he could gnaw the toes off naughty children.'

What is surprising, given Bergman's obvious identification with Borg, is that the story is told from Alma's perspective as much as it is from that of the tormented, mentally disintegrating artist. It's her face we see staring in fear and bewilderment as her husband's behaviour becomes ever more erratic. Early on, we see her perplexed as her husband stands in the dark, looking like Christopher Lee on leave from a Hammer horror film and declaring, 'in an hour or so it will be daylight and then I can sleep'. If this is a self-portrait, it is not a flattering one. Borg is not especially sympathetic. He may be a tortured, visionary artist, but he is also an abusive and self-absorbed husband, making his wife of seven years suffer with him. She has taken on his traits. She is prey to his hallucinations. (Alma is the one who first sees the sinister old lady in the aristocratic clothes who turns up at her cottage telling her not to let Borg tear up her sketches and encouraging her to read his diary, which contains the revelations about his former lover Veronica Vogler [Ingrid Thulin].)

In *Hour of the Wolf*, Bergman overlays a very simple story about an artist going mad with phantasmagoric elements. It's as if all the demons preying on Borg have sprung to life. The film combines horror elements with grotesque comedy. For example, Borg is preyed upon by an analyst called Heerbrand – a strange man in a mackintosh and beret who accosts him as he is striding across the island and tries to engage him in conversation. This analyst is like a more desperate version of Monsieur Hulot, the Jacques Tati clown Bergman so admired. Heerbrand pesters Borg, tries to offer him advice and boasts about his job. ('I examine souls and turn them inside out.') Borg reacts to this interfering busybody much as Bergman did to critics he didn't like – by giving him a good wallop.

Bergman borrows from the rhetoric of horror films, throwing in distorted close-ups, flashy camera movements and eerie point-of-view shots. The seemingly deserted island on which Borg and Alma arrive by rowing a boat turns out to be inhabited by a very sinister Baron Von Merken, who lives in a castle and whose friends are all sneering aristocratic types. The men are dressed like Bella Lugosi in *Dracula*. The women are caked in make-up. They talk about having their 'fangs intact'. Bergman, a connoisseur of all kinds of humiliation, relishes showing Borg's discomfiture at a dinner in their presence – the way he sweats, flounders in conversation, forever itches at his shirt collar and tries to seek solace in wine.

The stylisation and manipulation are far more evident than in Bergman's earlier films. We are always aware that Bergman is the presence pulling the strings behind the scenes. The macabre puppet show in which we see a strangely lifelike performance of Mozart's opera, *The Magic Flute*, adds to the sense that the artistry here is intended to be self-conscious. 'The loveliest and most disturbing music that has ever been written' is what the Baron (and master of ceremonies) calls the music.

The Baron and Borg embody different facets of Bergman, the director. The former represents his showy and sadistic side: the magician enrapturing and bullying the audience with trick effects. Borg, by contrast, stands for a knotted integrity. His art isn't a matter of special effects but of compulsion. He is not driven by a desire for riches or social status.

In the film's most famous scene, Borg is attacked by a beatific-looking little boy who accosts him on the rocks.

The richness of the scene – as in so many of Bergman's other dream sequences – lies in its ambiguity. What does the boy stand for and why does he appear? Is he a representation of Borg's childhood self? Does he represent the artist's creative urge? Is he the child that Borg and Alma never had? Is he simply an unlikely and therefore all the more potent embodiment of evil? Bergman doesn't answer any of these questions directly, but instead presents us with a sequence which we might expect to find in a David Cronenberg horror movie. The near-naked boy first shadows Borg as he is fishing by the rocks and then suddenly bites him and clings to him as if trying to throttle him. Borg's reaction is to bludgeon him furiously with a rock. We then see him carry the boy's body and drop it in the ocean. The scene has a biblical undertow – it is like a distorted version of the Abraham and Isaac myth.

There is a balance to be struck, Bergman seems to argue, between using the demons to fire his creative imagination and allowing them to distort and destroy his life. As he put it in a late interview:

> Of course the demons have to be around. It would be very dangerous not to have them there. But they need to be kept under control. As long as I am in the studio or theatre, I control the universe. And so the demons are automatically under control. I mean, the passions are under control.[2]

If *Hour of the Wolf* is an allegory about an artist's torments, it can also be read as a coded account of a relationship falling apart. Borg and Alma are the couple who are losing their ability to communicate. Borg – like Bergman – is unwilling to make any concessions to cosy, bourgeois domesticity. As a result, he is impossible to live with. There is also the other woman in the shape of Veronica Vogler, as mysterious and alluring as Alma is homely.

'The vampire motif is nothing new for Bergman, but here we find it in a gothic horror story which is at once both inaccessibly personal and entertainingly brilliant', wrote Lasse Bergstrom in a perceptive review in *Expressen*. 'The magician suffers yet finds delight in his tricks. And that is the paradox in this esoteric, beautiful film.'[3]

Yes, Borg is tormented, but on some primal level, he is enjoying his rich, grotesque and often erotic nightmares. He half relishes his own debasement.

Bergman and his team (especially cinematographer Sven Nykvist) clearly enjoyed the experience of making a film which combined high arthouse elements with motifs from B horror movies (ravens fluttering and squawking, chases down the labyrinthine castle corridors, lots of chiaroscuro lighting and even one scene in which a character walks on the ceiling).

In his next film, *The Shame* (1968), the magus made another island-based allegory, but this time using elements of the action thriller rather than of the horror movie.

At the press conference on Faro for *The Shame*, Bergman said: 'I'm not showing any political commitment in the film. I'm only striving to be absolutely true to reality.' Nonetheless, critics couldn't help but see references to political events of the time – the US war in Vietnam, the threat of a nuclear Armageddon and the possibility of a Europe under totalitarian, Soviet-style control. The very fact that Bergman had called his original screenplay *The War* emphasised what appeared to many to be an obvious political subtext.

This, though, wasn't a film about how war impacted on nations or armies. The focus was deliberately very specific. How – the film asked – would a bourgeois, middle-class couple react to being caught up in the middle of such upheaval? This was similar to the conceit of Jean-Luc Godard's *Weekend* (1967), made the year before, in which a Paris couple go for what they hope will be an idyllic weekend in the countryside, but are then confronted at first hand with bloodletting and violence, which hitherto they had been able to distance themselves from as something happening somewhere else and which they merely saw now and then on their TV screens. What starts with a traffic jam takes in class and gender struggle, murder and even cannibalism.

Bergman detested Godard and wasn't interested in his brand of showy agit-prop and formal trickery. 'I have never been able to connect with any of his films', he commented in a 2002 interview. 'I have never understood them either ... I find Godard's films affected, intellectual, full of themselves, and, from a cinematographic point of view, pointless and frankly tedious. Endless, dull, Godard is desperately boring.'[4]

The Godard bashing was hardly charitable, given that the French director had been one of Bergman's earliest and most ardent champions. There were also some overlaps between their work, especially in the late 1960s when both were becoming ever more self-reflexive and finding ways to lay bare their own devices. Just as Godard opened *Tout Va Bien* (1972) by showing cheques being written to cast and crew, Bergman's features included film catching fire and sequences of characters talking directly to camera.

The Shame was less formally radical than Godard's *Weekend*. On one level, it was an action thriller. However, even far away on the isle of Faro (where he shot the movie), the director was reacting to the political turbulence of the times. Bergman later reflected in *Images*:

> To make a war film is to depict violence committed toward both groups and individuals. In American film, the depiction of violence has a long tradition. In Japan, it has developed into a masterful ritual, matchlessly choreographed. When I made *Shame*, I felt an intense desire to expose the violence of war without restraint. I did not understand that a modern portrayer of war needs a totally different fortitude and professional precision than what I could provide.[5]

Once the outer violence stopped and the inner violence began, the director argued, *The Shame* became a much better film.

When society can no longer function, the main characters lose their frame
of reference. Their social relations cease. The people crumble. The weak
man becomes ruthless. The woman, who had been the stronger, falls apart.
Everything slips away into a dream play that ends on board a refugee boat.
Everything is shown in pictures, as in a nightmare. In a nightmare, I felt at
home. In the reality of war, I was lost.[6]

In his remarks, Bergman is drawing attention to a key tension running throughout his work. Whereas other filmmakers looked at outer
events – war, crime and social and political upheaval – Bergman's instinct was always to turn inward, to displace the drama onto the personal
sphere. Even so, in *The Shame*, he offers an effective enough account of
individuals having their identities stripped from them by militarism. At
the start of the film, Jan and Eva Rosenberg (Max Von Sydow and Liv
Ullmann) are a typical couple. They bicker. They love art and culture.
They enjoy their life of relative seclusion. They think they are outside
politics. Once the planes come, the soldiers invade and they are forced
into a battle for survival, their personalities withering away. Sex becomes
a bartering tool. They no longer have qualms about betraying those who
used to be close to them. The stooped, elderly looking couple wheeling
their meagre possessions past a burned-out church are virtually unrecog-
nisable from the attractive man and woman seen at the beginning of the
film. *The Shame* ends with another of Bergman's sequences blurring the
lines between real life and nightmare. The couple has secured a place on
a small boat and is trying to flee the island, but death is all around and
the boat is becalmed.

Some critics were very harsh towards *The Shame*. It was called 'soul
shit'. Certain reviewers saw it as Bergman's belated and feeble attempt
to engage with contemporary events. Swedish novelist Sara Lidman, who
protested actively against the Vietnam War, was especially outspoken in
her denunciation of Bergman.

Such attacks didn't dissuade Bergman from continuing to probe away
at the inner violence couples are capable of wreaking on each other's
lives. This was the subject of his 1969 film *The Passion of Anna*, again
shot on the isle of Faro. Max Von Sydow played the 48-year-old Andreas
Winkleman, a hermit-like character, living alone on the island, determined to get away from the world.

Conveniently – for students of the film – Bergman includes sequences
in which all the main protagonists are invited to give a gloss on their own
characters. 'As an actor, what is your personal view of Andreas
Winkleman?' – we hear the director ask his leading man. 'He is awfully

difficult in one way because he has tried to hide from the world around him', Von Sydow replies on camera.

> His unhappy marriage and his legal worries have driven him into a blind alley where he tries to conceal his identity. He tries to wipe out his means of expression so that, without his being aware of it, that hiding place has become a prison. The hard thing for me is to try and express a lack of expression.

Bergman and cinematographer Sven Nykvist use colour in a very different way than they had done in *All These Women*. The emphasis is on dark reds and browns as well as on the cold blue of the skies. They show the autumnal beauty of the island and its austere quality.

The plot is set in motion when a neighbour, Anna (Liv Ullmann), asks to make a phone call at Andreas's house. She leaves her bag by mistake, and he reads a private letter that appears to herald the break-up of her marriage.

> Dearest Anna, I can no longer live with you. I've been pushing this truth aside for some time because I love you. I can't, I won't live with you any more. I don't believe in new attempts as neither of us wants to change.

Anna, we subsequently discover, has lost her husband and son in a car accident.

Andreas goes to return the bag, thereby meeting the neighbouring couple, Eva and Elis Vergerus (Bibi Andersson and Erland Josephson).

This was evidently a wretched film to make. Bergman has written of a crew member – infused with the spirit of 1960s rebelliousness – telling the director and cinematographer that they were dictators and demanding a more collective approach to decision-making. His stomach ulcer was playing up. Out of either boredom or a desire to test himself and bring more spontaneity to his working method, Bergman had left his screenplay open ended. Some of the formal problems were to be solved during shooting – or so Bergman hoped. He recalled:

> The screenplay had been written in a white heat. It was more a description of a series of moods than a traditional, dramatic film sequence. Ordinarily, I solved any anticipated technical problems immediately in the writing stage. But here I chose to deal with the problems during filming.[7]

Wars don't intrude. They're healthy, affluent and cultured. Nonetheless, they find plenty of ways in which to torment one another. 'My philosophy (even today) is that there exists an evil – and humans are the only animals to possess it', Bergman wrote. 'An evil that is irrational and not bound by law. Cosmic. Causeless. Nothing frightens people more than incomprehensible, unexplainable evil.' He claimed that *The Passion* was essentially the same story as *The Shame*, but told more credibly.[8]

The two main male characters shared some of the director's traits. Elis Vergerus (played with sleek malevolence by Josephson) shares Bergman's voyeurism and his sadism. He collects photographs. His huge private archive encompasses everything from images of people eating to people asleep to people in the grip of violent emotions. He may be a bourgeois Swedish professional, but he shares many of the traits (and the surname) of the Mengele-like Nazi scientist Bergman portrayed a few years later in *The Serpent's Egg*.

Andreas, meanwhile, shares some of the director's neuroses: his moral cowardice, his reclusiveness and his capacity for betrayal.

Von Sydow highlighted *The Passion of Anna* as a perfect example of a Bergman film in which there is an undertow of subtle humiliation.

> I, as Andreas, visit the other man, Elis, in his studio and he keeps photographing me. The way he does it becomes a strange, terrible torture – again and again, keeps on forever – till there is an eerie quality in it. 'Don't move. No. No. Turn your head like that. Look that way. Hold your breath' – and you are kind of hypnotised and humiliated.[9]

Elis, in Von Sydow's description, is like the puppetmaster – a role Bergman often ascribed to himself. Von Sydow described Bergman as someone

> very sensitive and very afraid of being handled by other people. A man who is very anxious to stay in command and who is very good at being in command – who worries terribly beforehand when, for example, he makes a movie; who is so terribly well prepared from every angle about every little detail just in order to avoid every risk of being caught off hand by situations – to keep control of everything.

In *The Passion of Anna*, the humiliation works in more than one direction. Elis is cuckolded by Andreas and so has reason to be cruel to him. Eva, meanwhile, has experienced the loss of a child during her only pregnancy – an incident which drove a wedge between her and her husband. There is a madman on the island who has been slaughtering animals for no discernible reason. (Bergman and Nykvist relish showing the blood against the snow.) All this violence seems like an outward manifestation of the damage and suffering that the four protagonists are wreaking on one another.

In his own life, Bergman was a jealous and possessive figure. Kabi Laretei recalls that when she was away on trips as a concert pianist, he was constantly suspicious that she was unfaithful. Liv Ullmann has spoken of the jealousy still 'cooking within him' about a lover years before who slept with someone, which impelled him, in his 80s, to write the screenplay for *Faithless* (which Ullmann directed). He was able to harness this jealousy in his work. Bergman had an uncanny ability to analyse and dramatise his own feelings. It was as if he was the outsider looking in at somebody else's life – he was his own subject.

Bergman was surely wrong to complain about his own mistake in *The Passion* of leaving so many traces of the 1960s. He felt that the mini-skirts and hair-dos dated the film and that audiences watching it in later years would immediately place it as a product of its era. As so often in his work, the most powerful sequences are those in which faces are foregrounded. During the extraordinary monologue in which Anna – seen in a big close-up – reminisces about the car accident in which her husband and child were killed, her clothes and hairstyle are immaterial – it's her words and expressions which matter. Her suffering can be read in her forlorn gaze and in the subtlest changes in her expression.

Equally unsettling is the scene in which Andreas confesses to Anna his self-loathing and sense of disgust at the world around him. Again, the scene is deceptively simple – a single close-up of Von Sydow held for a small eternity in which he looks more and more forlorn.

Another of the film's strongest scenes simply involves Von Sydow reading a letter. The eccentric old man Johan Andersson has been found dead. It appears he has committed suicide after being beaten up by thugs who were sure he was the man killing the livestock. They dragged him by the hair, spat on him, bludgeoned him with a stone and taunted him. He protested his innocence before finally confessing in order to stop the punishment. Then, when he was left slumped on the ground, one of them pissed on his face. His sense of shame was such that he didn't want to go on living – he could no longer 'look anyone in the face'. He has therefore written the letter – his death note – to Andreas, the only man on the island to have treated him with kindness. Bergman could have tried to portray Johan's humiliation on screen. Instead, by having Von Sydow read out the letter, he leaves it to the audience to imagine the man's degradation. Just as with Bibi Andersson's erotic confessions in *Persona*, the spoken word here carries every bit as much impact as any visual recreation would have done.

Bergman treated actors with such respect and intelligence that he was often able to elicit searing performances from them. They trusted him and were therefore prepared to expose themselves on screen on his behalf. The bond between the director and the cast members was intimate. However, once a film was over, if Bergman wasn't happy with how it had turned out, he would cut ties in a way that some collaborators felt brutal and peremptory. This was what happened with US star Elliot Gould in *The Touch* (1971). Gould played an American archaeologist who embarked on an intense affair with a doctor's wife, the conventional wife and mother Karin Vergerus (Bibi Andersson). The affair was destructive and violent and yet still had a liberating effect on Karin, enabling her to see herself as more than just the bourgeois homebody, deferring to her husband Andreas (Max Von Sydow).

When Bergman was courting Gould to star in the film – the director's first in English – and to play such a sexually frank role, he was sensitive, flattering and tactful. Gould was nervous about doing the film, but Bergman gradually talked him around. 'He was just too reassuring, so interested, so enthusiastic', Gould later recalled to *Life* magazine.

> I knew that I trusted him. I felt that, regardless of my feelings. You never heard an eagerer man than myself, and on the other end of the phone a man more desirous of making me comfortable. He was just so sensitive, terrific.[10]

Before shooting began, they spent time together in Stockholm and on the isle of Faro. Gould was instantly accepted and liked by Bergman's crew. *The Touch* had all the makings of a happy collaboration. 'He never talks to you about psychology, only specifics', Gould enthused of his director.

> He is never patronising. When there were really neurotic, complicated things to be done, he would say something. On the next take I would feel almost as if my ribs opened a little bit and something that maybe happened to me when I was 2 would fill in the cracks between the lines.[11]

Gould described one occasion on which the two men hugged each other and Bergman gave him the following words of wisdom: 'don't contract your muscles. Be open even to emptiness because then whatever does come will be real'. Gould claimed he almost burst into tears at the guru's wisdom. 'It was just so simple and true.'[12]

However, once the film was completed, Bergman had little desire to maintain the friendship with the American star he had called his 'favourite little brother in the world'. When Gould called him to ask about meeting up, Bergman refused to see him. He was warmer to Gould on a subsequent call, but *The Touch* was evidently not a film he felt any pride in at all. 'The story I bungled so badly was based on something extremely personal to me: the secret life of someone who loves becomes gradually the only real life and the real life becomes an illusion', he wrote.[13] Having exposed something so private and seen it held up to ridicule in certain quarters, he was keen to move on. Financially and creatively, he appeared at a low ebb.

The mid-1970s saw Bergman make two films which brought him – thanks to Swedish television – to a far wider audience than he had ever reached before: *Scenes from a Marriage* (1973) and *The Magic Flute* (1975). The former turned into a full-blown phenomenon both in Sweden, where it was shown as a six-part series, and internationally, where it was released as a 168-minute feature. 'What is long, Swedish, deeply depressing, humourless and enormously boring?' asked the British critic Ian Christie in the *Daily Express*.[14] The answer, inevitably, was Bergman's film. Perhaps his discomfiture was understandable. British reviewers weren't used to lengthy marital psychodramas with little action, but to an abundance of talk. Bergman's film was essentially a two-hander. The faces of the couple Johan (Erland Josephson) and Marianne (Liv Ullmann) dominate the screen and are often seen in close-up. They seem like the typical bourgeois Swedish couple with a comfortable and affluent lifestyle, but in true Bergman fashion, they manage to torment one another. As Marianne puts it, 'their lack of problems is a serious problem'. The paradox is that they have all the outward trappings of happiness and yet still contrive to make one another wretched.

The film begins in deceptively cheerful and upbeat fashion with Johan (a professor) and Marianne (ironically a divorce lawyer) giving a magazine interview. Sitting on a sofa holding hands, they are asked some trite questions about their relationship, but in answering them, they uncover tensions.

Immediately afterwards comes one of the most explosive scenes. They are having a dinner party with their good friends Katarina and Peter. All seems well in their luxurious dining room, which is decked out with roses, decanters, silver candelabra and even a chandelier. The couple are proudly boasting about the flattering interview with them that has appeared in the magazine. The journalist has characterised them as 'people who have never forgotten to give love pride of place'. The mood very rapidly sours when Peter reveals how 'rotten' his relationship with Katarina has become. She calls him a spineless jellyfish. He complains about her cooking. That is just the prelude to a full-blown marital spat that ends with Peter quoting a line from Strindberg: 'I wonder if there is anything more horrible than a man and wife who hate each other.'

During this searing row, Johan smokes his pipe and looks askance while Marianne makes her excuses and goes off to do the washing up. They are shocked that their close friends can behave so cruelly to one another. However, this row anticipates the deterioration in their own marriage.

Bergman is alert to the misery that the feuding spouses inflict on one another. He also shows the comic absurdity of their behaviour. There is even the sense that they enjoy tearing strips off one another. Meanwhile, the more vicious they become, the more evident it is that they still have strong feelings for one another. If they didn't, they wouldn't be able to affect one another so deeply. Ullmann and Josephson give immensely subtle and affecting performances. In one scene, Johan mentions in a matter-of-fact fashion to his wife as they lie in bed before going to sleep that he wants 'a clean break'. Marianne reacts as if she has just been hit. She flinches and groans.

It is a familiar tale of a couple who can't live with each other but struggle to live apart. There is no real resolution, although the film ends in surprisingly tender fashion with Johan and Marianne back in each others' arms 'in the middle of the night in a dark house somewhere in the world.' Bergman clearly didn't see it as his role to solve the characters' problems, but merely to state those problems clearly.

The film had been self-financed and shot quickly on a small budget as a form of spiritual 'spring cleaning', but turned into a huge hit in Scandinavia. Bergman found himself cast in the unlikely role of a marriage guidance counsellor. Strangers would approach him for advice about their relationships. He was obliged to change his telephone number to escape entreaties from miserable husbands and wives. In the wake of the film, there were widespread debates about the institution of marriage. Divorce rates went up.

Bergman's film version contained the same six episodes as the TV series, but its focus was far more intently on Johan and Marianne. What made it such a compelling experience – even for viewers who wouldn't normally go near Bergman's work – was its combination of soap opera elements, cinematic and theatrical conventions, and a depth of characterisation you wouldn't normally find outside a novel. Bergman's script was subsequently published as a play and has been performed many times. Johan and Marianne didn't seem so different from the bickering couples found in TV series and magazine articles of the time. The film seemed very contemporary. However, Bergman was also evoking the spirit of Strindberg and his famously lacerating plays about relationships that have turned into living hells.

Seven years later, when he was in exile in Germany, Bergman resurrected Peter and Katarina, the couple from the beginning of *Scenes from a Marriage*, in *From the Life of the Marionettes* (1980). Here, though, the drama wasn't played out in the dining rooms. ('Screw those dinner parties!' Peter says.) Instead, we are confronted with murder and necrophilia. This was one of Bergman's boldest and least characteristic films. It was as if the director was trying to emulate the brazen aggression of the German director Rainer Werner Fassbinder and to move as far away from the cosy bourgeois domesticity of *Scenes from a Marriage* as he could. He was working with German actors. Peter was played by Robert Atzorn and Katarina by Christine Buchegger.

At the start of the film, we see the drunken Peter assault a prostitute. She flees into a gaudy red room. He follows her and strangles her. At this point, the film switches from colour to black and white. He kills her and has sex with her. Peter Egermann, a hard-working, conscientious career man, has somehow been transformed into a Jack the Ripper-like psychopath. (In his early career, Bergman had been obsessed with Jack the Ripper, portraying him in plays as an adolescent anti-hero, 'constantly forced to tear open his own heart and show himself as he really is to the audience'.)

Fourteen days before the 'catastrophe', Peter Egermann went to see Professor Mogens Jensen at his office. He was in the grips of a destructive depression and has morbid fantasies about killing his wife with a razor and about suicide. Jensen prescribes a long walk, a coffee and a few cognacs as the cure for depression.

Jensen is a Mephistophelian figure with designs on Katarina. She, meanwhile, remains in love with Peter. 'I carry him inside of me, no matter where I go.'

From the Life of the Marionettes was Bergman at his darkest and most destructive. The harsh black-and-white cinematography, the leaps back and forth in time, the use of pounding disco music and the morbid dream sequences are disorienting. In Bergman's work, the protagonists often have androgynous traits, but this is one of his few films with an openly gay character, the self-loathing fashion designer Tim (Walter Schmidinger), Katarina's colleague and friend.

'When I close my eyes, I feel like a ten year old, even physically. Then I open my eyes again ... and look in the mirror ... and there I see this old

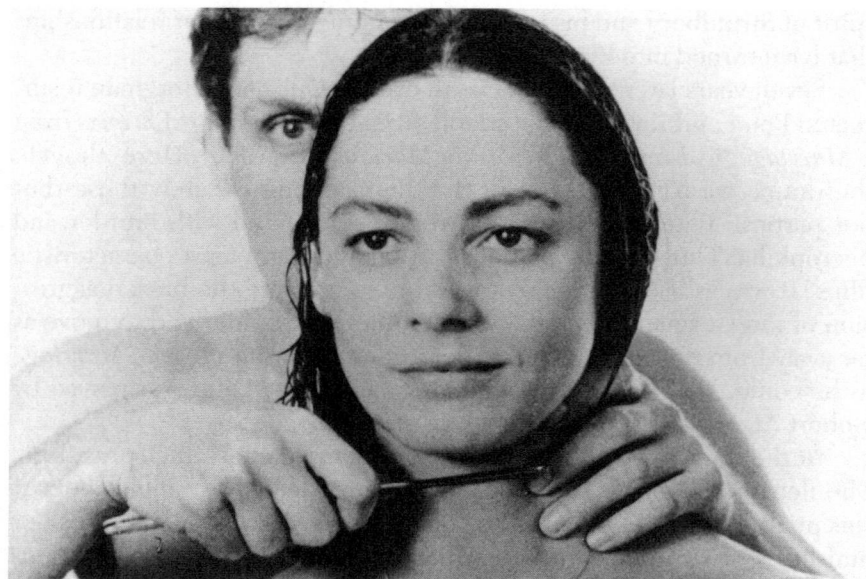

Bergman's underrated *From the Life of the Marionettes*. Katarina (Christine Buchegger) and Peter (Robert Atzom) in a jarring fantasy sequence.

fogey.' Tim bemoans his ageing and the loss of his childhood self. He is disgusted by himself and by his own sexual drive. 'When you get your orgasm, your nose is so deep in shit that you almost suffocate.' He is a sympathetic figure who craves intimacy but knows he will never find it.

At times, the film is like a police procedural drama and at times like a psychoanalytic case study. The project is to work out just why Peter has committed such a hideous act. Was it his childhood? (His mother talks of his fear of the dark.) Was it his marriage or the stress of work? Was it his latent homosexuality? (Tim had loved him and had tried to lure him away from his married life.) Whatever the case, he ends up silent and alone, locked up in the asylum.

From the Life of the Marionettes gives vent to the rage that Bergman still clearly felt at the actions of the Swedish tax authorities that had forced him into exile. It is a messy, inchoate film, but one with real edge. There is no obvious explanation for Peter's behaviour. That is why the film is so unsettling. The title suggests a deep pessimism – a sense that none of the characters can mould their own fates. Their behaviour is pre-ordained. They are like puppets.

Unsurprisingly, such a barbed and difficult film was given a mixed response. Eva af Geijerstam in *Dagens Nyheter* called it 'a chamber play ... full of references to, and parallels with, his earlier films. But ... with such tightly-closed doors, that I, at least, feel compelled to peer through the keyhole. And that is not an entirely pleasant experience.'[15]

Bergman's attitude towards his audience seemed to oscillate during the 1970s and early 1980s. He made some of his most accessible films alongside some of his most hermetic work. *Face to Face* (1976), like *From the Life of the Marionettes*, fell firmly into the latter category. It was about Dr Jenni Isaksson (Liv Ullmann), a psychiatrist who comes close to a suicidal breakdown. Trying to portray his main character's troubled psyche, Bergman mixed reality with dream sequences. Audiences were often baffled. As critic David Parkinson noted, 'the symbolism was deemed as confused as Jenny's character shifts were contrived'.

Alongside such forbidding work, Bergman directed a big-budget TV version of *The Magic Flute* that was shown on the TV over the Christmas holiday period and attracted a huge audience. (Many young Swedes who know little of Bergman's other work still regard it with huge fondness.)

In *Autumn Sonata* (1977), which he shot in Norway during his exile from Sweden, Bergman at last worked with his namesake (and one of the biggest stars in post-war Hollywood), Ingrid Bergman. As the director acknowledged, this was Bergman (Ingmar) 'doing a Bergman'. In other words, it was a case of the director living up to outside preconceptions of what a Bergman film ought to be like rather than striking out on any new path.

Bergman had first expressed his interest in working with Ingrid Bergman many years before. In the early 1960s, they both shared the same agent – Katharine Brown at MCA. Bergman had written to Brown telling her how keen he was to collaborate with the great star.

The film was the study of a relationship between a mother and a daughter. The mother Charlotte (Ingrid Bergman) is a brilliant concert pianist who has neglected her children in pursuit of her career. The daughter Eva (Liv Ullmann) is a shy, slightly dowdy figure, living a quiet life as the wife of a parish priest and still scarred by the loss of one of her own daughters. Eva's sister Helena is severely handicapped. Eva has been looking after her – another source of friction between mother and daughter.

The conflict in *Autumn Sonata* isn't just between mother and daughter; it is between different generations of actors with very different preconceptions about what cinema should be. On the one hand, Ingrid Bergman is the 'grande dame', representing the Hollywood idea of a 'star performance'. On the other, there was Ullmann – intense, naturalistic and determined to get under the skin of any character she played and to convey that character's doubt and insecurity.

At first, the director and leading lady had little rapport. As Bergman later noted in *Images*, they spoke different languages.

> Starting on the first day when we all read the script together in the rehearsal studio, I discovered that she had rehearsed her entire part in front of the mirror, complete with intonations and self-conscious gestures. It was clear that she had a different approach to her profession than the rest of us. She was still living in the 1940s.[16]

Ingrid Bergman was brusque and haughty. She suggested the script was on the dreary side and ought to be enlivened by a few choice witticisms. At one stage, she even slapped her director. He, in turn, took a more aggressive approach with her than he would normally have done with his regular repertory of actors. In the end, the two came to respect one another. *Autumn Sonata* is a rarity in Bergman's work in that the star's performance defines the film as much as the work of the director. The fact that this was one of Ingrid Bergman's last performances before her death from cancer a few years later only added to the sense that she was the centre of the movie.

Either Bergman elicited a magnificent performance from his actress or she delivered one through instinct. The director didn't normally work with stars (although several of his actors became international names on the back of their roles for him). There was clearly a clash of egos as well as of acting styles. However, Bergman soon grew to admire her generosity and talent.

Ullmann was equally good, staring at her mother with a mix of affection and dread through a pair of huge round spectacles and eventually expressing the anger she has kept pent up about the mother's neglect. Ullmann, as she showed again and again in her work with Bergman, had an extraordinarily expressive face. She could convey so much with the smallest changes in expression. As Sven Nykvist wrote of her, 'Liv has a radiance which penetrates the steel shield of the camera.'[17] Like Ingrid Thulin in *Winter Light*, she is made to appear mousy and even ugly – to wear unflattering dresses and put her hair in a bun.

The director was drawing on personal material. As he acknowledged, he had been 'family lazy' throughout his life. He had always put his work first. He understood perfectly Charlotte's egotism. When she discovers that her disabled daughter, whom she has ignored for so long, is living with Eva rather than in an institution, her reaction is purely selfish. It's her own pain she focuses on rather than that of her disabled child – she seems to blame the daughter for chafing at her conscience and making her feel guilty.

Autumn Sonata reflected Bergman's passion for classical music and the way he drew on it in his own work. In one revealing scene, Charlotte tries to show her daughter how to play a piano piece. Her instructions echo Bergman's feelings about performance. Chopin, she tells her daughter, was 'emotional, not sentimental'. Kabi Laretei recalls an incident in her married life with Bergman when he made a similar point to her, very forcefully.

> I was practicing Beethoven's *Apasionata*. The last movement starts harshly. He came running down saying what are you doing – you want to make it softer, you want to make it beautiful. It isn't. It is cruel. It is terrible. That was a lesson. He said that Beethoven had tenderness and cruelty side by side and that you mustn't soften it. He (Bergman) could be very loving and very angry just like that, within one second and you had to know him very well to take it.[18]

Be calm, clear and austere – that was Charlotte's motto. At the time he made *Autumn Sonata*, Bergman was none of these things. He was riled by his exile. There is a sense of an artist casting around for a style in which to express himself best. He lurched from the relative simplicity of *Autumn Sonata* to the decadent frenzy of *A Serpent's Egg*, from the febrile intensity of *Face to Face* to the effervescence and theatricality of *The Magic Flute*. The metaphor he used to illustrate his search was taken from mining. 'I am drilling, and either the drill breaks or else I don't dare drill deeply enough. Or else it is because I don't have the strength, or else I don't realise that I should drill deeper', he wrote in *Images*. 'Then I pull up the drill and don't take that extra dizzying step. I pull up the drill and declare myself satisfied. That is an unerring symptom of creative exhaustion, exceedingly dangerous because it doesn't hurt.'[19]

Bergman was in danger of losing the edge in his work – that element of perversity and surprise that characterised his best films. In his search for creative renewal, the director eventually turned his gaze back towards the world of his childhood.

10

Prospero in Retreat: Back to Faro, Back to Childhood

'WHEN I ARRIVED here 40 years ago, there were hardly any roads', Barbro Hiort af Ornas recalled of her first arrival on the isle of Faro, which she discovered only a few years after Bergman. There were just gravel roads and paths, and fences to keep the sheep in. On the island, you could find absolute peace.

> No one to see and nothing to disturb you, just nature. I have often been here in the winter time, at Christmas. At night there is just you and the stars – they are so close. There are no lights. Dark everywhere.[1]

Although she had worked regularly with Bergman over a period of almost half a century, Hiort af Ornas rarely met the director. He had come to the island to be on his own.

> It is sort of a shelter. He doesn't have to meet people here. He can be alone with the stones and the heavens. It is good for the soul. I don't know if it is something intrinsically Swedish, loving the sea and the wind so much? Maybe it is.[2]

During his exile in Germany, Bergman pined for Faro. One of the most affecting passages in his autobiography describes an evening, not long after he had left Sweden, when he and his wife Ingrid once chartered a private plane in order to be able to fly to Visby and then travel on to Faro. They got there late, but it was still light. 'The huge lilac hedge outside the old house at Damba Water was in full bloom. We sat on the steps of the house until dawn, enveloped in the heavy fragrance, then early in the morning, we flew back to Copenhagen.'[3]

There was a harsh side to life on Faro. It may have been Bergman's refuge from the world, but for the inhabitants, there was always the consciousness that they were looked down upon by the residents of the nearby island Gotland, who in turn were condescended to by those on the mainland. Farmers on Faro regularly complained that they were paid less for their sheep than the farmers on the mainland. The permanent dwellers on the island resented the influx of tourists who appeared every summer, leaving rubbish on the beach. Facilities were often shocking. In his two documentaries about Faro, which he described as his gift to the island, Bergman recounted horrific stories about the islanders' experiences. In *Faro Dokument* (1970), there is a grim story about a woman who continued working with a broken leg. Finally, the leg went rotten and was chopped off. Her son was institutionalised, but that was partly so that the son could eat. The population was dwindling. The local fishing industry was almost dead. There was little for the young people to do.

Faro was too dark and repressive a place to be classified as a paradise. Nonetheless, in *Faro Dokument* and its follow-up *Faro Dokument* (1979), Bergman showed huge curiosity about the lives of these tough and fatalistic islanders. His affection for them was self-evident. He seemed fascinated by the primal, sometimes violent, nature of their struggle for survival. His camera showed them slaughtering livestock. They had no fancy abattoirs. They killed animals with knives in their backyards.

Bergman, the restless artist, found a contentment on the island that he simply didn't experience anywhere else. He commented at the time of *Faro Dokument* (1979):

> My community spirit lies in Faro. Since my childhood I've felt rootless wherever I happen to have been. It was only when I first went to Faro in 1960 and moved there 13 years ago that I felt at home somewhere in the world. That's where my roots are, where I feel that I belong. When I've finished my work down here [in Munich], or finished my work full stop, then I'll go back there and become a Faro man.[4]

Faro was where he went to escape. It wasn't his only refuge. His other great solaces were memory and imagination. As he grew older, he was constantly looking back to his childhood.

As his son-in-law, the crime writer Henning Mankell, wrote in the weeks after his death, this was where his creativity was rooted.

> I believe that the true artist is the child. When we grow up, before school starts reproaching us if we show too much trust in imagination and fantasy, when reality's letters and mathematical formulas must rule, we lose a lot of what we had by nature before. We lose that unfettered faith in the forces of fantasy and imagination. But not only because it could help us in building inventive wooden huts or rafts, or making pirate ships out of pieces of bark. We

need fantasy and imagination to deal with the difficulty that so often comes with life.[5]

It was little surprise that his 'final' film as a director, *Fanny and Alexander* (1982), took him right back to where he had started. 'Yes, there is some kind of ferocious autobiographical material in there,'[6] he said of the film, which is about a young boy with a fervid imagination who loathes his stepfather, a sadistic bishop with more than a hint of Bergman's own father. The film, which won four Oscars, is set over a single year. It's a rich, over-determined affair in which the director's admiration for Charles Dickens, E. T. A. Hoffman, Shakespeare, Ibsen and *The Phantom Carriage* come together with his love of magic, his interest in supernaturalism and – of course – the events of his own childhood. It's a chronicle which self-consciously mixes joy and terror.

Bergman famously tried to make each film as if it was his last. His relentless perfectionism went hand in hand with a sense of deep fatalism. If he didn't get it right now, would he ever get the chance again?

'I think that anything I have done of any value is rooted in my childhood', Bergman told his friend Jorn Donner, the producer of *Fanny and Alexander*. 'Or in dialectic terms, it is a dialogue with my childhood. I've never distanced myself from my childhood but have continued a dialogue with it'.[7]

In the film, this dialogue is far more direct and less filtered than in Bergman's other work. What was remarkable about *Fanny and Alexander*, though, was that this was not just a very personal look back at childhood by the director. It was also a costume epic with a huge cast and full of elaborate set-pieces. Like much of Bergman's later work, it exists in two versions – a five-hour cut made for TV and a shorter theatrical version shown internationally.

There was something fetishistic about the way that Bergman set out at the beginning of the film to recreate the Christmases he remembered from his childhood in every last detail. The production and costume design are mind-boggling – the pots and pans in the kitchen, baubles on the Christmas tree, sherry glasses, bric-a-brac and ornaments, plants, drapes, cushions, clocks, mirrors, toys etc. This was Bergman in Cecil B. DeMille mode. He was telling the story of his own childhood, not of Moses parting the Red Sea, but he saw that as no reason why his movie shouldn't be on an utterly epic scale.

The film offered an evocation of childhood. It was also his tribute to the transformative power of theatre. Early on, we see stage production – a nativity play. We hear Alexander's father Oscar (Allan Edwall) making a speech:

> My only talent, if you can call it a talent, is that I love this little world within the thick walls of the playhouse. And I am fond of the people who work in this little world. Outside is the big world ... and sometimes the little world reflects the big world for a moment so that we understand it better. Or is it, perhaps, that we give the people who come here the chance of forgetting for a while, for a few short moments, the harsh world outside.

The speech has a double pathos. Not only is Oscar very shortly to die, Bergman seems to be speaking through him. There is a carnival-esque mood at the Christmas feast of the Ekdahl family, their friends and servants. The kids misbehave. The elderly relatives get drunk and flirt with the younger women. Everyone holds hands and forms a long line, dancing through the house. Uncle Carl takes the kids off to watch his 'fireworks' display – an exhibition of very noisy farting on the staircase. The Christmas sequence captures the full range of yuletide emotions – the joy, the boredom, the lust, the self-indulgence and all the petty squab-bling. Little Alexander has his magic lantern to play with. Bergman be-ing Bergman, there is also an undertow of gloom. We know that death is not far away. In Alexander's first magic lantern show, the story he tells is ghostly and macabre, about a woman alone in a big, dark house. 'Her mother is dead and her father is carousing with loose companions.' Come midnight, a white figure floats into view, being carried on moonbeams. It is yet another of Bergman's manifestations of death. The figure, we're told just as the kids' illicit show is interrupted, is the girl's dead mother.

The tone of the first part of the film is reminiscent of that found a year or two later in John Huston's final feature, *The Dead* (1987). Adapted from James Joyce's story, Huston's film likewise contrasted Christmas cel-ebration with asides about loss and bereavement. 'The Dead confronts you with certain facts of life – love, passion, marriage and death – and forces you to face them', Huston noted of his source material. His obser-vations could have been applied equally well to *Fanny and Alexander*. Just as Bergman had recreated turn-of-the-century Stockholm at Christ-mas time, complete with snow and hansom cabs, Huston had done some-thing similar with the Dublin of the same era. The party held by two elderly spinsters and their unmarried daughter isn't so different from the great Christmas gathering that opens a Bergman's film. *The Dead* too ends on a Bergmanesque note, with Gretta (Anjelica Huston) re-membering a former lover, a young man of 17, who died of tuberculosis. It is apparent she still pines for him. As her husband listens to her, it dawns on him that he doesn't really know her or understand her feelings at all.

Such mutual incomprehension is felt by the couples in Bergman's films as well. In *Fanny and Alexander*, always intended as a final summing up, he revisits characters and ideas from both his life and his work. Old actors are seen in familiar guises, but their performances are lent extra poignance by the way time has caught up with them. Jarl Kulle, the roistering seducer from *The Devil's Eye* and *Smiles of a Summer's Night*, is still preying on women as Gustav Ekdahl, but with his greying beard, he looks a little bit absurd. Erland Josephson, who had appeared in a Bergman stage production of *The Merchant of Venice* at the start of the Second World War, is playing the kindly Jewish antique dealer Isak Jacobi. Other familiar faces also appeared in minor roles, among them Harriet Andersson as a maid and Gunnar Bjornstrand as one of the characters in the theatre troupe. The dying agonies of Oscar Ekdahl (Allan Edwall), as his family hover around him, inevitably rekindle memories of Harriet Andersson's equally tortured and prolonged death throes in *Cries and Whispers*.

To play Alexander, Bergman had recruited a 10-year-old called Bertil Guve. He had spotted Guve in a bit part in a Lasse Hallstrom film on TV and dispatched two assistants to Guve's school to check out the boy's credentials. Guve recalls how odd it was to have Bergman's associates turn up in his classroom to look him over. Guve hadn't much enjoyed his experience on the Hallstrom film and was far from certain that he wanted to audition for *Fanny and Alexander*. His mother explained to him that the Swedish director was, in his way, as famous as Bertil's then idols, the Swedish tennis star Bjorn Borg and the Hollywood cowboy John Wayne. She also told her son that he could audition for the role safe in the knowledge that he had very little chance of landing into it.

In the event, Bertil was chosen. Bergman later told him that he liked the way he 'acted with his eyes'. It helped, too, that Guve had a dreamy, slightly melancholy quality as well as a vivid imagination. (During his audition, he told a tall tale about having killed his grandfather which appealed to Bergman greatly.) Bergman could clearly see traces of the child he had once been in the face of his young lead. Guve, who sang in a choir, shared his love of music. He appeared to his colleagues 'old beyond his years'.

There were great expectations about *Fanny and Alexander*. Bergman had recruited the cream of Swedish actors and technicians. This was the

biggest project in the country's cinema history. Guve recalls the atmosphere on set as being happy and high spirited. (Not that the production was without its problems, with technicians injuring themselves and
cast and crew falling prey to flu. Appropriately enough, the disease that
had almost killed Bergman as a child laid him low when he was mid-way
through his last big film.) Bergman didn't tell Guve what the film was
about. Every day, he would be given a few pages of screenplay. The production was shot chronologically – so the young actor had the sense he
was living through the story being told.

Initially, Guve didn't get on with Pernilla Allwin, who played his sister
Fanny. The two were suspicious of one another and jostled for position.
Given Bergman's vexed relationships with his own siblings, their rivalry
and rancour seemed oddly fitting. Tensions were short lived. As they grew
more accustomed to one another, the child actors became firm friends.
Between shots, they would get up to mischief. Guve recalls racing around
on an old pedal bike, often getting his clothes covered with soot or mud
and thereby sending the film crew into a panic. He had a strong rapport
with his director. The 10-year-old boy and the director, by then into his
60s, struck up an unlikely friendship.

Only once did Guve fall foul of Bergman and witness his ferocious
temper. During one sequence, when he hadn't at first understood his
lines, Guve laughed nervously on camera. As he stood there tittering,
Bergman exploded. 'He jumped up and grabbed my arm and said this
is the most outrageous, the most unprofessional behaviour I have ever
seen.' The child star was left in tears and the crew was in a state of shock.
The next take went just as badly. Guve wasn't laughing – now he was
crying. Bergman eventually took Guve into another room. 'He put his
arm around me. I cried. We talked. Everything was sorted out.'[8]

Bergman was digging back into his childhood, re-evoking old joys and
bringing some of his dreaded demons back to life. At around the time he
made the film, he was also working on his autobiography. To many critics,
the book and the film seemed like companion pieces. Michiko Kakutani
wrote perceptively in the *New York Times* that Bergman had taken 'the
mirror of his personality' in *Fanny and Alexander* and 'broken it into
shards'.[9]

Fanny and Alexander also represented Bergman's final assault on his
father. The sadistic stepfather Bishop Edvard Vergerus (Jan Malmsjo)
was one of the most hostile of his many representations of characters
based on Erik Bergman. (He would depict him again in *The Best Intentions* and *Sunday's Children*, but in a far more forgiving light.) What

is immediately striking about the bishop is his immense conceit. He is playing a role. His chilly egotism is contrasted with the conviviality and camaraderie of the amateur actors, putting on their productions of Shakespeare and Christmas plays. He is cold and formal – a cruel and narcissistic man who delights in always being right.

There was something strangely masochistic about the most distinguished filmmaker in Swedish cinema ritually revisiting the boyhood traumas of 60 years before. 'Can you tell me what is a lie and what is the truth', the bishop asks his stepson. Of course, it is a loaded question, a prelude to a punishment he plans to inflict on the boy simply because he can't understand Alexander's imagination. All Alexander has done is cook up a few far-fetched stories about running away to the circus. The bishop reacts as if he is guilty of a heinous crime. Like a Gestapo officer in a Second World War movie, he is sleek in his malevolence, presenting his own behaviour as selfless and well-meaning. He is as terrifying as any figure in Bergman's work. He presents his punishments as if they are gifts. 'Do you choose the cane, castor oil, or the bogey-hole', he asks young Alexander, as if offering him a choice of sweets. When Alexander opts for the cane, he gives him an enthusiastic thrashing – and then, having meted out the punishment, insists that the tearful boy ask for forgiveness.

Fanny and Alexander was rapturously received. The knowledge that this was his 'last' film added to the reverence with which the critics treated it. The UK press's response was instructive. 'Bergman's resounding farewell to cinema', pronounced the *Daily Telegraph*. 'A film to treasure', chimed in *The Daily Mail*.

Perhaps *Fanny and Alexander* risked distorting Bergman's reputation. It enjoyed such extraordinary success that audiences thought it summed up and defined Bergman. A beautifully made and very tasteful costume drama, it was the kind of movie that appeals to a mainstream audience who might have found films like *Persona* and *The Hour of the Wolf* repulsive. On one level, it was Bergman's most personal work. On another, it was evasive. Bergman may have been sharing his innermost secrets, but he also knew how much was at risk. Jorn Donner had not committed so much public money to a private confessional.

Like the boy who cried wolf too many times and then saw the wolf for real, Bergman had conjured up a demon that, on this occasion, he couldn't exorcise. It had long been his conceit that every film was his last. This one really was. It had long been his complaint that filmmaking left him emotionally and physically in tatters. This time it really did. In an evocative passage in *The Magic Lantern*, he describes a typical day's filming in 1982. He makes it sound so grim that a spell in Stalin's Gulag would have been welcoming by comparison. The temperature was freezing. It went without saying that he couldn't sleep and that his bowels were playing up. 'I went over my actual situation', he writes. 'How was my body, how was my soul, and, most of all, what had got to be done today?' With a valetudinarian's relish, he listed his ailments. Nose blocked. Left testicle aching. (Cancer, he guessed.) A ringing in his ear.[10]

Other filmmakers have talked about the crippling sense of responsibility that a director feels. Ang Lee, for example, has pointed out that it is hugely stressful when a small army of people look up to you and rely on you for guidance. There is nobody for the director to confide in. The buck stops with him. Of course, the work itself can be enormously rewarding. In the same passage in *The Magic Lantern* in which he bemoans his illnesses and worries, Bergman talks about the quiet delight that he experiences when working with trusted and talented collaborators. He is like a pearl fisher. Just occasionally, he and his crew capture something gleaming and magical that makes their efforts all worthwhile. The stress, though, was becoming too much.

Moreover, Bergman had always been competitive. He was like an athlete who had begun to fear he was losing his physical edge. He was terrified of turning out inferior work and being eclipsed by those he had always regarded as lesser rivals.

Bergman's 'retirement' from filmmaking lasted a very long time – it was a quarter of a century from the completion of *Fanny and Alexander* in 1982 to his death in the summer of 2007. In that period, he assumed a role in Swedish cinema culture roughly akin to that of the ghost in *Hamlet* – or, indeed, the ghost of Alexander's father in *Fanny and Alexander*, who appears again and again and seems to look over his family. Even when he couldn't be seen, Bergman's presence could always be detected.

The director in retirement became an emblem of a kind of arthouse cinema that seemed increasingly under threat. As he wrote scripts for Bille August, his son Daniel Bergman and his former partner Liv Ullmann to direct, there was still the sense that he was the puppetmaster. *Best Intentions, Sunday's Children* and *Faithless* may not have had his name above the title, but to critics and audiences alike, they still seemed like Bergman films.

Liv Ullmann's *Faithless* (2001) saw Bergman, by then in his 80s, still probing away at personal, deeply uncomfortable episodes in his past. Yet again, he was revisiting his own infidelity and the beginning of his relationship with Gun Hagberg. It's a languorously paced film, heavy on talk, but with an excoriating emotional intensity. A Prospero-like old man, 'Bergman' (Erland Josephson) living by the sea listens, rapt, as a 'voice' tells him a story. The voice takes the form of Marianne Vogler (Lena Endre), a beautiful actress and mother married to Markus (Thomas Hanzon), a successful composer. Almost as a dare or on a whim, without any thoughts of the consequences, she begins an affair with Markus' best friend David (Krister Henriksson), a crumpled, charming, curmudgeonly, twice-divorced writer. What starts as a casual romance has a devastating effect on the lives of all the protagonists.

'I don't know what so obsessed him (Bergman) about that relationship because he has met so many (women), he has left so many. He has imparted tragedy in so many of their lives', Ullmann told me when I interviewed her before the film's British release.[11]

What was striking was the sexual jealousy that Bergman still seemed to feel, 50 years after his relationship with Hagberg had begun. Ullmann speculated:

> What he says hurt him was the time that she came home after having been with her husband. He became so angry. That is what he cannot forgive himself for. My theory is that it's the jealousy that is still cooking within him. In spite of what the two of them had experienced in Paris, she slept not once with her husband. She was with him in a car, then outside the car, then in his flat. I think it is this boiling jealousy that he cannot get over. I think that for the only time in his life he was confronted with somebody else doing what he had been doing all his life.[12]

She suggested that many young people watching *Faithless* agreed that David has grounds for anger when Marianne 'betrays' him with her husband. (The fact that he has already cuckolded the husband adds an extra layer of discomfort and irony.)

> I have had young people seeing this film and they say of course he should be furious. She didn't sleep with her husband once. It was many times. How many times do you rape somebody? You can rape somebody once, but you can't go up to their apartment after and be raped again, and then you sit for a while and you are raped again. It doesn't happen. And it doesn't happen that he (the husband) says now I want you to have an orgasm and you are raped into an orgasm. It doesn't happen.

Ullmann spoke of her initial trepidation at tackling screenplays so personal to Bergman.

> At first, when we were working on the storyboard, I felt that this was not necessarily the subject that I would have wanted to make a movie on. It is

dark and it doesn't have forgiveness. The first year was difficult. I said to him
'I'll do the shooting in the studio but you can do the preproduction and the
post-production because it is so personal.' He didn't want to do that. I said
then it was my film and it would have to be my vision. He said that was what
he wanted.[13]

It became apparent that the writer and the director had different
conceptions about the project. The film begins with a quote by German
author Botho Strauss, which spells out Bergman's obsessions.

No common failure, whether it be sickness or bankruptcy or personal misfortune, will reverberate so cruelly and deeply in the unconscious as a divorce.
It penetrates the seat of all anguish, forcing it to life.

Faithless begins with Bergman (Josephson) alone on his island, con-
juring up demons from his past. We see him sitting at his desk, looking at
old photographs. As he does so, the characters from those photographs
gradually spring to life. The film looks set to turn into a brooding psy-
chodrama about regret, old age, sexual jealousy and betrayal. However,
Ullmann interprets Bergman's material in a way that he would not have
done. In particular, she foregrounds the role of the child.

The absence of children in Bergman's dramas about warring spouses
is striking. We don't see them in *Scenes from a Marriage* or *From the Life
of the Marionettes*. In *Faithless*, however, the child is central.

'You can't damage a grown-up life. We've all had people leave us',
Ullmann explained her choice to place so much emphasis on Marianne
and Markus' child.

He (Bergman) has given people sorrow but I'm sure people have given him
sorrow. I don't think he has really damaged any woman's life by leaving her.
I don't know who else was involved. If there were children, that might have
had a worse effect. When we love people, we are going to be in for some unhappiness. We know that. Each story we hear in life is subjective ... I thought
about the child because I couldn't make a movie making this woman the
heroine. To me, she made so many strange choices that I can't feel sorry for
her. That was why I showed so much more of the child in the movie. The
child is the only victim. The child didn't make any choice. The child is almost faithless to everybody too. The child knows this about the father and
doesn't tell the mother, and knows this about the mother and doesn't tell
the father, and is part of a really horrendous dance. The others are unhappy
because unhappiness comes with love, but they made the choice; they said,
'OK, I want to go to Paris to have fun.' Marianne is unhappy, but she made
that choice. She didn't involve the child in that choice at all except for saying
stay with your grandmother while I'm in Paris. She was not really contemplating what this affair might do with the child. In all his former films about

the father and the mother, the victim is the person who is writing the film, which is Ingmar. It is very tough for me because this happened. Who is the victim? It's the child because the child grew up and became Bergman and wrote these movies[14].

When he wrote his screenplay, Bergman had barely thought about Markus and Marianne's daughter. She certainly wasn't a major character. This may seem surprising, given Bergman's very vexed relationship with his own father. However, he belonged to a generation which had a very different notion about fatherhood than that of young parents in the Sweden of 2001. Bergman – as he admitted – had never paid much attention to family life. His focus had always been on his work – on fulfilling himself as an artist, on the one hand, and on raising enough money to pay maintenance to his ex-wives and children, on the other.

In *The Magic Lantern*, Bergman wrote a strangely forlorn account of attending Gun Hagberg's funeral after she had died in a car crash. He went together with his son, Ingmar Jr., who was then 19 years old. They hadn't seen each other for many years. The son was hostile to him. They couldn't find common ground on which to communicate. Bergman recognised himself in the younger man but was unable to reach out to him. This sad little episode stands out in his autobiography because it is virtually the only moment in which he mentions his children in any depth at all. They just weren't on his mind.

With *Faithless*, Bergman accepted Ullmann's emphasis on the plight of the child. 'Ingmar himself when he saw the movie said "Shit! Why didn't I think of that?" He liked that', Ullmann recalled.

The film, which premiered at the Cannes Festival in 2001, was respectfully received. However, there was a sense that Bergman was a man out of another time. 'Admirers of the great Swedish director Ingmar Bergman will find much to enjoy in this personal and revelatory film about the destructive forces unleashed by thoughtless sexual misbehavior', wrote *Variety*, praising Liv Ullmann for extracting 'every nuance from the tantalising material'. Still, *Variety*'s reviewer pointed out that this was a film for those who already knew and liked Bergman, not new converts. 'For non-aficionados, the slow pacing, familiar themes and alienating performance of the principal male actor will prove irritants.'[15]

Bergman's final film as director, *Saraband*, saw him embracing digital technology. Right at the end of his career, Bergman was again a pioneer, albeit a querulous and demanding one. The film was shot when Bergman was 84, in the autumn of 2002, and was shown on TV in Sweden a year later, but didn't surface abroad until two years later. Bergman only wanted it to be shown in venues that had the proper facilities for HD digital projection. He had been unhappy with the quality of the transfer from HD to film and had therefore vetoed the original plans for theatrical distribution.

'The film was made on high-def video and he didn't like that', the film's star Liv Ullmann noted of his battle for the best technical results.

> First, it was with four cameras. Then, after two days, it was with only one camera. He hated that he couldn't sit by the camera like he usually does. He had been guaranteed that it would look like a film if copied right. But it didn't look like a film and so he said it wouldn't be shown as a film. Only when he was promised that it would be shown digitally would he give his approval. I like all that. He doesn't give up. He just sticks to what is right for him. He is professional. In our world where no-one seems to care about so much, here is someone who cares.[16]

The director's drive and perfectionism hadn't diminished at all. 'I demand the same thing of others as I do of myself: the absolute best', he declared before shooting began. 'You set all other considerations aside. You have only one loyalty – to the work itself.'

A fascinating documentary – *Behind Saraband* – was made about the shooting of the film. Bergman may have been hard of hearing in one ear and very elderly, but his crew was clearly in awe of him. A balding, stooped but still physically imposing figure, he prowled around the set. In rehearsals for the scene in which the daughter, a talented musician, attacks her wastrel father, Bergman was right beside his actors, whispering instructions, almost joining in the fight himself. He passed on tips to his actors he had learned from Alf Sjoberg more than half a century before on the set of *Frenzy*. 'Sjoberg said to me, "Remember this, Bergman. What is half-hidden is far more suggestive, more seductive more exciting than what is fully visible." '

Bergman remained extraordinarily fussy about the props, inspecting and replacing chairs, glasses, mugs and flowers. What shone through was his determination to make sure that all his collaborators felt their work was worthwhile. 'They shouldn't feel that this is fruitless', he stated. 'It's so easy, in this profession, to feel what you are doing is meaningless. That it's just a bunch of hassle. That it's monotonous. So it's very important to me that the actors feel that what we're doing is meaningful.'

Saraband reunited Marianne (Liv Ullmann) and Johan (Erland Josephson), the couple from *Scenes from a Marriage*. Marianne goes to visit her ex-partner in the countryside and finds herself caught in the middle as Johan feuds with his son Henrik (Borje Ahlstedt). Johan loathes and despises his son, but is very close to his granddaughter, the talented musician Karin (Julia Dufvenius).

For all the bitterness that runs through *Saraband*, there is also a vein of forgiveness. The film was dedicated to Ingrid Van Rosen, Bergman's beloved fifth wife who had died in 1995. Her passing away had changed his own attitude towards death. Fear of death, rage against it, had been the defining theme in many of his films. In *Saraband*, there was an acceptance of death. Bergman used to say that he could feel Ingrid's presence, especially when he was on Faro, where they had lived together. The old terror seemed to have abated. In *Saraband*, Henrik's late wife Anna is likewise a benign and living presence. The memory and respect for her enable the bickering protagonists to transcend their differences.

'Saraband is autobiographical in that he had a son who died and they never got to make up', Ullmann said.

> It's tough because that was horrible for him. You would think this film would be everything he would like to say – I love you, I care for you etc., but (in the film) it's still as if they can't talk. That is very brave. He is saying this is who I am. This is my music and I am going to play it again and again. I am sure that much of the film has to do with the wife (Ingrid Van Rosen) that he lost 10 years ago, but also it has to do with the idea that for some people, the easiest person to love is someone who has gone. That picture (of the dead wife) in the film is not of Ingrid. It's a lady who works in costumes in the theatre. But she looks like Ingmar's mother.[17]

Saraband was given a mixed reception when it screened first on Swedish TV. It was austere and reserved, full of musical motifs and a little old-fashioned for the taste of the television audience. Internationally, the film was greeted far more warmly. Critics admired the searing intensity and lack of compromise.

> It's not unusual for veteran directors to end their careers with intimate minor-key statements, which are often marked by near-minimalist formal austerity, *Saraband* very nearly fits this category, except that we're used to calling such farewell films 'autumnal'. It comes as no surprise that Bergman's is militantly wintry.[18]

Bergman had seemed on the brink of silence before, only to write or direct new plays and films, but *Saraband* really was his last film. In early 2004, he also cut his ties with the Royal Dramatic Theatre in Stockholm, emptying the office that he had kept there for so many years. His plan was to spend whatever time remained with him on Faro. He retreated to his island. He lived there alone, with music, films and books as his companions. His children came to see him in the summer, but he didn't have many other visitors. He kept in touch with old friends by telephone. New films were dispatched to him regularly. He watched these in the barn/studio/cinema where, 30 years before, he had shot *Scenes from a Marriage*. 'He sits there with this woman who keeps cows and horses. She knows everything now about showing films. He sits there with her showing the films. Every new film. He knows everything that is being made', Liv Ullmann noted with wry amusement.[19]

At the time of writing (the spring of 2008), it is coming up to a year since Bergman's death. The tributes are still being paid to him. Film festivals throughout the world have staged retrospectives. His plays (notably the stage version of *Scenes from a Marriage*) have been frequently revived. There are websites devoted to him. New prints of his films are being struck. The Bergman 'industry' is in full flow. As the archive is studied in further depth and more details of his life and work emerge, new books and scholarly articles are inevitable.

Sometimes, when respected filmmakers die, there is an initial flurry of interest in their work that soon wanes. When the Polish master Krzysztof Kieslowski died in 1996, eulogies, retrospectives and new publications quickly followed. A decade on, though, and his films have passed – at least temporarily – out of fashion. Bergman is unlikely to suffer any such lapses from critical grace. What is surprising is how much mystery still surrounds him and how much there is left to discover. His work often appeared nakedly confessional, but he was a showman too. His art was as much to do with magic, concealment, trompe l'oeil effects and suspension of disbelief as with simply laying bare his own biography in dramatic form. The more that people thought they knew about him, the more inscrutable he became. The term 'Bergmanesque' may have gained currency as a way of describing a certain strand of brooding, self-conscious arthouse cinema. Certain themes, characters and even names (all those people called Vergerus or Borg) may have recurred again and again in his work, but he remained an elusive and protean figure.

When the US academic Raphael Shargel edited together a selection of Bergman interviews in 2007, he noted in his introduction the vastly contradictory ways in which Bergman's interviewers characterised him. Some call him tall, others medium-sized. Some say that he is physically imposing, others that he is nondescript. They all have their preconceptions about Bergman, and invariably they manage to get him to fulfil them. From the late 1950s onwards, from the time of *The Seventh Seal* and *The Virgin Spring*, he was regarded internationally as one of the masters of world cinema. Critics seemed to find it unseemly or intimidating to peer behind his public image as saturnine artist, wrestling with questions of faith and the devil, and ask such prosaic questions as: how did he finance his films, how were they distributed, how much money did they make? Economic and technical questions were ignored in favour of treating him as some kind of mystical Scandinavian visionary. This study has attempted to offer a more grounded account of his career: to look at that mix of cunning, pragmatism and luck he needed to establish himself as a filmmaker in the post-war Swedish industry and to trace his influences. As he once told an interviewer, 'I don't think somebody just becomes a director . . . we are like stones in a building, all of us. We all depend on the people coming before.'[20] It has also tried to explore the way he evolved a 'personal' style by drawing so heavily on his own past while also borrowing ideas from other artists and filmmakers. The argument here is that any real understanding of Bergman's extraordinary achievements can't come from simply focusing on his films alone, but must ask how and why those films came to be made. The transformation of the unhappy parson's son playing with his magic lantern into arguably the most revered European auteur of his era didn't come about simply through Bergman's imaginative powers and flair for self-dramatisation. It was always his insistence that he was a craftsman as much as he was an artist. The aim here has been to look at how he learned his craft.

Notes

Introduction

1. Pergament, Danielle, 'Faro: The enchanted island that Bergman called home', *International Herald Tribune*, 8 October 2007.
2. Interview with the author, June 2007.
3. Ibid.
4. Interview with the author, July 1996.
5. Interview with the author, June 2007.
6. Macnab, Geoffrey, 'Ingmar Bergman: The Swedish master who hides away on a small island', *Independent*, 13 July 2007.
7. Macnab, Geoffrey, 'House rules', *Sight & Sound*, June 2001.
8. Bergdahl, Gunnar (ed.), *20th Century of Bergman* (Gothenburg 1999).
9. Von Trier, Lars, 'An artist to prove yourself against', *Cahiers du Cinema*, Special issue 2007.
10. Quoted on Wikipedia: en.wikipedia.org/wiki/Bo_Widerberg.
11. Bergman, Ingmar, *Images: My Life in Film* (London 1995), pp. 304–11.
12. Ingmar Bergman interviewed on *The South Bank Show*, 1978.
13. Neyrat, Cyril, 'The demon tamer', *Cahiers du Cinema*, Special issue 2007, pp. 111–14.
14. Rosenbaum, Jonathan, 'Scenes from an overrated career', *The New York Times*, 4 August 2007.
15. Ibid.
16. Ibid.
17. Bergman, Ingmar, *The Magic Lantern*. Translated by Joan Tate (London 1988), p. 68.
18. Bergman, Ingmar, 'What it means to make a film', lecture given at the University of Lund, Sweden. Translated by P. E. Burke and Britt Halvarson, 1959.
19. Ibid.
20. Baxter, Brian, 'Obituary: Ingmar Bergman', the *Guardian*, 31 July 2007.
21. Cox, Alex, 'A sentimental education', the *Guardian*, 7 January 2006.
22. Schrader, Paul, 'The master Ingmar Bergman 1918–2007', *Independent*, 31 July 2007.
23. Allen, Woody, 'The man who asked hard questions', *The New York Times*, 12 August 2007.
24. Interview available to be downloaded at vikingfilms.streamburst.tv/catalogue.
25. Interview with the author, 2005.

26. Ibid.
27. Interview with the author, 2006.
28. Ibid.
29. Bertolucci, Bernardo, 'Cinema will end up killing me', *Cahiers du Cinema*, Special issue 2007, p. 14.
30. Interview with the author, 2005.
31. Interview with the author, 2007.
32. Ibid.
33. Interview with the author, 2005.
34. Lee, Ang, 'My flavour of strawberries', *The Ingmar Bergman Notebook: Talks & Seminars*, 'Bergman Week 2006' (Gothenburg 2006).
35. Bergman, Ingmar (1995), p. 14.
36. Interview with the author, 2005.
37. Ibid.
38. Nyrerod, Marie, *Bergman Island*, Sveriges Television, 2006.
39. Bergman, Ingmar (1995).
40. Bergman, Ingmar (1988), p. 16.
41. Pergament, Danielle (2007).
42. Cited in Ash, Adam, 'After a full artistic life, Ingmar Bergman lets death checkmate him', 1 August 2007 (www.blogcritics.org/archives/2007/08/01/214407.php).

Chapter 1: A Portrait of the Young Filmmaker

1. Bergdahl, Gunnar (ed.), *20th Century of Bergman* (Gothenburg 1999).
2. Ibid.
3. Bergman, Ingmar, *The Magic Lantern* (London 1988), p. 8.
4. Interview with the author, 2007.
5. Ibid.
6. Interview with the author, 2007.
7. Nyrerod, Marie, *Bergman Island*, Sveriges Television, 2006.
8. Lahr, John, *Show and Tell* (London 2001), pp. 227–51.
9. Bergman, Ingmar, *Sunday's Children*. Translated by Joan Tate (London 1994).
10. Ibid.
11. Ibid, p. 92.
12. Interview with the author, 2005.
13. Bergman, Ingmar (1988), p. 34.
14. Nyrerod, Marie (2006).
15. Interview with the author, 2007.
16. Ibid.
17. Ibid.
18. Bergman, Ingmar (1994), p. 17.
19. Donner, Jorn, 'Ingmar Bergman: On life and work', Made ARTE 1998.

20. Winterbottom, Michael, *The Magic Lantern*, Thames TV, 1989.
21. Donner, Jorn (1998).
22. Bergman, Ingmar (1988), p. 1.
23. Donner, Jorn (1998).
24. Bergman, Ingmar (1988), pp. 12–25.
25. Interview with the author, 2007.
26. Interview with the author, 2001.
27. Interview with the author, 2007.
28. Ibid.
29. Donner, Jorn (1998).
30. Interview with the author, 2007.
31. From workbook to *A Serpent's Egg*.
32. Bergman, Ingmar (1988), p. 13.
33. Bergman, Ingmar (1988), p. 16.
34. Bergman, Ingmar, 'What it means to make a film', lecture given at the University of Lund, Sweden. Translated by P. E. Burke and Britt Halvarson, 1959.
35. Ibid.
36. Ibid.
37. Bergman, Ingmar (1988), p. 32.
38. Ibid, p. 77.
39. Ibid, p. 203.
40. Referenced in Winterbottom, Michael (1989).
41. Annan, Gabrielle, 'Review of *The Magic Lantern*', *Sunday Telegraph*, 1988.
42. Bergman, Ingmar (1988), p. 109.
43. Nyrerod, Marie, *Bergman and the Cinema*, BBC 2007/SVT 2004.
44. Bergman, Ingmar (1959).
45. Donner, Jorn (1998).
46. Interview with the author, 2007.
47. Bergman, Ingmar (1988), p. 35.
48. Referenced in Winterbottom, Michael (1989).

Chapter 2: Early Work

1. *Bergman Notebook*, Included in an exhibition at the Swedish Film Institute, 2007.
2. Bergman, Ingmar, *Images: My Life in Film* (London 1995), p. 118.
3. Henning L. Hakanson, letter to *Aftonbladet*, quoted on www.ingmarbergman.se.
4. Quoted on www.ingmarbergman.se.
5. Bergman, Ingmar, *The Magic Lantern* (London 1988), p. 66.
6. Katz, Ephraim, *The International Film Encyclopaedia* (London 1987), p. 109.
7. Quoted on www.bergmanorama.com/films/crisis.htm.

8. *Bergman Notebook* (2007).
9. Quoted on www.ingmarbergman.se.
10. Ibid.
11. Steene, Birgitta, 'The landscapes of Ingmar Bergman', lecture delivered during Bergman Week on the isle of Faro, June 2007.
12. Ibid.
13. Bergman, Ingmar (1995), p. 137.
14. Ibid, p. 139.
15. Hedlund, Oscar, 'Ingmar Bergman, the listener', Saturday Review, 29 February 1964.
16. Quoted on www.ingmarbergman.se.
17. Bjorkman, Stig, Manns, Torsten, and Sima, Jonas, *Bergman on Bergman: Interviews with Ingmar Bergman* (New Jersey 1986).
18. Dymling, Carl-Anders, 'Rebel with a cause', Saturday Review, 27 August 1960.
19. Bergman, Ingmar (1995), p. 146.
20. Shargel, Raphael, *Ingmar Bergman Interviews* (Mississippi 2007), p. 8. 'The tensions of Ingmar Bergman' by Vilgot Sjoman, 1957.
21. Bergman, Ingmar (1995), p. 278.
22. Ibid, p. 277.
23. Ibid.
24. Beyer, Nils, *Morgontidningen*, quoted on www.ingmarbergman.se.
25. Quoted in *To Joy, Film Notes*, by Philip Strick, Tartan DVD.
26. Nyrerod, Marie, *Bergman and the Cinema*, BBC 2007/SVT 2004.
27. Nyrerod, Marie, *Bergman Island*, Sveriges Television, 2006.
28. Nyrerod, Marie, *Bergman and the Theatre*, BBC 2007/SVT 2004.
29. Bergman, Ingmar (1995), p. 283.
30. Bergman, Ingmar (1988), p. 34.
31. Godard, Jean-Luc, 'Bergmanorama', reprinted in *Cahiers du Cinema*, e-special issue 2007.
32. Interview with the author, 2003.
33. Bergman, Ingmar (1995), p. 285.

Chapter 3: The 'Middle Period': 1953–60

1. Nyrerod, Marie, *Bergman and the Cinema*, BBC 2007/SVT 2004.
2. Ibid.
3. Bergman, Ingmar, *Images: My Life in Film* (London 1995), p. 291.
4. Ibid, p. 340.
5. Ekwall, Karl, *Aftontidningen*, quoted on www.ingmarbergman.se.
6. 'Summer with Harriet', Jannike Ahlund talks to Harriet Andersson, Ingmar Bergman in the audience. In the village hall, Faro Island, Sweden, 29 June. *The Ingmar Bergman Notebook: Talks & Seminars*, 'Bergman Week 2006' (Gothenburg 2006).

7. Interview with the author, 2007.
8. Bergman, Ingmar (1995), p. 291.
9. Ibid, p. 295.
10. Ibid, p. 296.
11. Ibid, p. 185.
12. *Aftonbladet*, quoted on www.ingmarbergman.se.
13. Shargel, Raphael, *Ingmar Bergman Interviews* (Mississippi 2007), p. 7. 'The tensions of Ingmar Bergman' by Vilgot Sjoman, 1957.
14. Interview with the author, 2007.
15. Ibid.
16. Ibid.
17. Dymling, Carl-Anders, 'Rebel with a cause', Saturday Review, 27 August 1960.
18. Interview with the author, 2007.
19. Donner, Jorn, 'Ingmar Bergman: On life and work', Made ARTE 1998.
20. Bergman, Ingmar, *The Magic Lantern* (London 1988), p. 155.
21. Scorsese, Martin, and Wilson, Michael Henry, *A Personal Journey Through American Cinema* (London 1997), p. 17.
22. Interview with the author, 2007.
23. Ibid.
24. Ibid.
25. Bjorkman, Stig, Manns, Torsten, and Sima, Jonas, *Bergman on Bergman: Interviews with Ingmar Bergman*. Translated by Paul Britten Austin (Simon & Schuster: New York 1973).
26. Shargel, Raphael (2007), p. 7. 'Conversation with Bergman' by John Simon, 1971, p. 89.
27. Interview with the author, 2007.
28. Bergman, Ingmar (1995), p. 20.
29. Ibid.
30. Anton Chekhov's short stories, selected and edited by Ralph E. Matlaw (W. W. Norton & Company: New York), ISBN 0-393-09002-7, PZ3.C3985Cg 1979 [PG3456.A15] 891.7'3'3, 78-17052, pp. 235–47.
31. Interview with the author, 2007.
32. Bergman, Ingmar (1995), p. 24.
33. Quoted on www.ingmarbergman.se.
34. Bergman, Ingmar (1995), p. 313.
35. Ibid.
36. Quoted on www.ingmarbergman.se.
37. Ibid.
38. Quoted in *Sight & Sound*, October 2005.
39. Bergman, Ingmar (1995), p. 161.
40. Ibid, p. 164.
41. Parkinson, David, *Bergman: A Life in Films*, booklet included with Tartan's *The Ingmar Bergman Collection*, 2006.

42. Quoted on www.ingmarbergman.se.
43. Ibid.
44. Ibid.
45. Ibid.
46. *Playboy*, Vol. II, No. 6, June 1964.
47. Bergman, Ingmar (1995), p. 167.
48. Ibid, p. 170.

Chapter 4: Bergman and Hollywood

1. Bergman, Ingmar, 'What it means to make a film', lecture given at the University of Lund, Sweden. Translated by P. E. Burke and Britt Halvarson, 1959.
2. Ibid.
3. Dymling, Carl-Anders, 'Rebel with a cause', Saturday Review, 27 August 1960.
4. Bergman, Ingmar (1959).
5. Interview with the author, 2007.
6. Ingmar Bergman, the Swedish auteur was courted by the American studios *Independent*, 12 October 2007.
7. Ibid.
8. Ibid.
9. Ibid.
10. Ibid.
11. Ibid.
12. Ibid.
13. Ibid.
14. 'Sweden's Ingmar Bergman not committed to anybody – but Janus', *Variety*, 6 July 1960.
15. From the correspondence between Bergman and Janus Films, The Bergman Archive.
16. Ibid.
17. Neyrat, Cyril, 'The demon tamer', *Cahiers du Cinema*, Special issue 2007, pp. 111–14.
18. Rohmer, Eric, 'Dreams: As long as we have the rapture', *Cahiers du Cinema*, Special issue 2007, pp. 27–8.
19. Rose, Steve, 'Bergman? Dodgy bowels, you know', the *Guardian*, 3 March 2001.
20. Quoted on www.ingmarbergman.se.
21. 'Bergman upsets the Swedes', *Birmingham Post*, 14 December 1963.
22. 'Interview: Ingmar Bergman', *Playboy*, Vol. II, No. 6, June 1964.

23. Ibid.
24. Ingmar Bergman, the Swedish auteur was courted by the American studios *Independent*, 12 October 2007.

Chapter 5: Tax and Politics

1. Bergman, Ingmar, *The Magic Lantern*. Translated by Joan Tate (London 1988), p. 124.
2. Ibid, p. 123.
3. Jones, William G. (ed.), *Talking with Ingmar Bergman* (Dallas 1983), Seminar 1: 'A spear into the darkness', p. 15.
4. Interview with the author, July 2007.
5. Hobsbawm, Eric J., *Age of Extremes: The Short Twentieth Century 1914–1991* (London 1995).
6. Quoted in *Pandora, The Independent* (London 16 September 1999).
7. Bergman, Ingmar (1988), p. 124.
8. Bergman, Ingmar, *Images: My Life in Film* (London 1995), p. 290.
9. Interview with the author, July 2007.
10. Press notes for *The Serpent's Egg*.
11. From material on *The Serpent's Egg*, The Bergman Archive.
12. Bergman, Ingmar (1995), p. 207.
13. Bergman, Ingmar (1988), pp. 100–1.
14. 'Cries and whimpers in socialism's showcase', *Time* magazine, 7 June 1976.
15. Ibid.
16. Ibid.
17. Bergman, Ingmar (1988), p. 88.
18. *Time* magazine, 7 June 1976.
19. The Bergman Archive.
20. Winterbottom, Michael, *The Magic Lantern*, Thames TV, 1989.
21. *Time* magazine, 7 June 1976.
22. Ibid.

Chapter 6: Bergman's Actresses

1. BBC Arena, 'Encountering Bergman', directed by David Thompson, broadcast 13 July 2007.
2. Lawton, Heather, 'Darling buds of May', the *Guardian*, 9 January 1985.
3. Interview with the author, July 2007.
4. Hirschberg, Lynn, 'In the name of the father', *The New York Times*, 27 January 2008.
5. Ullmann, Liv, quoted in an interview included on Tartan Video's 2001 release on DVD of *Faithless*.

6. Interview with the author, 2001.

7. Bergman, Ingmar, *The Magic Lantern*. Translated by Joan Tate (London 1988), p. 42.

8. Interview with the author, 2001.

9. Ibid.

10. Quoted in programme notes for Ibsen's Nora at the Court Theatre, Chicago.

11. Interview with the author, 2001.

12. Interview with the author, July 2007.

13. Ibid.

14. Quoted on www.ingmarbergman.se.

15. Quoted in the production notes of José Luis Borau's *The Sabina* (1979).

16. Interview with the author, 2006.

17. Bibi Andersson interviewed, American Film, March 1977.

18. 'Take five', interview with Bibi Andersson, Issue 633, *Time Out New York*, 15–21 November 2007.

19. 'Summer with Harriet', interview with Harriet Andersson. *The Ingmar Bergman Notebook: Talks & Seminars*, 'Bergman Week 2006' (Gothenburg 2006).

20. Nyrerod, Marie, *Bergman and the Cinema*, BBC 2007/SVT 2004.

21. Bergman, Ingmar, 'The snakeskin', *Sight & Sound*, August 1965.

22. Strindberg, August, *The Stronger*. Translated by Edith and Warner Oland (London 1890).

23. Ibid.

24. Bergman, Ingmar, 'What it means to make a film', lecture given at the University of Lund, Sweden. Translated by P. E. Burke and Britt Halvarson, 1959.

25. Ibid.

26. Ullmann, Liv, *Changing* (New York 1977).

27. Quoted on www.ingmarbergman.se.

28. Bergman, Ingmar, *Images: My Life in Film* (London 1995), p. 64.

29. Nyrerod, Marie, BBC 2007/SVT 2004.

30. Ibid.

31. 'Back from the cold', the *Guardian*, 23 September 2005.

32. Bergman, Ingmar (1988), p. 7.

Chapter 7: Religious Faith – the Trilogy: *Through a Glass Darkly, Winter Light, The Silence*

1. Interview with the author, 2007. 'Inside the container', *Independent*, 16 February 2007.

2. Interview with the author, July 2007.

3. Bergman, Ingmar, *The Magic Lantern*. Translated by Joan Tate (London 1988), p. 273.

4. Ahndoril, Alexander, *The Director*. Translated by Sarah Death (London 2008).

5. Sjoman, Vilgot, 'L136, diary with Ingmar Bergman'. Translated by Alan Blair (Ann Arbor 1978), referenced on www.ingmarbergman.se.

6. 'The face of the divine', Bishop Lennart Koskinen on *Winter Light*, *The Ingmar Bergman Notebook: Talks & Seminars*, 'Bergman Week 2006' (Gothenburg 2006), p. 21.

7. Bergman, Ingmar, *Images: My Life in Film* (London 1995), p. 265.

8. Nyrerod, Marie, *Bergman and the Cinema*, BBC 2007/SVT 2004.

9. Bjorkman, Stig, Manns, Torsten, and Sima, Jonas, *Bergman on Bergman: Interviews with Ingmar Bergman*. Translated by Paul Britten Austin (New York 1973).

10. Bergman speaking on Swedish Television, clip included in Winterbottom, Michael, *The Magic Lantern*, Thames TV, 1989.

11. Letter to Janus Films, The Bergman Archive.

12. Shargel, Raphael, *Ingmar Bergman Interviews* (Mississippi 2007), p. 29. 'L136, diary with Ingmar Bergman' by Vilgot Sjoman, 1963.

13. Bergman, Ingmar (1995), p. 245.

14. Interview with the author, July 2007.

15. Ibid.

16. Bergman, Ingmar (1995), p. 248.

17. Shargel, Raphael (2007), p. 31. 'L136, diary with Ingmar Bergman'.

18. Bergman, Ingmar (1995), pp. 343–4.

19. Cowie, Peter, *Max Von Sydow – from* The Seventh Seal *to* Pelle the Conqueror (Stockholm 1989).

20. Bergman, Ingmar (1995), p. 104.

21. Shargel, Raphael (2007), p. 38. '*Playboy* interview' by Cynthia Grenier, Vol. II, No. 6, June 1964.

22. Bergman, Ingmar (1995), p. 112.

23. Interview with the author, 2000.

24. Shargel, Raphael (2007), p. 44. '*Playboy* interview'.

25. Bergman, Ingmar (1988), p. 161.

26. Bjorkman, Stig, Manns, Torsten, and Sima, Jonas (1973).

27. Ibid.

28. Bergman, Ingmar (1988), p. 222.

Chapter 8: Bergman the Polymath

1. Kakutani, Michiko, 'Ingmar Bergman: Summing up a life in film', *The New York Times* magazine, 28 June 1983.

2. Nyrerod, Marie, *Bergman and the Theatre*, BBC 2007/SVT 2004.

3. Marker, Lise-Lone, and Marker, Fredrick J., *Ingmar Bergman: A Life in the Theatre* (Cambridge 1992).

4. Nyrerod, Marie, BBC 2007/SVT 2004.

5. 'Coup de theatre', the *Guardian*, 14 May 1969.

6. Nyrerod, Marie, BBC 2007/SVT 2004.
7. Interview with the author, July 2007.
8. 'A Hamlet for the '80s', *Time* magazine, 30 March 1987.
9. Bergman, Ingmar, *Images: My Life in Film* (London 1995), p. 221.
10. Quoted on www.ingmarbergman.se.
11. Lahr, John, 'Review of *The Misanthrope*', *New Yorker*, 8 May 1995.
12. Interview with the author, July 2007.
13. Bergman, Ingmar, *Sunday's Children*. Translated by Joan Tate (London 1994).
14. Goodridge, Mike, Obituary for Anthony Minghella, *Screen International*, 28 March 2008.
15. *Moving Pictures International*, May 2007.

Chapter 9: The Magus

1. Bjorkman, Stig, Manns, Torsten, and Sima, Jonas, *Bergman on Bergman: Interviews with Ingmar Bergman*. Translated by Paul Britten Austin (New York 1973).
2. Donner, Jorn, 'Ingmar Bergman: On life and work', Made ARTE 1998.
3. Quoted on www.ingmarbergman.se.
4. Ibid.
5. Bergman, Ingmar, *Images: My Life in Film* (London 1995), p. 300.
6. Ibid, p. 299.
7. Ibid, p. 307.
8. Ibid.
9. Merryman, Richard, 'I live at the edge of a very strange country', *Life*, 15 October 1971.
10. Ibid.
11. Ibid.
12. Ibid.
13. Bergman, Ingmar (1995), p. 85.
14. British Film Institute, microfiche service of cuttings from Bergman's films.
15. Quoted on www.ingmarbergman.se.
16. Bergman, Ingmar (1995), p. 332.
17. Quoted on www.ingmarbergman.se.
18. Interview with the author, July 2007.
19. Bergman, Ingmar (1995).

Chapter 10: Prospero in Retreat: Back to Faro, Back to Childhood

1. Interview with the author, July 2007.
2. Ibid.

3. Bergman, Ingmar, *The Magic Lantern*. Translated by Joan Tate (London 1988), p. 104.

4. Quoted on www.ingmarbergman.se.

5. Mankell, Henning, 'To the end, a man of music', the *Guardian*, 6 August 2007.

6. Nyrerod, Marie, *Bergman and the Cinema*, BBC 2007/SVT 2004.

7. Donner, Jorn, 'Ingmar Bergman: On life and work', Made ARTE 1998.

8. Interview with the author, 2008.

9. Kakutani, Michiko, 'Ingmar Bergman: Summing up a life in film', *The New York Times* magazine, 28 June 1983.

10. Bergman, Ingmar (1988), p. 64.

11. Interview with the author, 2000.

12. Ibid.

13. Ibid.

14. Ibid.

15. *Variety*, May 2000.

16. Interview with the author, 2005.

17. Ibid.

18. Romney, Jonathan, 'Review of *Saraband*', *Sight & Sound*, October 2005.

19. Interview with the author, 2005.

20. Shargel, Raphael, *Ingmar Bergman Interviews* (Mississippi 2007), p. 77. 'Conversation with Bergman' by John Simon, in *Ingmar Bergman Directs* (New York 1972).

Index